D0849691

Is There Anything Good About Men?

"On second thought—you hunt, I'll gather."

Is There Anything Good About Men?

HOW CULTURES FLOURISH
BY EXPLOITING MEN

Roy F. Baumeister

OXFORD
UNIVERSITY PRESS
2010

OXFORD
UNIVERSITY PRESS

Oxford University Press, Inc., publishes works that further
Oxford University's objective of excellence in research,
scholarship, and education.

Oxford   New York
Auckland   Cape Town   Dar es Salaam   Hong Kong   Karachi
Kuala Lumpur   Madrid   Melbourne   Mexico City   Nairobi
New Delhi   Shanghai   Taipei   Toronto

With offices in
Argentina   Austria   Brazil   Chile   Czech Republic   France   Greece
Guatemala   Hungary   Italy   Japan   Poland   Portugal   Singapore
South Korea   Switzerland   Thailand   Turkey   Ukraine   Vietnam

Published by Oxford University Press, Inc.
198 Madison Avenue, New York, New York 10016

www.oup.com

Oxford is a registered trademark of Oxford University Press, Inc.

Library of Congress Cataloging-in-Publication Data

Baumeister, Roy F.
  Is there anything good about men?: how cultures flourish by exploiting men / by Roy F. Baumeister.
     p. cm.
  Includes bibliographical references and index.
  ISBN 978-0-19-537410-0 (hardcover)
    1. Men. 2. Men in popular culture. 3. Equality. I. Title.
  HQ1090.B38 2010
    305.3109—dc22   2010018772
  ISBN-13: 978-0-19-537410-0
  ISBN-10: 0-19-537410-X

9 8 7 6 5 4 3 2 1
Printed in the United States of America
on acid-free paper

Dedicated, with deepest appreciation,
To the women who have loved me

Acknowledgments

I have worked on this book for years. During that time I have spoken about it with many people. I cannot begin to thank them all. Many of them have helped, although, to be honest, quite a few advised me not to write this book. They thought that saying anything favorable about men is taboo and could seriously damage my career. I hope they are wrong.

Three sources of encouragement are therefore particularly welcome and deserve special thanks. The first is my longtime friend and colleague Professor Kathleen Vohs. She supported the project, gave ample constructive criticism of the various ideas, and made many useful suggestions. She also read the entire manuscript and offered detailed and very helpful feedback.

Next, I also wish to mention my editor at Oxford, Lori Handelman. She's been delightful to work with and has provided crucial editorial guidance at several key steps along the way.

Last, I wish to thank the many men and women who have written to me during this project to express their support and encouragement. Early writings and talks on this topic generated some publicity for it, and many people read those preliminary works and wrote to me about how much better they felt about male–female relations and manhood after reading my thoughts. I have written many books and articles and given many talks, but none of them generated anywhere near the popular response as this work did. The warm messages from total strangers helped me keep going during the more difficult stages of getting this book done.

Two important sources of support also deserve special thanks. My wife Dianne did much toward maintaining a home and life in which this sort of intellectual work could thrive. She also read the entire book and talked about ideas with me, helping to steer me through some of the more difficult and sensitive issues. The other is my employer, Florida State University, which also has helped considerably by creating an environment conducive to this sort of prolonged exercise of reading, thinking, and writing.

I wish also to thank others who read the manuscript and offered valuable comments, especially Tyler Stillman and C. Nathan DeWall.

Contents

Is There Anything Good About Men?

CHAPTER 1

An Odd, Unseasonal Question

I S THERE ANYTHING GOOD ABOUT MEN? The question is provocative today, because hardly anyone dares to suggest that men are superior to women in any respect. Political correctness permits us to say that women are better than men at one thing or another. But it's mostly taboo even to suggest men are better at anything more important than opening jars and killing bugs.

In this book, I develop a somewhat radical theory about men and women. It holds that differences are rooted mainly in tradeoffs. If one gender is better at something, the superior ability will probably be linked to being worse at something else. Otherwise, it would be reasonable to expect that nature would have made both genders equally good at most things.

That is not the main point, however. I intend to go far beyond the questions of who is better at what. We want to know not just what men are good *at*—but also what men are good *for*.

One of the most important traits that make us human is our ability to create and sustain giant social systems that can evolve and adapt and compete against each other. These systems are called *cultures*. I shall suggest that cultures routinely exploit men in certain ways, which is to say cultures find men more useful than women for certain tasks. We shall ask what those tasks are and why cultures pick men for those.

The reasons that it has recently become taboo to say positive things about men are rooted in the women's movement and its wide-ranging influence. That, in turn, is grounded in the way men and women relate to each other in our society and culture. Men and women occupy different positions in society, and always have. If anything, the separate worlds that men and women have long occupied have become merged to a degree that would have astonished many of our ancestors. But all is not yet quite equal, to the dismay of many. Why not?

One might instead ask, who cares? But people do care. In particular, men have long held higher positions in society than women have. Most rulers throughout history have been men. Even today, most countries are governed by groups consisting mostly of men. Elsewhere in society, men rule also: in corporate boardrooms, on town councils; even within families, men seem to have more authority. The Global World Forum recently rated most nations on various dimensions of equality, and it found not a single country in which women generally enjoy superior status over men. Nor did the Forum find full equality was reached in any. Thus, men have higher status than women in every country in the world today.

To simplify broadly, two main explanations have been put forward for why men have dominated culture and ruled the world. The first was accepted nearly everywhere until the twentieth century: that men were naturally superior to women. The forces that created human beings, whether they involved a divine power or the natural processes of evolution (or some combination), made men to be better and created women to help and serve men.

The second explanation was a reaction against the first. It said that women were not inferior to men on any meaningful dimension. Possibly women are superior, but definitely not inferior. Therefore, the difference in social standing had to be explained as oppression. Men must somehow be working together to keep women down. Men devised a clever system for themselves, called patriarchy, and they used it to share rewards and to oppress women.

This book offers a third explanation.

It's not that men are smarter than women (the first theory). It's not that men are wicked conspirators against women (the second theory). It's about some basic likes and dislikes. It's rooted in how men treat other men, and how that is different from the way women relate to other women. It's about how culture works. Due to an accident that just happened to be lucky for men, culture grew out of the way the men related to each other, more than out of women's relationships. There were crucial tradeoffs: Women's relationships were vital for some other things. Just not for constructing large systems, like a market economy, or a large team. Because culture grew out of men's relationships—including competition, trading and communicating with strangers, and ample doses of violence—men were always in charge of it.

Gradually things are changing. Women have asked, and occasionally demanded, to be allowed into the giant systems that men built, and to varying degrees they have been let in.

Meanwhile, there are hardly any places in the world where men are asking (or demanding) to be allowed into giant social systems built up by women. That in itself is not surprising, because such systems hardly exist. But the lack of such female-created social systems is something worth pondering.

What this Book Isn't

Before we get started, let's clear up a few things. This book is not against women. It is not even particularly in favor of men. Along the way I will have various, mostly positive things to say about both genders, but those are not the main point.

One core interest of the book is to examine how culture exploits men. This does not mean I am denying that culture exploits women too. Many cultures do exploit women, some more than others, and sometimes cruelly.

This is not a book based on personal experience. It is certainly not a complaint. I don't regard myself as a victim, either of women or of culture. Women have been very good to me, with a few minor exceptions. Culture has been good to me also, and also with a few minor exceptions.

Nor is this book a pitch to gain victim status for men. The modern widespread eagerness to claim victim status for one's own group makes me ill. If you read this book and end up thinking the main point was that men instead of women should be considered victims, or even assume this status alongside women, then you have completely missed my point, and I have failed to get my message across.

I don't want to be on anybody's side.

Many women are exploited and victimized in their culture. Many unfortunate women have had their lives compromised by society. But men are used and exploited too. We are perhaps more accustomed to seeing how society exploits women, but perhaps that is all the more reason to take a look at the other side too.

The point is how a giant system of social roles, ideas, and conventions can push people to behave in certain ways, including ways that are not in their best interests. These may include working at a job you detest, putting up with being mistreated, or giving up some of your hard-earned money to support people or projects you may not like. It can even include marching across a field toward people who are trying to shoot you, instead of away from them, like any sensible animal would. Culture uses men in some ways and women in others.

If there is a message, it's that it would be better for men and women to appreciate each other's contributions more. Men and women have been partners throughout human history, mostly working together for the good of both. As partners, they have often done quite different things, thereby making different contributions to each other's welfare. That, after all, is how nearly all partnerships work. A bit of mutual gratitude would be quite appropriate.

Gender Warriors Please Go Home

This book is not about the "battle of the sexes." I'm not trying to score points for men against women, or vice versa. I don't think the "battle" approach is healthy. In fact, I think the idea that men and women are natural enemies who conspire deviously to exploit and oppress each other is one of the most misguided and harmful myths that is distorting our current views about men and women.

Feminist theory has had the unfortunate side effect of accustoming us all to thinking of gender in terms of conflict: mainly men oppressing women, and men being threatened by female successes. Instead, I think men and women for the most part work together. Any time people work together, there are occasional conflicts, but these are not the main story. One goal of this book is to reinterpret the relations between men and women as more cooperative and complementary than antagonistic. I think most women don't really see men as the enemy, except as taught by some highly politicized Women's Studies classes. Likewise, most men don't see women as their enemy.

Several years ago, when I first began to give talks about how culture uses men, a fellow came up to me after a major speech. He identified himself as a group therapist who had been conducting all-male group therapy sessions for more than twenty years. He said something that has stuck with me ever since. In all those years of men's groups, he had never once heard any group of men talk about women as the enemy. It wasn't that there was no talk of women—on the contrary, men talked endlessly about women. And plenty of problems were brought up. But their talking was about how can we learn to understand women, how can we get along with women, how can we give them what they want and satisfy them, and how can we build or repair our relationships with women. It was never about how to exploit women or oppress them or "put them in their place," or keep them from being successful at work. The feminist view of what male society is all about is wildly off the mark.

It is possible that women's groups sometimes discuss men as the enemy. Even so, I don't think that is as common as the gender warriors want us to think.

I spent many years teaching and doing my research at a fine private university in Ohio named Case Western Reserve University. It suited me well for many reasons, not least of which was most of the faculty and students seemed indifferent to politics. But the national politics did occasionally or eventually make an impact there. At one of these points, the university administration woke up to the idea that women faculty needed encouragement and support, and they proposed to set up a program to help the women junior faculty get help and advice in launching their careers.

"Junior faculty" is a technical term referring to young professors who do not yet have tenure. It's often a difficult phase of life, because for the first time you are no longer a student and so nobody gives you advice or tells you what to do, and you have to figure out how to juggle all the complicated demands of the job: teaching classes, serving on committees, advising students, running a laboratory and collecting data, and publishing instead of perishing. Across the nation, there were claims that women were finding this an especially difficult time, sometimes complicated by the rush to start a family before one reached the age of 40 and perhaps not getting enough help from the older, tenured (mostly male) professors. Hence, many universities were setting up special programs to help these young women get their careers going. Somebody at my university finally noticed the trend and thought we should have one too.

The university polled the women faculty and contacted the campus women's center to solicit suggestions and comments to find out what the female junior faculty would most like from such a program. The women had a big meeting, discussed the proposal at length, and then voted to approve the plan with one major change: The university should offer it to both men and women.

Obviously, they thought that giving young professors a bit of help and advice was a good thing. But the women didn't think it was fair or necessary that only the female junior faculty should benefit from this. They came out strongly in favor of creating the program to be available to all junior faculty, male and female.

The point of this story is that there is often much less than meets the eye to the so-called Battle of the Sexes. From reading feminist accounts of gender politics one gets the impression that men and women have been collective enemies throughout history (and still are). Instead, I think that in general men and women look upon each other rather favorably and try to treat each other fairly. The generosity of these women professors in wanting to share their programs with their male colleagues is hardly an isolated incident. Nor is such fairness one-sided. Men, too, have been actively and vocally in favor of extending their rights and privileges to women. Even in that story, it was male deans and administrators who had first raised the idea of starting a program for the women faculty.

About Feminism

Any fair assessment of modern American feminism would have to assert that on the one hand, there has been some brilliant and insightful scholarship that has advanced our collective understanding of the truth. Likewise, it would have to acknowledge, on the other hand, that some of it has fostered hatred and readily sacrificed the pursuit of truth for the sake of self-interested political gain. Feminism is a big tent, covering many different views and attitudes.

Many of us, especially those of us past a certain age, have affectionate memories of the feminist movement in the 1970s. We associated feminism with promoting equality, challenging entrenched wisdom, touting openness to free thought and new ideas, and searching in an idealistic spirit for positive views toward both genders. These days many people associate feminism with something quite different, even the opposite: promoting women at the expense of men, defending dogmas, stifling new thought, and deploring men. I used to call myself a feminist but, like many men *and* women, I have grown uncomfortable with the label, given what it has come to mean.

Quite possibly both the old and the new views have something to them. In her book *Who Stole Feminism?* Christina Hoff Sommers argued that the feminist movement had indeed changed from a men-welcoming, idealistic movement promoting one kind of utopia into an antagonistic and often stridently anti-male movement. The very success of the 1960s–1970s feminism at achieving many of its reasonable goals caused many to think the job was done. Fewer moderate women joined, and this left the movement to be taken over by the more radical and fanatical types.

Although feminist ideas are mentioned from time to time in this book, I want to emphasize from the start that I am not debating any actual feminist scholars or the movement of feminist thought itself. In fact, I strongly suspect there is no point in debating with feminists.

The business of feminism was aptly summarized by Daphne Patai and Noretta Koertge, two scholars who have spent their careers in Women's Studies programs and who wrote a thoughtful book, *Professing Feminism*, on what passes for scholarly activity in those departments. Crucially, they pointed out that most feminists do not pay any attention to criticisms from non-feminists. They listen a little bit to criticism from each other—but that mainly concerns the purity of their commitment to feminist politics and doctrine. When scientists criticize each other, they focus mainly on research methods and how well different possible theories fit the data. That sort of thing is not common in Women's Studies, according to Patai and Koertge.

That means that even if an outsider like me made the most brilliant, correct, and insightful point against some feminist claim, the feminists wouldn't listen or change their views one iota. So why bother?

Meet the Imaginary Feminist

There is however one reason I will occasionally need to mention feminist views. For better or worse, feminists have dominated discourse about gender and how men and women relate to each other. Their views have become the standard, conventional wisdom. Many readers will automatically think of standard feminist views when I bring up issues like why women earn less money than men (e.g., the system of patriarchy oppresses women by not giving them a fair wage).

My argument is not with actual feminist scholars, and especially not with the most open-minded and thoughtful among them. Indeed, my thinking has been informed by them, some of whom are quite brilliant. Rather, my argument is with a certain stereotyped feminist outlook. I am arguing not with actual feminists, but with *feminists as they are perceived by men*.

Let me therefore introduce a character, the Imaginary Feminist, who will crop up from time to time to remind us of the established wisdom. The most advanced intellectual feminists may object to what she says and to my depiction of her. They may say, "that's not necessarily what all feminists assert." I agree. I don't care. I need to address the misconceptions that many men have about gender relations. The Imaginary Feminist represents these. The extent to which actual feminists are responsible for these views is debatable,: it might be extensive or it might be less. But before you dismiss the views of the Imaginary Feminist as irrelevant, ask a few men whether her comments are indeed those they would expect many feminists to express.

Again, I freely admit she doesn't speak for all feminists (as if anybody does). She represents the sorts that men notice the most. These include the ones who have campaigned to have urinals removed from public lavatories so that men will be forced to sit down to urinate, on the grounds that when men urinate standing up they are dominating and oppressing women. These include the ones who cheered the news that Title IX accomplished more in the way of canceling men's sports teams than promoting women's teams. They include the leaders who urged women to become lesbians because sex with men was "sleeping with the enemy." They include the ones who insult men who hold the door for them or, more generally, who attack anything men say and ultimately try to intimidate men from having or expressing opinions. In short, these are the grumpy and simplistic ones who explain everything in terms of male wickedness and oppression.

Who Stands Out?

When I proposed this book, I said that the hostility between the sexes had been overstated. I mentioned as an example the women's suffrage movement. I pointed out that women got the vote because a majority of men, only men, voted to extend the vote to women. That was hardly resistance. I said compared to the way men react when they really do want to resist somebody—such as when men fight a military invasion by an enemy—men had essentially welcomed women with open arms and affirmative action.

One reviewer objected strenuously. She said I should learn some history. The campaigners for women's suffrage had endured verbal and occasionally physical abuse. Hunger strikers had been force-fed, and so on.

She was right about those particulars, of course. On the other hand, I was also right about the voting. To understand the correctness of both views, one has to distinguish between the general pattern and the most salient and confrontational minority. It works both ways.

The actions of the male majority are indisputable, because the election depended on them. Most men voted to extend the vote to women. These men were not conquered or overwhelmed by invaders, nor were they cowed into submission.

To the suffragettes and others, however, the support from the relatively silent majority of men was less visible perhaps than the overt hostility and occasionally violent abuse from the most vocal minority. Hence, one can understand that many women saw men in general as actively resisting them. The nasty few left much more of an impression than the friendly many.

The same logic applies, with roles reversed, to the way men today perceive feminists. No doubt there are many women who identify themselves as feminists yet who do not hate men and may even like them, who may believe in equal opportunity for everyone rather than advancing the cause of their gender at the expense of men, who believe in telling the truth even if it is not favorable to their cause, and who do not resort to moral intimidation to silence men and dominate any debate. Yet these are not the feminists who stand out to men. The confrontational minority of feminists act as if they represent all feminists (indeed all women), and men have had much more contact with them than with the more harmoniously and peaceably inclined ones, precisely because they are outspoken and confrontational. It is with their views that I will occasionally need to take issue. They are the ones for whom the Imaginary Feminist speaks.

Oppression and Prejudice

One main theme that the Imaginary Feminist will bring up over and over is that society is riddled with prejudice against women and that the history of male–female relations consists of various ways in which men have oppressed women. This has become a standard view. If you question it, the Imaginary Feminist does not typically respond with carefully reasoned arguments or clear data. Instead, she accuses you of being prejudiced and oppressive even for questioning the point.

If she does point to evidence, it will be something like "women earn less money than men" or "people prefer sons to daughters." These are supposed to qualify as proof.

In science, especially social science, statistical data are often a bit slippery and there are often several possible explanations for any finding. Having spent my career engaged in this business, I can vouch for what goes on when you try to publish the results of experiments you have done: There is debate among the reviewers chiefly as to whether you have ruled out all other possible explanations, other than your preferred one, for your findings.

Yet sometimes claims about oppression and prejudice seem immune to this process. They are not treated with the same strict discipline that other scientific theories must encounter.

Take the difference in salary. This will be discussed at several points in this book, but for now we are concerned with the simple question: Do women's generally lower salaries prove that society oppresses women?

Other researchers have examined this question, and the oppression hypothesis routinely has taken a beating. There are multiple possible explanations for the gender salary gap, and several have much clearer support than oppression. Men are more likely than women to work full-time rather than part-time. On average across the population, men are more ambitious than women. They work harder and put in hundreds more hours per year. Men are less likely than women to take a few years off during the crucial career-building years of their thirties. Men take bigger risks than women. Men are more willing to sacrifice other sorts of career benefits, such as freedom from travel requirements, low stress, and even personal safety, for a higher salary. Men are more likely than women to negotiate for a higher salary. All these contribute to higher male salaries.

The preference for boy babies is an interesting case, particularly to me because early in my career, I used to lecture about this in connection with prejudice against girls and women. The research finding I read when I was writing my first lectures back in 1979 was that parents were more likely to have another child if their first or previous child had been a girl than a boy. The explanation given at that time was that parents really want sons, and so if they have a girl, they regard the reproductive event as a failure and are eager to try again, whereas if they have a son, they are satisfied and so they stop. It made sense to me. As a trusting young member of the field, I believed what was in the journals, and I passed that interpretation along in my lectures.

But in fact, there are alternative explanations. I have seen multiple sets of parents, even some who obviously had strong pro-female sentiments, go through the same pattern of having another child after a daughter but stopping after a son, and it seemed absurd to accuse them of anti-female bias. They loved their daughters. What they said, and what research evidence also shows (if anyone had bothered to look before attributing parental choices to sexism), is that girl babies are generally easier than boy babies. Not always, of course, but often enough to account for the pattern we are describing.

Many couples are apprehensive as the birth of their first child approaches. How will their lives change? Will they be good parents? Will they be able to cope? And then a sweet little girl baby arrives. A bit of adjustment here and there, and the couple thinks, hey, this is not bad at all! What was everyone warning and complaining about? Having a baby is easy and so very satisfying. Let's have another!

Boy babies are more trouble. They scream and cry more often than girl babies, and louder too. (Incidentally, this well-documented finding has been recognized as an important challenge to the conventional claim that females are more emotional than males.) Once they start crawling and walking, they get into things. They make bigger messes. They climb the furniture and pull the draperies. They fight with other kids. Parents who have boys think, this is difficult. Let's not have any more of these.

Recently I visited China. The preference for boys there is well entrenched in the culture and it is hard to deny that there is overt preference, to the point of prejudice. Today, with the one-child policy preventing parents from trying again if they have a daughter, it has been necessary to make it illegal to determine a baby's gender before birth, because of selective abortion of female fetuses. When a couple has a son, my Chinese colleagues told me, everyone congratulates them: "That's great!" If the couple has a daughter, friends carefully say, "Also good!" In rural areas, where laws are somewhat less stringent, couples who have a daughter are sometimes permitted to try again for a son, whereas if the first child is a son, no more children are allowed.

Yet even there, it may be overly hasty to attribute these attitudes to oppression and prejudice. My Chinese colleagues pointed out that Chinese tradition and law stipulate that a son is responsible for taking care of his parents in their old age. A daughter is not. If your son does not provide for you, you can sue him, and there were such cases in the courts, as reported in the newspapers I read while I was there. You cannot sue your daughter, though. In a society that does not have reliable pensions, Social Security, and other provisions for the elderly, this is extremely important. The desire for a son is not necessarily a sign of some irrational bigoted hatred of the female gender. It may simply be a prudent concern with who is going to feed you when you are too old to work. You can't count on your employer or the government to do it. You can't even force your daughter to do it. But you can force your son to do it.

The law and tradition are themselves quite relevant to one theme of this book. Males are required to support their parents, while females are exempt from this requirement. This is not to say that Chinese society is full of laws that favor females across the board. But it is one small sign of what we shall focus on in this book, namely how societies choose to use men. If that law applied to women and not men, our Imaginary Feminist would quickly use the word "exploit," as in society is exploiting women by making them do things that it does not require men to do. If we want to understand gender and culture, we need to have our eyes open to how society exploits men as well as women.

He, She, and It

I shall propose that men and women are different in some basic ways and that some cultures—successful ones—capitalize on these differences to outperform rival cultures. The Imaginary Feminist asks, why not matriarchy? Why can't women rule? I say, yes, why not? Whatever works is likely to be tried, eventually, and what works best will prevail over rival systems.

It has been tried. Unfortunately, those matriarchal cultures and societies did not stand the test of time. There is probably a good reason. In fact, I shall suggest that women can rule, and even quite effectively. But usually they don't. It's not a matter of competence or capability. More likely, it has to do with the willingness to take the risks and make the sacrifices that are involved in competing for power.

To understand why men and women have the lives they do, it is necessary to move beyond thinking of them as enemies. A more useful way of thinking will include at least three entities rather than the duo of men against women. The third is the cultural system itself.

The system is not exactly an independent force. But humans use systems to make their lives better. In other writings, I have gone so far as to conclude that culture is humankind's biological strategy. It is how people attempt to solve the basic biological problems that all species face: survival and reproduction. We have culture, a system that shares information, coordinates different tasks, and increases wealth. In general, we live vastly better in culture than we would live if we were suddenly left by ourselves in the forest and had to scrape by with our own muscles and wits.

Some might object to the need to talk about the culture or the system as a separate entity. Isn't the system just something made up by people? In a sense, yes, but that does not imply that people can simply dissolve it or change it. When the bank forecloses your house, or your firm's economic outlook leads to downsizing and you lose your job, or war is declared and you are summoned to put on a uniform and risk your life—then it becomes quite obvious that the system has power that individuals cannot deny or even very effectively resist. Almost everybody wishes the great economic collapse of 2008 could be reversed, but it can't. The system is not a fiction at our command.

The system uses people in different ways. People put up with this because, mostly, they are better off with it than without it. True, the system is created by people, but they also experience it as beyond their power to control. We may try to change our culture by voting, but that exercise reveals how little control we really have. You can vote in every election all your life and still remain dissatisfied with your culture.

This book seeks to understand the relationships and interactions among men, women, and culture. Even that simple triangle is not a complete explanation, however. Most cultures have had to compete against other cultures. To survive, a culture has to do more than provide decent lives for the men and women in it. It may have to accumulate the wherewithal to compete against other cultures. Competition can be economic, military, technological, or intellectual. Often it has been simply demographic: Larger groups typically prevail over smaller ones.

In short, cultures have challenges. To survive, they must use their men and women effectively. That does not necessarily mean using men and women in the same ways. In fact, most cultures have used men and women in somewhat different ways.

How Can Men Be Exploited if They Run Everything?

Let's turn now to one of the most important and basic questions about this book's project. When I tell people I'm studying how culture exploits men, the first response is often to question how anyone could possibly think that society exploits men, given that men are in charge of everything. This is a fair objection, and we should take it seriously.

How, indeed, can we say that men are exploited by society? On the one hand, it is true that men dominate society. They occupy the vast majority of power positions as presidents, prime ministers, and other rulers. Except for those few countries that have constitutions requiring half of the legislature to be female, the parliament or congress is generally full of men. The private sector is no different. Most large corporations are headed by men. There is some debate as to whether there is a real "glass ceiling" that actually prevents women from rising to the top, but regardless of how it comes about, the power elite is full of men.

This is a standard riposte if anyone starts to point out the problems or difficulties men have. Certainly, the Imaginary Feminist won't listen to any talk about men being oppressed. Men shouldn't complain. Only women have the right to complain. It seems a straightforward step from noting that men are on top of the elite power structures to saying that it must be great to be a man and that society is set up to favor men with privileges and advantages, not to exploit them. The Imaginary Feminist gets quite angry at any insistence that culture victimizes men, and she would point to evidence of male rule.

In the United States, at last count, men occupy the presidency and vice presidency. They hold all but one of the Supreme Court seats. They hold a bit over 80% of the seats in the Senate and in the House of Representatives. The same is true for the office of governor of specific states. Men occupy more than 90% of the CEO positions in the Fortune 500 top American corporations. And so on. Similar patterns occur throughout the world.

In short, and to oversimplify, men run the world. Seeing this, it is easy to think (as many feminists have) that society is set up to favor men. It must be great to be a man.

Hence the question, once again: How can you say men are exploited, if they run everything?

The answer to this is important, because it opens the door for many of the other points this book will make.

Meanwhile, at the Bottom

The mistake in that way of thinking is to look only at the top of society and draw conclusions about society as a whole. Yes, there are mostly men at the top. But if you look at the bottom, really at the bottom, you'll find mostly men there too. These are the worst outcomes society has to confer. And in each case, men far outnumber women.

Look at the prisons, for example. According to the U.S. Department of Justice statistics, nine out of ten prison inmates is a man. Life doesn't get much worse than being in prison, at least not in America. (If you really want to see worse than just being in prison, look specifically at Death Row. There are almost no women ever on Death Row. Is anyone calling for some affirmative action there? The courts demanded that other institutions, like universities and corporations, work toward equal representation of men and women. How about the courts applying the same criteria to themselves and insisting that women get half of seats in the electric chair? But of course that would be ridiculous.)

Moreover, the law-enforcement system has a strong bias against men. (Imagine if our society were half as indignant about the police engaging in gender profiling as it is about their racial profiling!) Warren Farrell documented this in his book *The Myth of Male Power*. When men and women are convicted of the same crimes, the men get much longer prison sentences than the women. This is on top of the fact that men are more likely to be charged and prosecuted in the first place, so that the few women who are convicted are probably much more serious offenders than the average male convict. For example, if a man and a woman are arrested together for some offense, the standard procedure is to get the woman to testify for the state and then grant her immunity or a reduced sentence, so that the man is held mainly responsible.

Another group at the bottom of society is the homeless. More men than women are homeless. In fact, for many years homeless people were almost exclusively men. Farrell has also noted how attitudes toward the homeless changed with gender makeup. When homeless people were almost entirely men, they were regarded as immoral trash, and they were called bums and tramps. The first homeless women were called bag ladies, and the "lady" term denotes a respect that was never accorded the males. Gradually, the increase in female homelessness made that population seen as a group deserving of support, care, and interventions, instead of contempt. But we still do not hear of "bag gentlemen."

Women are not 51% of the homeless. Exact numbers are elusive, of course, but the preponderance of males is indisputable. A recent Italian study on homelessness concluded that about 15% are women. The U.S. National Coalition for the Homeless notes that there are about three times as many single homeless men as women.

The point remains. Homelessness is another category of life at the bottom of society. And far more men than women are to be found there.

Let's now look at one place that's another kind of bottom and also clearly indicates societal exploitation. That's death on the job. Society needs people to do all its various jobs, and some of those jobs are dangerous. Somebody has to climb out on the roof, or exchange gunfire with the criminals, or run into burning buildings, or sail the stormy seas to rescue the desperate, or even just drive cars and trucks on the busy or dark roads that kill so many. Some of those people will end up injured or, in the worst case, killed. According to the U.S. Department of Labor Statistics, these days there is still a severe imbalance in death on the job, by about twelve to one: 92% of Americans who die in the line of work are men. This is true despite the fact that there are almost as many women as men employed in America.

One more spot at the bottom deserves mention: being killed in battle. Most societies in world history have needed to put warriors on the battlefield, and many have failed to come home. These casualties have overwhelmingly been men.

That's changing, one might say. Women are entering combat and sharing the risk. Although correct, it is beside the point. Women's progress in sharing the risk of combat death is accompanied by women sharing many of the rewards that society has also, such as prestigious and well-paying jobs. Plus, women's progress into high-paying jobs has been faster than their progress into risk and danger. Much has been made in the media about the second Iraq war, in which women did enter combat and take fire and, yes, get shot. Even so, it was hardly a matter of shouldering half the risk. In 2007, the Iraq war passed the sad milestone of 3,000 American deaths (including everything from being shot in combat to being killed in a traffic accident). Of those dead soldiers, 2,938 were men. The 62 women comprised about 2% of the deaths.

None of this is meant to minimize or ignore women's suffering. Women have suffered plenty of bad things over the centuries. Even those who were not killed in war have often found hardship, victimization, and sometimes death as a result of war. My first point is just that the conventional view of men enjoying lives of ease and privilege while women toil and suffer is not correct.

Men are more expendable than women, at least from the perspective of the cultural system. Actually, this will be one of the keys to understanding the different ways that culture uses men and women. The idea has several roots, some as deep as the basic ability to make babies for the next generation, to enable cultures to compete simply by outnumbering their rivals: a culture needs only a few men but as many women as possible.

Seeing Both Sides

Yes, there are more men than women at the top of society, but there are also far more men than women at the bottom. The two are related. Society uses men and women differently.

In this instance, the error that led to thinking society simply favors men was understandable. Women felt they were at the bottom of the power structure, and so they looked up toward the top and saw men there. It was easy to think that the whole system is set up to benefit men and make men superior. Even today, whenever someone starts to say that life can be hard for men, the quick and loud response stifles any further discussion: men are still in charge, so quit complaining.

Probably the one-sided conventional view had its roots in the feminist critique of society as patriarchy, which is to say a conspiracy by men to exploit women. Feminists have acknowledged that they look at the world from women's point of view. Sitting there, they looked up toward the top. They saw men at the top, and they thought, men are in charge of things, wow, it must be great to be a man. Society must be set up to benefit men.

They are right that men are generally in charge of things. These men may have some problems, but it is quite fair to say that they enjoy a large share of the rewards society has to offer. In that sense, some men really do have it good. It is even correct to say that throughout most of history (things may be slowly changing now), the men at the top have enjoyed rewards and benefits better than those women could hope to attain. But the other conclusions —that it's therefore great to be a man, and society is set up to benefit men—are biased by the error of ignoring the downside.

One of the most interesting books about gender in recent years was by Norah Vincent. She was a lesbian feminist who with some expert help could pass for a man, and so she went undercover, living as a man in several different social spheres for the better part of a year. The book, *Self-Made Man*, is her memoir. She is quite frank that she started out thinking she was going to find out how great men have it and write a shocking feminist expose of the fine life that the enemy (men) was enjoying.

Instead, she experienced a rude awakening of how hard it is to be a man. Her readings and classes in Women's Studies had not prepared her to realize that the ostensible advantages of the male role come at a high cost. She was glad when it was over, and in fact she cut the episode short in order to go back to what she concluded was a greatly preferable life as a woman. The book she wrote was far different from the one she planned, and any woman who thinks life is better for men will find it a sobering read.

We shall have plenty more to say about the men at the top. They are an important part of the story about how culture uses and, yes, exploits men. The men at the top do often enjoy a big share of the rewards culture offers, so some may be reluctant to say they are exploited. Culture does, however, use them for its own advantage, even while it dispenses big rewards to them. But for now, we need to balance our recognition of men at the top by also seeing the men at the bottom.

After all, if we simply made the same kind of reasoning error but in the opposite direction, we could focus exclusively on the men at the bottom. We could say, look at the people ground up by society, imprisoned, executed, unemployed, sent to early deaths, and we would see that they are mainly men. Extrapolating, we could reasonably conclude from them that society is set up to benefit women by protecting them from these miserable fates and by sacrificing men instead. We could say, it must be great to be a woman. This conclusion would be wrong and biased—just as wrong and biased as the conventional wisdom about how great men have it.

Making Different Choices

The fact that men outnumber women at both the top and bottom of society is an important clue to how culture uses the genders differently. Although in modern society women can be found in just about all walks of life, men still outnumber them at the extremes, and in the past this difference has been even greater.

It is simple but misleading to focus on one aspect and concentrate on that. Unfortunately, that's what conventional wisdom has done. If you follow the popular media, you see and hear plenty about the gender gap in pay and the general unfairness about women earning less than men. Meanwhile, you will see and hear very little about the gender gap in occupational death. I have yet to see anyone writing that it's unfair for men to be killed so much more often than women.

Very likely, those two gaps have some link. Society has to pay people more to take dangerous jobs. All else being equal, would you take a job that carried a significant risk of being killed or maimed, rather than a job with no such risks? Of course not. But there are such jobs, and the culture needs somebody to do them. It knows nobody will choose such jobs if all else is equal—so it has to make all else not equal. The standard way to do that is with pay. Society increases the pay for dangerous jobs in order to get people to take them. This is called a tradeoff.

Tradeoffs will be important throughout this book. In fact, I think gender theory needs to acknowledge tradeoffs much more than it has.

Consider, then, the tradeoff of money and danger. Suppose you were contemplating two jobs, identical in most respects, but one of which had a higher risk of injury and death. On that basis, as I've said, any rational person would choose the safe job. But now suppose the employer for the dangerous job was willing to increase the salary. How much more money would you want to compensate you for a slight increase in risk? Most likely, you would accept a slight increase in risk for a huge increase in salary. (After all, every time you drive on the highway you accept a slight risk of being killed, but the anticipated benefits of the trip make it worth it.) Therefore, the question becomes one of trading off money against risk: how much more money versus how much increase in risk.

Confronted with such tradeoffs, men and women tend to see different tipping points. I'm sure it is possible to pay the average woman enough extra to make her willing to take more risk. But the average man will take that same risk for a smaller increase in salary. And so the employing organizations tend to stop there. Many research studies have shown that men put more emphasis on money when choosing jobs and careers than women do. As a result, these men earn more than the women who took the safer careers. As another result, some of these men will end up injured or killed, more so than the women who took the safer careers.

Taking and doing those dangerous jobs is thus one thing men are good for. That is one way that most cultures use men more than women.

CHAPTER 2

Are Women Better than Men, or Vice Versa?

LL MY ADULT LIFE, I've heard a steady stream of information, largely uninterrupted, about how women are better than men. It's exceedingly rare to hear a news story about men being found to be superior to women in anything, but every so often there is another new set of findings on another area where women are better than men.

Certainly one doesn't hear much good news about men these days. Books with titles like *Men Are Not Cost Effective* speak for themselves. Maureen Dowd's book *Are Men Necessary?* never explicitly answered its titular question, but anyone who read the book knows her answer was fairly clearly no. She spent many gleeful pages saying women are better than men at this or that, but despite the title I couldn't find any sections devoted to what men were necessary for, except maybe the parts about paying for dates. And even there, she didn't think men were necessary, just suckers.

The news media are not much better. For example, as I write this, a recent issue of *The Economist*, my main source of news, had this to say. "Future generations might ask why a man can't be more like a woman.... Arguably, women are now the most powerful engine of global growth." The assumption of the superiority of women was hardly concealed there. "To make men feel even worse, researchers have also concluded that women make better investors than they do." Makes you wonder why stockbrokers aren't all women. "Studies have also suggested that women are often better than men at building teams." Watch out, NFL! The article ended by saying that it is time men did more of the housework.

A recent column in the highly respected *Chronicle of Higher Education* (that's what university presidents and deans read, among others) was called "Who needs men?" You get the idea. Actually it did make a feeble attempt at balance and conceded that men had done a few good things in the past, but it concluded that men had outlived their usefulness, and, apart from the logistical problem of getting rid of all men, said the world would be better off without them. Imagine anyone saying that about women!

On television, things are even worse. Back in the early 1990s my wife and I heard about a report on gender bias in advertising. The researchers in that study compiled all the commercials they could find depicting men and women competing against each other, such as when two people were trying to rush to get to their business meeting using cars they had rented from different companies. The researchers found that the women were depicted as winning these competitions 100% of the time. My wife and I were skeptical of this, because we are social scientists and know there is always variation. No pattern holds up 100% of the time! And so we've kept an eye on commercials ever since. Perhaps twice in more than a decade we may have seen saw a commercial that in a halfhearted way depicted the man being right and the woman wrong about something. But in general, the study was correct. Try it yourself. On television, when commercials pit men against women, the women always win.

That's advertising. The shows and situation comedies are hardly better. Older shows such as *My Three Sons* and *Father Knows Best* depicted fathers as intelligent, competent, caring human beings, but I haven't seen any such shows in a long time. Most Hollywood fathers are simply buffoons and caricatures. A few are downright evil, though more so in TV movies and dramas than in comedies. See if you can find a show that makes the woman look stupid while the man looks wise or kind. I doubt you'll succeed. But the reverse scenario, with only the man looking bad, is standard fare.

Children's books are much the same. Sometimes, to be sure, both parents are depicted as stupid, but if only one parent is depicted as wise and kind, it is almost always the mother. Fathers come across the worst in the stories that little children hear as they grow up.

You can hear it even in the way people talk. I recall listening to two literature professors discussing their interpretive strategies, and they bandied about the terms "masculinist" and "feminist." Although both of the professors were men, it was obvious that to them, "masculinist" was bad and "feminist" was good, and they were striving to outdo each other as to whose ideas were more feminist.

Maybe this can all be dismissed as propaganda, as political correctness, as fear of boycotts, as mere fiction and poetic license. What do real human beings actually believe?

The most thorough research on the question has been that conducted by Alice Eagly and her colleagues. They compiled mountains of data by asking large numbers of people, both men and women, about what traits they associated with men and women. In this age of political correctness, people are somewhat careful about what they say, but across thousands of questionnaires with dozens if not hundreds of ratings on each, one can gradually get an idea of what people really think. And despite any PC pressure to say that men and women are the same and to reject traditional stereotypes, Eagly's group found that people do indeed think men and women are different.

After wading through years' worth of questionnaire data and reams of statistical analyses, Eagly and her group concluded that there is one, overriding, general pattern. They called it "the WAW effect." WAW stands for "women are wonderful." That's the gist of the way people perceive differences between men and women today. Women are wonderful human beings. Or at least they seem wonderful in comparison to men.

Again, this is not the biased view of a small coterie of man-haters, but one emerging from multiple samples of mostly young people today, both men and women included. Both men and women think women are better people than men.

To be sure, men still outnumber women as top achievers in some domains. Does that mean that in some respects men are better than women? Hardly. We have all been taught to dismiss superior male achievement as evidence of prejudice and oppression.

Some do feel bad for the men, especially the young guys today, because they can't win. When men do worse than women, people say it's because women are better at this or that. When men do better than women, people say it's because women are oppressed, presumably by men, and so men are evil. Either way, men end up looking bad.

It Wasn't Always Thus

Some years ago there was a news story claiming that women were better than men at multitasking. Everyone seems to have heard of this and accepted it, though if you search for actual scientific evidence the conclusion is dubious. (Some brain scans offer reason to think women would be better at it, and an occasional study with an esoteric procedure finds it, but more systematic studies find no difference. Plus, recent evidence suggests that multitasking—doing several things at once—mainly leads to doing a worse job at all of them.) I even heard it mentioned on the reality show *Survivor*. But somebody said it once, and it was widely accepted. If someone had asserted that men were better at it, immediately there would have been skepticism and outrage and it would have been shot down pretty fast. A false statement about the superiority of women may go unchallenged.

Why the relentless stream of such stories? Student journalists are taught the "man bites dog" principle. Dogs bite people all the time, and so this is hardly news. But a man biting a dog, that is rare, and so deserves a headline and a story.

Obviously, many in the media still think that female superiority has a bit of the newsworthiness of man biting dog. They think people are still surprised to hear about women being superior to men. As this kind of story has become the norm and the established prejudice of the majority of people, its novelty has begun to fade, but it may also get a boost from precisely that prejudice, because people do like to hear news that confirms their stereotypes, and so women surpassing or outperforming men will be well received (and thus increase sales and advertising). Stories about the first woman this-or-that obviously do still qualify as man biting dog, because by definition the first woman to do something is unusual, even if hundreds or even thousands of men have done it before.

The point is that in the past, most people thought men were better than women—precisely the opposite of now. No doubt, the endless stream of stories about female superiority are still feeding off of this (increasingly quaint) assumption of male superiority.

In essence, we have been rebelling against the assumption of male superiority by going to the opposite extreme. After all, one of the great themes of the women's movement has been that women aren't inferior to men. Going back a bit in time, both men and women shared the assumption that men were superior. The most optimistic advocates of women thought that women could be almost as good as men at most things.

Prevailing Views About Men and Women

There are four possible answers to the question of whether men or women are better. At different times, three of them have reigned as the prevailing view. The fourth, somehow never popular, is probably the right one.

Up till the 1960s, psychology focused on men and used men as the model for the human psyche. Women were considered an inferior version. Psychologists, mainly men, studied mainly college students, who were also mainly men. Nobody much thought of this as a psychology of men. The goal was to build a psychology of people, and men were the obvious ones with which to get started. Periodically psychologists would suggest that one or another general principle might be slightly different for women. These differences sometimes took the form of implying that women lacked a bit of something, like ambition or resilience or a penis or logic or emotional restraint.

Then in the 1970s there was a brief period of denying that there were any real differences between the sexes. Supposedly it was cultural stereotypes and biased upbringing that made boys and girls turn out differently, but the differences, weren't even skin deep. If we could eliminate prejudices and discrimination and stereotypes from how we raised our children, then boys and girls would grow up to be the same.

This idealistic belief in how to fix parental prejudice led to one of the great surprises of my generation. As students, we learned and embraced the idea that gender inequalities and even gender differences were all due to socialization and so that if we simply treated our sons and daughters the same, they would grow up the same. A generation of modern, enlightened parents tried this as best they could. Surprise! It didn't work.

In one fairly typical story, two of my professional colleagues gave their five-year-old daughter a truck and their two-year-old son a big doll for Christmas, thereby reversing any stereotypical influences and teaching them that it was all right to play with different toys. The parents congratulated themselves on how progressive and forward-thinking they were, but it didn't last long. "They just swapped," as the adults tell the story with a mild laugh and shrug. Apparently there wasn't even any negotiation or discussion between the two little ones. Each just immediately preferred the other toy and somehow knew the other was feeling the same way.

Since the late 1970s, the field has largely taken the view that women are superior, and men are an inferior copy. In essence, it is the same approach that was used before 1960, but with the genders switched. Now women are the model and the ideal, and men are seen as the flawed version of the human species.

So we have had three different prevailing theories: men better than women, no difference, and women better than men. These require a bit of comment before we get to the fourth possible theory.

These shifts in theory came about more from political than scientific factors. The assumption of male superiority was central to our culture during most of its history, as in most cultures. The rebellion against it was largely political, and scientists climbed on the feminist bandwagon. Scientists make their careers by finding new patterns, and when it became acceptable to find proof of female superiority, there were plenty of things to find. There was a period of arguing that there were no differences other than products of stereotypes and socializing influences, fueled partly by the discovery that many differences were not so deep and ironclad as had been thought.

The study of gender differences attracted women and especially feminists. The early feminists wanted equality, and it served their goal to deny that there were any real gender differences. But female chauvinists were among them, those who resented and disliked men, and they gradually took control of the feminist movement. Hence, they embraced any findings of women being better than men, even if it went against the equality theme. Gradually the feminists in gender studies abandoned the idea of equality. Why settle for a tie when you can be sure of winning?

The Puzzling Thing

Much can be said about the switch from male superiority to female superiority as the predominant (though in both cases scientifically dubious) belief, but I here focus on a particular aspect. How could such a dramatic switch occur in such a short time? Why did men go from respected to despised beings in a little over a decade? How could society flip from one extreme to another so quickly and easily?

Obviously, an aspiring science such as psychology loses credibility when it just shifts from one theory to the opposite without convincing evidence. How could psychology jump from men being superior to women being superior? Part of the answer is that psychology's switch mirrored what was happening in the society at large, but that doesn't really answer the question. To begin with, how could society switch so fast?

The answer will provide a valuable first lesson about one important, basic difference between men and women. The next several sections will develop this point.

Women and Science

In January 2005, Lawrence Summers, at the time the president of Harvard University, ignited a national controversy by speculating about why there were more men than women among the tenured professors in the natural sciences departments at Harvard. As far as I can tell, he didn't actually say anything that constituted oppression or discrimination, nor did anyone accuse him of having been biased against women in his policies. His crimes were crimes of thought. He expressed some ideas that aren't permitted to be thought. He wondered whether there were more men than women at the highest levels of intellectual ability.

What followed has been described as a heated debate, though "debate" implies an exchange of views between two sides, and most of what was said was simply critical of him and his right to say what he did. "Scandal" would be a more appropriate word than "debate" or "controversy," because nobody was saying he was right. The only debate was as to how severely he should be punished for thinking and saying that there might be more men than women with the high level of innate ability required for making major breakthroughs in the natural sciences.

Summers was forced to back down and apologize and, not long after, he resigned, though the resignation was forced by multiple factors in the institutional politics of the university. Before he resigned, he had to go beyond apology and pledge to spend 50 million of Harvard's dollars to help solve the problem of the lack of women scientists. This was pledged in the name of "diversity," though as various pundits drily pointed out, it clearly wasn't for promoting diversity of opinion. On the contrary, the episode suggested that diversity of opinion is not welcome at Harvard.

Rather, the money was essentially to provide funding for women scientists and feminist administrators to analyze what is wrong with Harvard to cause it to have fewer women than men among its top scientists.

Our interest here is less in Summers' sorry saga than in the terms of the so-called debate. Almost everything I read about this discussion focused on the divisive issue of whether women are less capable than men at performing high-level science and math. He has been quoted, usually with derision, on that issue ever since.

Everyone insisted how wrong he was. For example, Louann Brizendine, in her book *The Female Brain*, says Summers was "dead wrong" to assert that men are better at science than women. Responsible scientists almost never use terms like "dead wrong," though self-righteous chauvinists, when they are confident of their political correctness and reader sympathy, don't mind using such language.

What do the data actually say? Summers' critics do have data to which they can point. To be precisely fair, there is a small difference between average male and female scores on math and science aptitude tests, with males scoring slightly higher. But it is hardly enough to explain the severe gender imbalance in Harvard physicists or Nobel Prize winners.

The main research finding toward which his detractors can point, I believe, is that on average, women and men are equally intelligent. Average IQ scores are about the same in men as in women. (Throughout childhood, girls score higher than boys, and then the boys catch up and move very slightly ahead in adulthood.) Anyone who says that on average men are meaningfully smarter than women overall is wrong. Depending on which studies you cite and how small a difference you will accept, there is either no difference at all or such a small difference that it is meaningless for practical purposes.

(Incidentally, the recently popular opinion that women are smarter than men is equally unjustified.)

Everybody agreed, of course, that there are in actual fact more men than women among Harvard's tenured professors in natural sciences. In this, Harvard is similar to most other places. Among top scientists all over the world, men outnumber the women.

And the question is why. Summers was pilloried for suggesting it might have to do with ability. The Imaginary Feminist is ready with an answer, of course. The only politically correct, socially acceptable explanation focuses on prejudice and discrimination. We all want to believe that women have just as much native ability as men but somehow are being kept out of these top jobs. Patriarchy—the idea that culture is a conspiracy by men to oppress women—is the preferred explanation whenever women don't perform as well as men.

Strictly Speaking

But Summers did not actually say that men are smarter than women. Nor did he say men are better at math and science than women are.

Math and science ability, like intelligence generally, is distributed along a continuum, with plenty of average people in the middle and small numbers scattered at the extremes. What Dr. Summers said was that at the high end—where the math and science genius-level intellects are found—there are more men than women.

This doesn't mean that men are on average smarter than women, though it could have meant that. After all, if men and women are found in roughly equal numbers all along the distribution except at the genius level, then the male average IQ would be higher.

But a surplus of men at the high end could also mean that there are more men at both extremes. It is possible to have more male than female geniuses even if the average IQ for men and women were exactly the same to the tenth decimal place—provided there are also more men than women at the other extreme, that is, with very low intelligence. In other words, it is statistically possible that there are more super-smart men than women, if there are also more hugely stupid men than women.

The crucial test case, therefore, is to look at the extreme low end. No one in the Summers debate brought this up or even asked whether there are more males at the bottom of the IQ distribution.

The data about low intelligence are indisputable, and far more definite than the data on genius, simply because researchers study mental retardation far more than they study giftedness.

There are more mentally retarded boys than girls. No matter what test or population you study, there are always more males.

There's no way around it. At the extreme low end of intelligence, males outnumber females.

In fact, as you move from the mildly retarded levels to the most severely retarded, the gender difference gets bigger—further evidence that it's a real effect. And, crucially, that is the same pattern found with genius: as you go from mild to moderate to extreme, there are fewer and fewer girls relative to the number of boys. Super-genius and severely retarded are both mostly boys' clubs, though a few exceptional girls do show up too.

All those retarded boys are not the handiwork of patriarchy! There is no conspiracy by men to make each other's sons mentally retarded. Somehow it just happens that there are more retarded boys than girls.

Nor is it some unlucky stereotype or the product of biased socialization. Nobody tries to bring up their children to be retarded. No parent wants to have a mentally handicapped child, whether a son or a daughter. The familiar litany of social causes, from expectations to selective pressures and socialization, hardly seems likely to be at work in producing all those boys who lack the ability to think, reason, and understand at a normal level. But more parents of sons than of daughters end up with a retarded child.

If the oversupply of retarded boys is not the result of men defending patriarchy, then quite likely the oversupply of genius boys isn't either. The most likely explanation is that some strong influence of Mother Nature produces both extremes. Something in the biology of maleness produces more cases at both extremes. (More about that later.)

Now, let's not overstate the case. There are plenty of female geniuses, just like there are plenty of mentally retarded females. Women can be found across the entire spectrum of intelligence, from the very top to the very bottom. But, in general, women cluster more in the middle, whereas men are spread out a little more to the extremes.

On this, Dr. Summers was quite right, at least in the sense of having a solid scientific basis for what he said.

Put another way, the average man and the average woman are almost exactly equal in intelligence. But across the population, men are both a little stupider and a little smarter than women. If you look only at the most and least intelligent people, you will find men outnumber women in both groups.

Men at the Extremes

More men at the top *and* at the bottom: This is a crucial fact to appreciate before we go spouting off about gender differences and patriarchal conspiracies and oppression and stereotypes. Men tend toward the extremes more than women, and that means both extremes. We will see this pattern in both culture and nature. As noted Chapter 1, we see male extremity through-out society: Just as more men than women are self-made millionaires, more men than women end up in prison. It is there in nature, too. In fact the data on height also show the male extremity pattern. Height is strongly dictated by one's genes, at least in places like the United States where nutrition is adequate in the majority of cases. On average, men are taller than women, but the distribution is flatter among men (as the statisticians say). There are more men at both extremes, far from the average male height, than there are women far from the average female height.

What about personality? This issue is not as contentious and fraught with political overtones as intelligence, and so less information is available. Still, there are some data that point to the same conclusion. For example, I recently visited the Positive Psychology Center at the University of Pennsylvania, where a group of top-level researchers are conducting groundbreaking research on humankind's strengths and virtues. They have recently and painstakingly created measures of the two dozen most impor-tant positive human traits and strengths, and they have now assessed several hundred thousand people on these. And what do they find? Men outnumber women at both extremes on these measures. Whether we are talking about kindness versus cruelty, curiosity versus closed-mindedness, wisdom versus immature pigheadedness, self-control versus self-indulgence, or humility versus narcissism, there are more men than women at both the good and the bad extremes.

There are exceptions. Current research in personality is dominated by the statistically constructed "Big Five" dimensions. On these, the experts do not find greater variation among men than women.

To avoid confusion, let me make clear that there are plenty of men in the middle too. In general, both men and women will be distributed according to a bell-shaped curve. There are more men (and women) in the middle than at the extremes.

Men and women are thus alike in that both are distributed with the greatest numbers in the middle range and fewer at the extremes. But there are more men than women at the extremes. (And so there are slightly fewer men than women at the middle.) This pattern will be found repeatedly, when you measure many different things. Though it sometimes does not occur, it is there often enough that we need to be alert to it.

What causes the male extremity pattern? We revisit the question later. It has roots in both nature and culture, and it has implications for the differences in how culture exploits men versus how it exploits women.

Damn Lies and Statistics

The male extremity pattern can produce all sorts of confusing and misleading findings. Even if men and women are exactly equal on average, almost paradoxically, you can get statistical data showing a difference between the male and female averages. All it takes is to use some kind of measure that is restricted at one end.

To make this clear, let's consider two examples. One is grades in college. The other is salary.

The point of this section is to show how statistics can mislead, especially in the hands of people with strong biases who want to mislead, but even in the hands of those who are trying hard to be fair. Mark Twain popularized the saying (though he did not originate it) that there are three kinds of lies: lies, damn lies, and statistics. The male extremity pattern can give rise to falsehoods of the last type and possibly of the other two. Even well-intentioned and unbiased people seeking the truth can be misled into asserting things that are unwarranted. And under the wilting or amplifying glare of political motivation, these statistical illusions can produce chagrin or alarm or glee—and can also provide abundant fuel for making all sorts of generalizations and claims and calls for political action.

Let's start with grades in college. Assume for the sake of argument that men in general, and male college students in particular, are equal on average in every relevant respect to women. That is, assume the men and women have the same average intelligence, work habits, ambition, conscientiousness. Also assume, crucially, that there are more men at both extremes. Of course, that entails that the extremes cancel each other out, so that the averages remain precisely equal.

What will the grades look like if those things are true? Will men and women earn the same average grades? That could happen. But now consider grade inflation, which has been a powerful pattern across the

United States in recent decades. Work that once earned a C now merits a B. In many college classes, the majority of students get A grades. Failure is increasingly rare.

The highest possible grade in most colleges, or what statisticians call the ceiling, is an A. The lowest (the floor) is an F. Over the last couple of decades, all grades have drifted upward toward the ceiling. The floor is far from the average, and the ceiling is close to it.

The low ceiling will affect the average grades of men and women. Remember, we have more men at both extremes of actual achievement. The really high achieving men, however, can no longer pull up the male average, because of the low ceiling. There is no grade above an A. (Curiously, many universities do not even permit A plus grades.) Lots of people get A's. And so the super-brilliant students get the same grade (A) as the moderately bright and conscientious ones.

Meanwhile, though, the low-achieving males will pull the male average down. There are more men than women getting the really low grades, and as these stand out more and more because of grade inflation, they will exert a strong downward pull on the men's average.

The result? Women will get better grades than men, on average. The important thing about this example is that we assumed that we got different results from the same (average) inputs. The average performance quality was exactly the same for men and women, but the average grade was different. That's because the distribution of grades in the era of grade inflation fails to appreciate really outstanding performance but is highly sensitive to really poor performance. In a sense, the surplus of males in the outstanding performance category doesn't really count for much, whereas the surplus of males in the dismally poor performance category does count.

Now let's turn to a different example with the opposite problem: salary. With grades, the ceiling was the statistical problem. With salary, the problem is the floor. There is a legal minimum wage. Of course, even if the legal minimum wage were not a factor, there would still be the de facto minimum of zero. Nobody works for a negative salary. A negative salary would mean, essentially, that if you were really incompetent you would pay the company to let you work for them.

Again assume that the average inputs are exactly the same for men and women: the same qualifications, the same abilities, the same efforts and sacrifices. Assume the average man and woman produce exactly the same quality and quantity of work. And assume that there are more men at both extremes.

There may be a minimum salary, but there is no maximum. And so at the high extreme, the top-achieving men can pull up the men's average salary. Meanwhile, at the low end, the floor (the minimum wage and the zero point) prevents the low-achieving men from pulling the male average back down. As a result, men's average salary will end up higher than women's—even if the average man is precisely equal to the average woman on every single factor that determines salary.

These differences are not temporary conditions that will go away. Nor are they problems needing to be solved. These differences will be permanent. Or at least, they will last as long as the assumptions are met: high grades with a low ceiling, a minimum salary, and men equal to women on average but cropping up more at both extremes.

In point of fact, in America today, women score higher grades than men in college and earn lower salaries. It is possible that there could be different causes. But that is all the more reason not to leap to conclusions. When these differences are mentioned in the mass media, they tend to get treated as if they point toward very different conclusions. It is common to infer from women's better grades that women are better students and perhaps even smarter than the men. Meanwhile, the higher earning power of men is not taken to mean that men are better workers than women. It is usually ascribed to some kind of evil conspiracy by men (patriarchy), and many people quickly think the gender gap in salary is proof of male wickedness and the oppression of women. Some argue that laws are needed to require women to earn as much as men.

Maybe. Let me point out that, in principle, one could just as well draw the opposite conclusions. Suppose someone were to say that women do better in college because colleges and the schools leading up to them discriminate against the young men and try extra hard to benefit the young women. The same person could say that men get higher salaries because they perform better than women in their jobs, or that they choose jobs that pay more, or because they work longer hours, or whatever.

My point is that neither conclusion is really justified. Until we rule out the very serious possibility that male extremity alone produces those differences, we cannot and should not conclude for certain that something else is responsible. Both the lower grades and the higher salaries of men could be nothing more than a statistical quirk stemming from male extremity.

Revisiting the Contradictory Stereotypes

Now we can return to the puzzle we noted earlier, namely how psychology in particular and Western society more generally could have switched from one prejudice to its opposite in a little more than a decade. The male extremity pattern can offer a seemingly solid basis for opposite conclusions.

For this, it is necessary to appreciate one simple fact about how stereotypes and prejudices are sustained. To be sure, there have been thousands of research studies on various aspects of prejudice, and there is no single or simple answer that explains all of them. But there are some broad conclusions. Most stereotypes are not just complete fabrications based on ignorance and hatred. Most of them have some fairly sizeable amounts of truth. Research by Lee Jussim and others has concluded that many stereotypes are far more accurate than most of us have been led to assume, though of course there are some that are wildly wrong and even in some cases intentionally devised to make some group of people look bad. More to the point, most people aren't bigots and are even somewhat careful about trying to find out whether the stereotypes they hold are true.

Unfortunately, perhaps, the way people check on whether their stereotypes are true is to look for confirming instances. You might say they try to establish whether their stereotypes are true but not whether they are false. This unfortunate trick of the mind has been dubbed *confirmation bias*. That is, people look for examples that confirm their beliefs more than they look for disconfirming evidence.

That's where male extremity comes in. It is ready-made for producing opposite stereotypes, by working with the confirmation bias. Whatever you expect might be true about men relative to women, you will be easily able to find plenty of real and valid examples to support your belief. Because men outnumber women at both extremes, everyone can easily find evidence to confirm good *and* bad stereotypes about men.

Want to believe men are superior to women? Easy. Just look at the top: the heroes, the philanthropists, the inventors, the geniuses, the statesmen.

Want to believe men are inferior to women? Easy. Just look at the bottom: the criminals, the junkies, the losers, the cheaters, the bullies, the warmongers, the mentally retarded, the abusers.

In an important sense, men really are better AND worse than women.

The Theory We've Never Tried

So theorizing about gender differences has featured three of the four possible theories. Once upon a time, and not so very long ago, it embraced the view that men were superior to women. The currently dominant view is that women are superior to men. And at times there have been strong arguments that there are no real or innate differences, just stereotypes and superficial differences caused by different upbringing.

What's missing from that list?

Different but equal is what hasn't been tried. In this view, neither gender is superior to the other across the board. But there are real differences. It's just that the differences cancel out in important ways.

This may sound like a namby-pamby compromise designed to please everyone. It is nothing of the sort. My argument for equality is an important basis for my broader argument about how culture exploits men.

Cultures exploit men and women differently. And they do this for a practical reason. Men and women are different and hence are useful to culture in different ways.

If there were no differences, then men and women would be interchangeable. Even if it were established that having different gender roles is helpful and useful for a culture—which I think is correct—it wouldn't really matter which gender played which role. Suppose most cultures needed somebody to fight in battles and also needed somebody to take care of the babies, and suppose (perhaps for obvious reasons) these tasks don't mix well, so it is best to assign them to different genders. We'd expect that some cultures would use men to take care of the babies and the women to fight the battles.

But if the genders are different, then successful cultures will figure out which gender is better suited to which of its tasks, and assign them thus.

The "different but equal" is a radical theory of gender equality. It gets to equality not by sameness but by tradeoffs. Differences survive because of these tradeoffs, in which a particular trait is well suited for one kind of task or contribution but its opposite has value for a different kind of task or contribution.

Gender and Tradeoffs

In the preceding section, I suggested that taking care of babies and fighting in battles are not fully compatible. I slipped that by rather fast. But now let's focus on it. The incompatibility might be a problem, if cultures need both of those jobs to be done. Why might those be incompatible?

One reason is the demands of the respective tasks. Babies need to be watched constantly and fed every day, indeed every few hours. Battles may require moving around frequently and unpredictably, taking chances, getting hurt, doing without regular meals and/or sleep, and sometimes being fully busy for a couple days. It's hard to imagine how the invasion of Normandy on D-Day in 1944 would have proceeded if the front-line American soldiers had had to return to camp to feed and change their babies every hour or two. The alternative of taking the babies along to Omaha Beach, perhaps strapped to the soldiers' backs, would also have had obvious drawbacks.

A more profound sort of incompatibility may have to do with the psychological and behavioral traits needed for those tasks. A gentle, loving nature may be best suited for taking care of babies, but it may be counterproductive on the battlefield. Being loud and intimidating may work wonders in hand-to-hand combat, whereas it won't put the baby to sleep. Being sensitive and attuned to others' feelings is ideal for someone caring for a baby, but it could cause a fatal hesitation when fighting someone with a spear or knife. Being able to shut off one's own inner feelings may be vital to enable a scared young person to march forward toward his possible death, but it would if anything make him less capable in caring for a baby.

The battle and baby issue is just one example. I don't mean to link everything to that. But it is chosen to illustrate an important point: tradeoffs.

My strong impression is that modern social scientists, and probably modern citizens in general, do not adequately recognize how pervasive tradeoffs are. I can't prove it, and it's only an impression. But there is a relentless quest to find the right fix, the right mix, the single solution to any problem. Why do we keep needing new laws? Shouldn't there be enough laws by now? But fixing one problem often creates another. Often there is no single correct solution to a social problem. That is because of tradeoffs. The better you make things in one respect, the more of a problem you create in something else.

My radical theory of gender equality is based on tradeoffs.

It means that there are real differences in the abilities of the two genders. But they are linked. Specifically, being better at one thing is linked to being worse at something else.

When first researching this book, I had wanted the multitasking difference to be true. I thought, if there is a tradeoff, then there has to be another side to that coin. If women's minds are naturally better suited for doing several different things at once, then there would be a corresponding deficit somewhere else. Men, perhaps, would be better at doing one thing at a time. This theory seemed intuitively quite plausible to me. Women juggle multiple tasks, simultaneously preparing the food for dinner, watching the children at play, and carrying on a conversation with each other. Men immerse themselves in single tasks, hence producing the great inventions and mathematical proofs. Unfortunately the multitasking difference between men and women is a myth. It could have been a fine illustration of the tradeoff approach.

Every time you hear of one gender being better at something, stop to think what is on the other side of that coin. What inferiority is tied to that superiority?

One Size Doesn't Fit All?

The tradeoff theory of gender says there are real, innate differences between men and women, including differences in capabilities and in inclinations. To say the differences are innate means that they are rooted in biology, that people are born with these differences (at least as tendencies). Perhaps these inborn tendencies can be overcome in some cases, but men and women start off different. Culture can reduce the effects of nature, but in most cases, culture builds on nature. Small natural differences in inclination may become giant differences in society, such as ones in which women are all kept at home to care for children and men are all required to earn a living.

Biologically based differences are put there by evolution. Evolution proceeds across generations, because the more successful versions do better than their rivals. They live longer and better and, most important, they reproduce more.

This is why it is implausible that one gender is innately better than the other across the board. When there is a good way to be, everyone will be it. Two legs are better than one or three, and so everybody has two legs. (Across multiple species, there are of course many four-legged and six-legged varieties, but I know of no mammals having an odd number of legs.)

Evolution thus naturally eliminates differences in favor of making every member resemble the better version.

Evolution will, however, preserve differences across many generations under one very specific condition: when there is a tradeoff.

If it is always better to be A than B, then gradually the members of the species with trait A will survive and reproduce better than the ones with trait B, until eventually most or even all the newborn babies have trait A instead of B.

However, if the A trait is better for some things while its opposite, B, is better for others, then there will be no permanent evolutionary victor. Both A and B will continue to reproduce and occur in each new generation.

Every time you hear that one gender is better than the other, ask yourself: Why would nature make one gender better than the other? Why would it preserve that difference, especially since the two genders mix their genes every single time a baby is made? Again, if there is a difference, most likely it is tied to a tradeoff. Nature will make one gender better at one thing, and keep it that way, if not having that ability makes people better able to do something else—indeed, something else that is too valuable to give up.

We are almost ready to start asking what these differences are. Then we can survey the differences between men and women with an eye to asking what nature and culture are likely to find men good for.

CHAPTER 3

Can't or Won't?

Where the Real Differences Are Found

THAT HUMAN BEINGS MAKE MUSIC IS ASTONISHING. The animals from which we evolved don't make music, and it's hard even to imagine how the idea of making music ever got started. I can't begin to count the hours I've spent listening to music, practicing and playing instruments, shopping for music, and the rest. I played in several small-time bands, and as anyone who has done so knows, whatever degree of success you have in that endeavor (and mine was fairly limited), you become a connoisseur of professional music, able to notice and appreciate things others miss and full of strong opinions about who is brilliant and who is wildly overrated by the musically unsophisticated public. And like many people who play instruments, I quickly became impatient with the layman's attitude that music is all about words and lyrics. If I ask people why they like some particular music, and they respond by saying something about the lyrics, they have lost all credibility as far as I'm concerned. Go read some book of poems if you want words.

One thing that has puzzled me over the years of focusing on the musical part of music is the gender difference. It is most obvious in jazz, which is in some respects the most advanced form of improvisational, instrumental music. When I was young and poor, I spent hours thumbing through the discount bins of albums, and I learned quite early that if the artist featured on the album was a woman, it almost inevitably meant she was a singer. A man on the cover might mean anything—guitar, sax, trumpet, piano. Some men sing too. Men do it all. But I'd say well over 90% of female jazz albums are by female singers. And even on those albums, most of the music was played by men, who worked their instruments in the background while the woman sang.

It's not that women can't play musical instruments. If you look at classical music, there are plenty of women who play, including at the top levels of ability. At the entry levels, such as the music schools where my daughter takes lessons, one sees more girls than boys, and they show just as much talent if not more. Nationwide, more girls than boys take music lessons. Women can and do play all manner of musical instruments superbly. They just don't play jazz.

What sets jazz apart is of course the creative challenge of improvising. The person who is playing has to make up what to play, moment by moment.

Is the deficit really in creativity? After or alongside improvising, the other most creative job in music is composing. Here again, men predominate. Women play music far more than they compose or improvise it. Creativity really seems to be where the difference lies.

One possible explanation is that women aren't creative. For a time, the pattern of female absence in composition and improvisation led me to think it was a lack of creative ability among women. But the data from my own field have pushed me away from that view. When psychologists give tests of creativity, the males and females score about the same. Women have apparently just as much basic, general creative aptitude as men.

Why, then, don't women do more creative things in music? Here is where the Imaginary Feminist might be tempted to introduce the standard arguments about oppression and socialization. Women aren't encouraged to be creative, or something like that. Pop feminism has taught us all to think along those lines. This is the formula we saw in Chapter 1: if a difference can't be explained on the basis of males having more innate ability, then it must be that men have oppressed and stifled women.

Maybe jazz music and the world of composition is a macho culture that won't allow females to participate. But this seems implausible. I have known many jazz musicians, and they aren't remotely macho. On the contrary, they tend to be quiet, nerdy introverts. They'll play with anybody who can keep up. Most bands I knew, including all the ones I was in, were desperate for a decent bass player in particular and would have taken anyone, even a foul-smelling gorilla who helped itself to others' food and peed on the floor, if it would have been willing and able to play the music.

The prejudice or oppression argument is hard to sustain. Jazz broke racial boundaries long before the mainstream society had even made up its mind as to whether integration was a good idea. When a talented female instrumentalist has shown up, such as the late Emily Remler, she was very popular and never lacked for musical partners.

I do think there is an explanation. But it's not where we have looked yet. This chapter is going to suggest looking for gender differences in a very different place.

The No-Difference Position

Chapter 2 introduced the tradeoff theory of gender differences as a radical theory of gender equality. To get started on this chapter's argument, let's pause for a moment to look at the non-radical theory of gender equality, which is that men and women are basically the same. In this view, the differences are trivial and have been overstated.

Psychology has shifted its prevailing views about gender several times. Up till the 1960s or so, the experts did not devote much thought to gender differences, reflecting a dominant view that these were not all that extensive or important. When men and women did exhibit different behaviors or opinions in one study or another, researchers quietly noted it, but nobody paid a great deal of attention.

Things heated up in the late 1960s and especially in the early 1970s, as the women's movement and other changes called more attention to women. A landmark in the field was the publication in 1974 of Eleanor Maccoby and Carol Jacklin's book *The Psychology of Sex Differences*. Those two scholars had combed through volumes of studies and collected the many findings of gender differences that had been reported, often without much comment, in study after study. The effect was something like having somebody go out searching for a few coins underneath the seats at a movie theatre and return with thousands of dollars' worth.

Rather abruptly, gender differences became a major interest in the scientific community, and expert opinion came around to think that men and women were quite seriously different. This shift coincided oddly with the rising feminist assertion that men and women were basically the same and differences reflected only prejudices and socialization. The tentative compromise was to believe that men and women were brought up to be different, and so that became the predominant way of interpreting observed differences. For example, "boys are socialized to be aggressive" and "girls are taught to attend to other people's feelings." Fathers, and especially mothers, who were just starting to get off the Freudian hook that had held them responsible for all their grown children's neuroses and other short-comings, were now blamed for having raised their children to develop personalities in line with outmoded and oppressive gender stereotypes.

Not long after that, statisticians got a new toy. With their usual flair for catchy titles, they called it estimated effect sizes. Let me explain it in plain terms. Up until this point, the way social scientists had studied behavior was by testing all their data to see whether there was any real difference or not. Yes or no: that was the extent of what the main statistical analyses gave you. In terms of studying gender, this older approach simply said that, based on your data, you either can or cannot conclude that there is some actual difference between men and women out in the world as a whole. The research question was simply, are men and women different, or not?

The new analysis allowed them to ask, how big is that difference?

The tables turned rather abruptly when the new tool was applied to gender differences. Yes, as Maccoby and Jacklin had documented, there are many gender differences to be found, because men and women are different in a vast number of ways. But most of these differences turned out to be quite small. Often gender accounted for only 3% to 5% of the variation in behavior. It was rare for a difference to reach 10%.

Elizabeth Aries put this succinctly in her 1995 book that was a sweeping reappraisal of gender differences based on the size of the effects. She noted the popularity of works by authors such as Deborah Tannen and John Gray, who treated men and women as opposites—indeed, in the case of Gray's works, as from different planets (men from Mars, women from Venus). "Why have we constructed polarized conceptions of men and women when the similarities between them outweigh the differences?" Aries asked.

The new view, therefore, is that men and women are different in many respects—but most of these differences are so small as to be scarcely worth talking about. Even in important, sensitive domains like mathematical aptitude, effect sizes changed the discussion. It was true that across the USA, the results from many thousands of SAT tests showed that boys on average have a higher aptitude for math than girls—but the difference was only about 3%. That's hardly enough to justify a company saying they would prefer to hire a man rather than a woman for a numbers-crunching job, or even enough reason to advise your daughter to take biology instead of physics.

In recent years, some experts have taken these small differences to argue strongly against the whole enterprise of studying gender differences. Janet Shibley Hyde, for example, a respected and influential researcher, saw the effect size data as vindicating the feminist ideals of her youth that denounced and denied the idea that women were different from men. In particular, when mental abilities are studied—anything from moral reasoning to mathematical problem solving—men and women look far more similar than different.

As always, there are cautionary arguments. Men and women in today's America may be more similar than at most other times in history or in other places. Our society has been trying for decades to erase gender differences by offering boys and girls the same schooling, the same upbringing, and the same opportunities, and by extending this egalitarian treatment to adult men and women also. Most cultures in world history have probably done the opposite, which is to steer men and women into different life paths and thereby increase the differences between them. Usually culture builds on nature, and so most likely males and females come out of the womb slightly different and then, by virtue of their experiences in social life, become more different over the years. Modern American culture is a rare exception that seeks to make men and women more similar to each other. Hence the small size of American gender differences may be atypical.

But I think most of those analyses have focused on abilities. Hence let me introduce another radical idea. Those analyses are focusing on the wrong things.

Can versus Want

How well someone performs a task depends on two things about the person (plus some external factors such as luck). One is the person's ability. The other is how hard the person tries. The latter, effort, is largely a reflection of the broad category of *motivation*. In plain language, motivation means wanting.

Thus, in a nutshell, performance depends on two things, ability and motivation. Ability is what you *can* do. Motivation is what you *want* to do. All the ability in the world won't lead to success in, say, basket-weaving or race-car driving, if you aren't interested in engaging in that sphere of endeavor.

In sports, for example, both ability and motivation matter. During practice, the coaches focus mainly on increasing ability. That's what "practice" means, after all: working to increase your skills. During the game itself, however, there is not much opportunity to increase ability, and so the coach's speeches then usually focus on motivation, that is, on getting the players to want to win and to try harder.

Motivation in fact goes well beyond task performance. It encompasses everything that people want and like. Economists, for example, talk endlessly about people's preferences, but *"preferences"* is just another word for motivation. It's doing what you like to do or want to do, or buying what you want to have.

Motivation is somewhat neglected in psychology these days, for complicated reasons that have little to do with its importance. The field of gender differences is likewise more attuned to abilities than motivation. It carries on hot debates about whether men or women are better at something.

Somehow, the question of whether men or women differ in what they like to do is not debated as often or as intensely.

Where the Real Differences Are

Chapter 2 proposed that gender differences were likely tradeoffs.

The focus was on abilities: why nature might make one gender better than the other at doing something. To be good at one thing might detract from being good at something else.

This is after all the way gender differences have been debated: Who's better at what?

It is in some ways an unfortunate debate. People are very sensitive. Saying one gender is better at something has a strong value judgment. Saying it as a general principle also gives rise to policy implications, most of which are troubling if not offensive to various parties. If girls aren't as good at math as boys, then they maybe should steer clear. Employers might prefer to hire men and might even be justified in doing so. And so forth.

Moreover, as we saw there are now strong views based on data that the gender differences in abilities, though real enough, are pretty small.

So before we go too far down the path of analyzing gender differences as traded off abilities, let's look elsewhere.

Where might that be? As we have just seen, performance depends on not just ability but also on motivation. So perhaps if men and women don't differ much in ability, they will differ more in motivation.

There are several advantages to focusing on motivation when we talk about differences between men and women. For one thing, it's less poisonous to discuss. If men and women do different things, it's more a reflection of what they like and want to do, than of what they are capable of. Policy implications are also muted. If you thought women were less competent than men at something, you might be justified in not wanting to hire one. But if the differences arise because most women don't like to do something, then the one who's applying for your job is obviously different, and you don't need to worry.

Hey Larry

It's worth revisiting the Lawrence Summers scandal with motivation in mind. The outrage that greeted his remarks is one sign of how sensitive people are about ability. The remark that caused so much trouble was the one about ability: He suggested that there were more men than women with the high innate ability needed to do physics at the level of a Harvard professor.

He also said a little about motivation. Specifically, he suggested that fewer women than men were willing to put in the long hours and make the other sacrifices required for success in a highly demanding, highly competitive field. As far as I can make out, this comment didn't attract much attention except a bit of grumbling about how tough it is for women to do that kind of work without adequate daycare or partners who share the housework.

I didn't see anybody talk about the basic idea of motivation to do math and science. And this is most likely where the biggest part of the problem is. (I use the word "problem" tentatively, because I'm not really convinced that the shortage of female physics professors at Harvard qualifies as a real problem. What, exactly, is the downside of having equations solved and neutrinos tracked by more men than women?)

Almost everything said against Dr. Summers, and what little was said in his defense, as well as what was said subsequently by people attempting fresh and balanced approaches to the issue of women in science, focused on the question of whether women have less native ability than men to study science. Always ability. The whole argument about Summers and what he should be permitted to say and think was about ability.

What if the lack of women in top science jobs isn't a result of differences in ability after all? Could it be motivation?

Maybe women can do math and science perfectly well. Maybe they just don't like to.

After all, most men don't like math either. Only a small minority of people find it satisfying to work with numbers and equations and such things. Think about the people you know who do like that stuff. Most of them are guys.

A few years ago, researcher Patricia Hausman, speaking to a meeting of the National Academy of Engineering, expressed a politically incorrect conclusion about why women don't make their careers in the natural sciences. It's neither because of a lack of ability nor because prejudice and oppression stop them. Her summation was apt: "They don't want to."

If ability differences explained the shortfall of women in science and math, while motivation levels were the same, here's what we'd see. Boys and girls, and later on men and women, would sign up for science classes in equal numbers (because signing up shows that they are interested). If abilities were different, then the females would flunk out while the males garnered the top grades and moved on. But that's not what happens.

Instead, it's motivation. When women do take math and science, they generally do fine. But mostly they don't sign up. That shows the difference in motivation. Women are less interested in taking those courses in the first place.

One scholar who has studied gender differences in school performance for decades is Professor Jackie Eccles at the University of Michigan. She knows very well women don't end up majoring in math and science as much as men, but she doesn't think ability has anything to do with it. In fact, in high school math and science classes (some elective, some required), overall the female students get slightly better average grades than the young men. True, as we saw in the previous chapter, this could be partly or wholly due to the male extremity pattern, but it certainly doesn't permit any conclusion that the young women are seriously lacking in any kind of ability.

Instead, Eccles has found that motivation is the key. This isn't just an opinion (expert or otherwise). Rather, this is the result of years of research and huge amounts of data, including studies that tracked students' careers over many years and looked at both abilities and motivations as well as outcomes such as what they chose to study and how well they performed. Men and women end up in different fields, and more men than women end up in science, but it's mainly because of motivation.

Probably the most thorough attempt to answer the question was published in a major scientific journal just as I was finishing this book. It listed several explanations for women's underrepresentation in science. Motivation, it concluded, was first and foremost: Women who have the ability to do well in math typically prefer non-science fields. Second, more men than women score in the top ranges on the major math aptitude tests. To the dismay of the Imaginary Feminist, the researchers concluded that evidence for discrimination (oppression) was mostly weak, dated, and anecdotal, and the more reliable data suggested this was not much of a factor, if any. The overall conclusion was that women's preferences are the single strongest factor.

To quote Professor Hausman again, "Wherever you go, you will find females less likely than males to see what is so fascinating about ohms, carburetors, or quarks." She said that she finds people endlessly fascinating, just like other women do. But as for things, well, "things bore me!" And that's the main reason women don't flock into engineering, physics, chemistry, and other fields that seek to learn how things work.

What's Fun?

The point of this chapter is that differences between men and women— that is, the big, meaningful differences that have an impact on what happens in the world—are in motivation rather than ability. The argument about women and science is one illustration. The main reason there are more male than female scientists is that men like science more than women. Now let's look around for other evidence as to whether sex differences are in motivation or ability.

The marketplace is one useful source of information about people. It may be especially helpful in areas such as gender, where there are so many personal and political biases that it's hard to sort fact from opinion. If we follow the money, we can get some valuable clues as to what's really going on. Where real differences or problems exist, somebody is likely to step forward and figure out how to make money by providing the needed services.

For example, you might think that the differences between men's and women's bodies would entail that the two genders would have some separate medical needs. And you'd be right. There are now women's health centers and various other clinics that specialize by gender. Where the two bodies are most different, as in the sex organs themselves, entirely different medical specialties exist. OB/GYN doctors don't see male patients. There are other specialists who mainly or exclusively treat men, such as those who work with prostate diseases.

Once upon a time, perhaps, general practitioners handled everybody's problems, male or female. But the marketplace has responded to the different needs of men and women by creating specialists and other services that are based on this difference.

So, let's ask first, is anybody making money off of gender differences in abilities? It's hard to think of any. This is one clue that there aren't a great many such differences. If women really had a seriously different level of ability for math or foreign language or whatever, there would be more classes aimed specifically at them, with different teaching styles. Ditto for men: there would be specialized classes, or perhaps products to address these problems.

What about motivation? Here, it seems, plenty of people are making heaps of money based on the belief that men and women want and like different things.

The entertainment industry is an underused source of clues to learn about motivation. Leisure and entertainment show what people like to do when they have no obligations and can just satisfy their own desires. In a sense, the entertainment industry caters strongly and carefully to what people's motivations are. Entertainment is based on motivation.

Start with the magazine industry, which is a highly competitive field. To be sure, there are magazines that everybody reads. Still, there are also men's magazines and women's magazines. There are in fact plenty of both. Oddly, both of them tend to put pictures of women on the cover.

Beyond that, however, the content is different. If men and women wanted to read about the same things, there would be no market for specialized magazines aimed at one or the other gender. There is, however, demonstrably a very big market. You can probably guess, and probably correctly, which types of stories go with which gender's magazines: fashion tips; ball sports; celebrity gossip; power tools; guns; diets and recipes; home décor; and on and on.

Magazines are hardly the only way that people make money off of gender differences in motivation. There are separate cable television channels aimed at male and female audiences, some even explicitly calling themselves "the women's channel" or "entertainment for women." Advertisements and commercials often aim at different genders. (If a woman mainly watches television by herself or with her female friends and then one day sits down to watch a ballgame with her husband, she'll be surprised at how many beer and car ads there are.)

Let's not overstate the case. Men and women do have many similar motivations, and certainly the entertainment industry has plenty of gender-neutral offerings, from TV dramas to sea cruises. But the fact that there are many differences shows that gender differences in motivation have significant economic reality.

It's worth adding that the entertainment industry can even shed light on the math question. I haven't done or seen any systematic research on this, but it would be possible to do. Simply go through men's entertainments (cable shows, or magazines, or whatever) and count how often numbers are used, and then do the same for women's entertainments. If men like numbers more than women, you'll probably find more numbers in men's fun than in women's. Nobody is surprised to hear, say on a sports show, that the Green Bay football team has so far this year amassed a 65% success rate at converting third downs in short-yardage situations in the third quarter, or that a particular hitter has a .375 batting average in late innings with a runner in scoring position.

Even the action shows have numbers: how many soldiers, what gauge gun, and how much money. In contrast, did you ever hear anyone, even the published soap opera summaries, say that 37% of televised spouses have demanded a divorce upon finding out that their partner is having an affair? Or that medical crises on ABC soaps outnumber those on NBC soaps by 18%? When numbers do come up for women, they usually represent something bad, like calories. Mostly they don't come up. On the soap opera, when one character finds out that the spouse has been having an affair, nobody pops in to say "37% of discoveries of adultery lead to divorce," whereas when there are two men on base with two outs, you'll probably hear exactly what the team or the next hitter has done on average across similar situations.

Another revealing example involves video games. Modern video games are played by young men much more than women, and they are full of numbers. In the new games, the player typically has to keep track of multiple sets of numbers: not just a score, but health points, shield points, enemy strength, and more.

Numbers and math are woven into the fabric of men's entertainment.

Sex Drive

Sex is another revealing and important sphere of behavior. People do complain a bit about a general lack of skill or technique in one or the other gender, but I doubt there is any far-reaching difference in sexual ability. In motivation, there is a difference. We'll take a closer look at this in a later chapter devoted to sex. For now, the crucial point is simply that there are gender differences in sexuality, and they mostly involve motivation. As the critics of Lawrence Summers would be pleased to hear, there is not much evidence to argue that men and women have innately different abilities for having sex. The differences are to be found in desire. Men want sex more often than women.

If anything, one can argue that women have a higher natural ability than men for sex. Women are more capable than men of having multiple orgasms. Women can have intercourse without being aroused, whereas men cannot. Women can continue performing sexually immediately after orgasm, whereas men must wait out a refractory period before they are ready to go again. If one chooses to regard these as ability differences, then they all suggest that women have higher ability. But men have higher motivation.

Thus, one of the most basic and universal human motivations—the desire to have sex—differs by gender. This particular motivation is stronger among men than women. That's probably why men still pay for dates, even in this modern era of ostensible liberation and equality.

What About Work?

We talked about leisure and entertainment preferences. Now let's turn to work. Here too there are probably motivational differences. It seems very likely that men and women differ, and have long differed, in their attitudes about work.

There is a common view these days that women work more than men. However, this appears to be wrong. One recent and careful study concluded that men and women work almost exactly the same total hours, if you count all kinds of work, including housework (and if you believe what people say).

And even this study may overstate women's work. The now-standard view that women work more than men came from feminist researchers who interviewed mainly women about how much they worked and how much their husbands worked. There was a definite axe to grind, and questions were formulated to make it look like women did more. There were plenty of questions about housework, but few or none about yardwork and other things that men do. Crucially, most of the studies did not even ask men about how much they and their spouses worked. One definite research finding is that people in general, both male and female, overestimate their own work relative to other people's, if only because they are more aware of when they themselves are working than of when someone else is. (A friend once asked five college suitemates how often they took out the garbage, as percent of the total times it got taken out. Three of the five each claimed to do it 90% of the time. And despite the fact that the five of their responses added together yielded the impossibly high result that the garbage was taken out over 300% of the time, they still sometimes missed the garbage collection!)

Moreover, it appears that people's estimates of their own work are less than perfectly reliable. Believe it or not, people routinely say they work more than they actually do. A methodologically careful and painstaking study by J.P. Robinson and G. Godbey had people say how much they worked—and then had them keep a careful record of what they did each day. The daily diaries did not match up with the general reports people gave. It turns out that most people wildly overestimated how much they worked. Moreover, for unknown reasons, women overestimated more than men, by about two hours a week.

But in a sense, all of that is beside the point. The data on total amounts of work blur together housework and paid work. Let's talk for a minute about work at the job. Regardless of the debates about housework and child care, and how much work is involved, most researchers agree that men spend more time working at their jobs than women. One recent estimate put the average difference at 400 hours per year. Another study in Britain tallied up those who work long hours and found mainly men. More precisely, it concluded that 80% of the people who work at least 48 hours per week are men.

The term "workaholic" became fashionable in the 1980s. My former colleague Marilyn Machlowitz, a workaholic herself, published several groundbreaking studies on this topic. I asked her once what was the gender breakdown among workaholics. She seemed surprised by the question, but she was sure the answer was that far more men than women fall in that category. No exact answer can be given, because there are no definite criteria for what constitutes a workaholic and where one draws the line between someone who's just a hard worker and someone who's a full-blown workaholic. But in any case, it is mainly a man's pattern. Certainly the stories about workaholics that filled Machlowitz's books were mainly stories about men.

Workaholism has little or nothing to do with ability. It reflects motivation, pure and simple. Workaholics are people who feel compelled to work hard and want to work as much as they can.

The difference in work hours probably has a great deal to do with an issue we touched on earlier, namely the gender gap in salary. I suggested that the pattern of male extremity could well cause a difference in salaries, given that there is a minimum salary but no maximum. If salary depended solely on ability, the male extremity pattern would certainly produce higher salaries in men. But I suspect that a bigger cause of the gender gap in salary has to do with motivation.

If men work longer hours than women and have more ambition about making it to the top in their line of work, this is likely to get them higher average salaries.

The phrase "glass ceiling" became popular for a while in discussions of differences in levels of business success. Hillary Clinton used it in 2008 to explain her failure to become President of the United States. The idea of a glass ceiling is that there are hidden conspiracies (a glass ceiling is an invisible barrier) among men to keep women down. There is no evidence that such conspiracies exist, apart from the lack of women at the top of many organizations. Moreover, most serious social scientists recognize that conspiracy theories are generally wrong, and this one should be considered quite dubious.

We have no evidence of male conspiracies to keep women from being promoted. We do have plenty of evidence that men put in longer hours on the job. The latter should be the preferred explanation for the salary gap.

Some years ago, I dined with a Dutch researcher in my field, Professor Agneta Fischer at the University of Amsterdam. She and I had shared interests in the psychology of self-concept and related topics. At dinner, she mentioned that she had also recently conducted a big research project in a completely new direction. When I asked about it, she said it had to do with gender and success in corporations. She was trying to learn about the glass ceiling.

She had gotten involved with one of the major, large Dutch corporations, who had agreed to cooperate with her research. She said she had surveyed the entry-level new workers and the top executives. She was trying to see what she could learn about the glass ceiling and women's issues. I held my breath because I did not know whether she was going to give a strong women-as-victims rant or something else, but I knew she was a careful scientist, so I asked what she found.

She said at the entry level there were about equal numbers of men and women, but their attitudes about work and the corporation were different. At the entry level, men had much more ambition and identified much more strongly with the company than did women. In other words, men were more motivated, at least at this low level.

At the top level, there were no such differences. The men and women had the same attitudes and goals. Their motivations were indistinguishable. Only, there were many more men than women at this top level.

Professor Fischer smiled and shrugged. It's pretty obvious what's going on, she said. Men and women start working as equals, but more men than women want to make it to the top. The people who make it to the top, both men and women, have those strong ambitions and care deeply about succeeding in their work—enough to make the personal sacrifices that are necessary. Some women care that much, and they do succeed. There's no glass ceiling, she said, other than women's own widespread unwillingness to put in the long hours of planning and working to make it to the top. Women who are willing to pay that price succeed too, just like the men.

Recent research points increasingly to the same conclusion. The pharmacy industry, for example, is generally recognized as having essentially zero sex (or race) discrimination. Part of the reason is that there never seem to be enough people to take all the jobs, so anyone, male or female, can get the training and then pick, choose, and negotiate a job to his or her liking. Though men and women go into the field at similar rates, they tend to pick different kinds of jobs and careers. Women favor easier jobs with minimal travel and with fixed hours that can be accommodated to family life. Men tend to pick the jobs with greater responsibilities, longer hours, less flexible demands, but with higher earnings. Hence in this field, like many others, men on average earn 27% more than women.

Actually, there are additional factors that have nothing to do with either glass ceiling conspiracies or hours worked. For one, men choose their jobs on the basis of money more than women do. Would you take a highly stressful and unpleasant job that paid a huge salary? More men than women say yes to this question.

For another, men are more likely than women to negotiate for higher salaries. Multiple studies have documented this. When women get a salary offer, they tend to accept it. When men get one, they tend to bargain for a bit more. The same thing happens each year when raises are handed out. Men are more likely to make an argument about why they deserve more. Sometimes they succeed with this argument, sometimes not. But if you don't try, you never succeed. Over the years, these small differences add up.

All these things reflect motivation. Men want to succeed more, they work longer at it, they care about money more, they make decisions based on money more, they are more willing to make sacrifices to succeed, and they negotiate more extensively for money. No wonder they earn more.

Remember the numbers on death on the job in Chapter 1? At last count, 93% of Americans killed on the job in an average year are men. That means that men take more dangerous jobs than women do. Do you think men like jobs that get them killed? More likely, they accept the danger because it comes with a higher salary. Societies everywhere have to pay people a bit more to get them to do dangerous jobs. It's a tradeoff: safety versus money. And on average men and women trade it off a bit differently. It's the motivation for money that is higher in men. Men will accept more risk than women in order to get a higher paycheck.

And All that Jazz

By now, you've probably guessed the answer to the question that started this chapter, namely why don't women play jazz. I suspect it has little or nothing to do with a lack of ability or a gender difference in creativity. It's because they don't really want to. That doesn't mean women are actively opposed to it. They merely are not as driven as men are to perform this sort of demanding, creative music.

I suppose the stock explanation for any such difference is that women were not encouraged, or were not appreciated, or were discouraged from being creative. That's certainly what the Imaginary Feminist will tell us. As usual, when one rejects the idea that men have ability than women, one is left with the explanation that men must have oppressed women.

But I don't think this stock explanation fits the facts very well. In the 19th century in America, middle-class girls and women played piano far more than men. Yet all that piano playing failed to result in much creative output. There were no great women composers, no new directions in style of music or how to play, or anything like that. All those female pianists entertained their families and their dinner guests but did not seem motivated to create anything new.

Meanwhile, around the same time in history, black men in America created blues and then jazz, both of which changed the way the world experiences music. By any measure, those black men, mostly just emerging from slavery, were far more disadvantaged than the middle-class white women. Even getting their hands on a musical instrument must have been considerably harder. And remember, I'm saying that the creative abilities are probably about equal. But somehow the men were driven to create something new, more than the women.

Our tour of various motivational differences has been somewhat haphazard. The point was just to establish the conclusion that the differences between men and women are most likely based primarily in motivation. If culture is to use men and women differently, it will likely do so on the basis of the differing inclinations and preferences that men and women have.

That raises the question, then, of what the centrally important differences are. The next two chapters will develop two big and key motivational differences.

CHAPTER 4

The Most Underappreciated Fact About Men

Here's a riddle for you: What percentage of our ancestors were men?

It's not a trick question, and the answer isn't 50%. True, perhaps half of all the humans who were ever born were male, but that's not the question. We're not asking about everyone who ever lived. We're asking about everyone who lived *and* who also has a descendant alive in the world today.

While you ponder that, let's consider life among the herds of wild horses. Males and females are born at about the same rate, and as youngsters their lives are similar, but when they reach adulthood their paths diverge. The mating season is in the summer, and when the females are old enough, they are soon busy with the reproductive process. The alpha male horse in each herd—the most powerful adult male who has risen to the top of the hierarchy—will be checking them out and, if they are fertile, will be having sex with them. They become pregnant and create offspring.

Each summer thereafter, the mare's story is about the same. She stays in the herd with the others as the alpha male works his way through them. When it's her turn, she submits to intercourse. (It doesn't seem very gentle or romantic by human standards, but probably human standards aren't really relevant here.) Over the years, she'll have a fair number of offspring, mostly sired by different stallions, depending on which male has won the coveted top spot that year.

Now consider the life of the male horse. As he approaches adulthood, he definitely does not find older females seeking him out to initiate sex with him. He starts to desire sex with the females, old or young or in between, but he quickly learns that sex is forbidden to him. The females belong to the alpha male, and if he starts to flirt, he risks being beaten up rather severely by the alpha male.

Assuming there is enough food, the young male then has plenty of energy but cannot put it into sex. Instead, he puts it into playing rough, competitive games with the other young males. Over time, it becomes clear which of them are the strongest and fiercest competitors.

Every male is descended from mostly alpha males. Occasionally a lesser male can manage to copulate and make a baby, but these are exceptions, and the line of ancestors consists mainly of the alphas. This is important to keep in mind: Every horse is descended from those that fought their way to the top of the male hierarchy. The competitive drive that propelled alpha males to the top is passed on to the next generation. As the blood of dominance heats in his veins, the young horse begins to hanker to become the dominant male himself. After he has bested his peers and playmates, at some point he will challenge the alpha male to a nasty fight. If he loses and survives, he may settle into a minor role on the periphery of the herd. If he wins, he takes over and becomes the alpha male.

Most male horses will never be the alpha male. They may never have sex at all, let alone reproduce. True, there is a bit of surreptitious hanky-panky, such as if a female consents to have a go with him when they are out of sight of the alpha male. But most females would rather have the alpha male as a mate: After all, her own offspring will be stronger and faster if its father was the strongest and fastest one rather than an also-ran. So consensual sex is fairly uncommon for these also-ran males. As for nonconsensual sex—what humans call rape—well, there may be a bit of that once in a while. In general, though, the fate of most males is to live in nearly total celibacy and to be a biological dead end.

And what about the strong and lucky one that becomes the alpha male? For that summer, he is the king, and he can have all the sex he wants. It's not all fun and games, however. He has to fight to stay on top, and so as long as he wears the figurative crown he has to be ready, almost at a moment's notice, to have strenuous and dangerous battles with challengers, at a time and place of their choosing, and over time these battles will wear his body down.

Moreover, he knows the other males don't stop wanting sex just because he defeated them once. Maintaining his harem requires constant vigilance.

He has to be ready to run the other males off and make sure the females stay together where he can watch them. He hardly sleeps that summer. He eats prodigiously to keep up his energy for the huge demands of sex, combat, and guarding.

By the end of his summer of love (to put it politely), he may be physically exhausted, perhaps so severely he will never recover. If he is exceptionally strong, and if there are not too many challengers, he may be able to repeat as alpha male next year and even in rare cases manage a third summer. But that will be all. The young challengers keep coming, and eventually one of them will take his place. After this, he is reduced to a humble, celibate life among the loser males. He had his brief season of glory, and it is over.

Counting Ancestors

Let's return now to the question of what percentage of our ancestors were women. Yes, each baby has one mother and one father, so each baby's parents were 50% male. But some of those parents had multiple children, and not necessarily always with the same partner. Every baby's parents are 50% male, but you can't extrapolate from that to conclude that today's human population has an ancestry that is 50% male.

The correct answer has recently begun to emerge from DNA studies, notably those by Jason Wilder and his colleagues. They concluded that among the ancestors of today's human population, women outnumbered men about two to one.

Two to one!

In percentage terms, then, humanity's ancestors were about 67% female and 33% male.

To illustrate how this could be possible, imagine a desert island at the start of time with just four people: Jack, Jim, Sally, and Sonya. Thus the population is 50% female. Let's assume Jack is rich and handsome, while Jim is poor and unattractive, so Jack marries both Sally and Sonya. Thus, Jack and Sally's baby, Doug, has ancestors who are 50% female (i.e., Jack and Sally). The same can be said for Jack and Sonya's baby, Lucy. But if you take Doug and Lucy together, their combined ancestors are 67% female (because their total ancestors are Jack, Sally, and Sonya).

Most people are surprised to hear that humankind today had twice as many female ancestors as male ones, because they thought it would be closer to 50:50. When experts hear about this, they are surprised too, but often for the opposite reason: They thought the imbalance would be even more severe. That is, they thought it would be maybe 75% to 85% female. Probably it was more severe through much of history, and especially prehistory. In many animal species, close to 90% of the females but only 20% of the males reproduce. The way the human population has ballooned in recent centuries means that most people who ever lived are either alive today or were alive recently, and in modern times the rule of monogamy has spread over large parts of the globe. In past eras, when polygamy (one husband, multiple wives) was the norm, the reproductive imbalance would have been even more severe. *Hence whatever conclusions we draw about the differences between men and women based on the two-to-one ancestor difference are probably understatements.* If we had done the research even just a few centuries ago, the ratio might have been three female ancestors to every male one, or four to one.

What does it mean that we are descended from twice as many women as men? It can be explained like this. Of all the people who ever reached adulthood, maybe 80% of the women but only 40% of the men reproduced. Or perhaps the numbers were 60% versus 30%. But one way or another, a woman's odds of having a line of descendants down to the present were *double* those of a man.

Also, crucially, the majority outcome is different—the most common outcome of normal life. Most women who ever lived to adulthood probably had at least one baby and in fact have a descendant alive today. *Most men did not.* Most men who ever lived, like all the wild horses that did not ascend to the alpha male's top spot, left behind no genetic traces of themselves.

That's a stunning difference. Of all humans ever born, most women became mothers, but most men did not become fathers. You wouldn't realize this by walking through an American suburb today with its tidy couples. But it is an important fact. I consider it the single most underappreciated fact about the differences between men and women.

In Chapter 3 I mentioned that the crucial differences between men and women are more likely to be found in terms of what they want (motivation) than in their abilities. The dramatically greater proportion of women among our ancestors provides a vital basis for understanding some of these motivational differences. To appreciate these, it is necessary to consider exactly how evolution works.

How Nature Measures Success

Darwin's theory of evolution has long dominated the study of biology, but lately it has come to exert a powerful influence on psychology as well. Psychologists have had to accept the fact that many behavioral tendencies are hard-wired, and that usually means they have been stamped in by the evolutionary processes.

To be sure, debates rage in many areas as to how much of behavior is a direct result of innate tendencies versus how much depends on what your mother made you do, what you copied from your peers, what you saw on Oprah, and other aspects of socialization and learning, as opposed to being prompted by your genes. It is increasingly fashionable to explore how innate and environmental factors work together, which, after all, is the essence of this book's approach to understanding how culture exploits men.

But if evolutionary theory is right about anything, it is right about reproduction. Making babies is at the core of it. Hence, when we talk about what produced success at making babies, we are likely to be on grounds where nature outweighs nurture.

The term "survival of the fittest" is often erroneously repeated as a one-line summary of Darwin's theory. The phrase was actually coined by Herbert Spencer, not Darwin. More important, though, it has now become regarded as misleading. Survival has come to be regarded as secondary by the recent generations of evolutionary theorists. Reproduction is the key.

It's all about reproduction. The bottom line in natural selection, which drives evolution, is reproducing., Actually, even that isn't even quite precisely right. Oak trees produce thousands of acorns every year, but not all of them become trees, and many that start growing don't survive to make more acorns and more trees.

The real bottom line is making new babies who will succeed in making more babies. If you do that, you are a success in evolutionary terms at passing along your genes, regardless of how long you live.

Followed to its extreme, we can look at the world population of humankind today as the result of evolution. Many people have walked the Earth in the past couple hundred thousand years. Some of them passed along their genes, which continue to be reproduced in today's population. Others were dead ends. Either they didn't have children, or their children died before reproducing, or their grandchildren did.

Looking back across the entire history of the human race, and taking nature's criterion of success as passing on your life to others, we can say that most of the men were failures. Most of the women were successes. Being male goes with biological failure in a way that being female doesn't.

Facing Different Odds

The difference in reproductive success is crucially important. It provides a powerful basis for understanding why men and women act differently.

Remember, if evolutionary theory is right about anything, it's right about reproduction. That's the core of the theory. Nature will most favor traits that lead to success at reproducing. But for thousands of years, men and women have faced vastly different odds and problems in reproducing.

The psychology of men and women, at least as set up by evolution, thus starts from very different prospects. Nature made life to seek to create more life. On this basic task, women faced good odds of success, whereas men were born to face looming failure.

We are descended, obviously, only from the women and men who succeeded, that is, the ones who passed on their genes. But men and women had to take different routes to success. It would be wrong to say it was easy for women, because childbirth and nursing placed heavy demands and took their toll. Nonetheless, throughout human history, women have seen the odds in their favor, while men have seen the odds against them. Nature molded the psyches of men and women accordingly.

That's a powerful basis for saying that men and women are built to want different things, in different ways.

The men and women who lived before us may not have thought about it in those terms of success and failure, but nature was choosing among them by whether they succeeded, and today's humankind is descended from the men and women who succeeded at passing on their genes. Today's humanity therefore has the traits that went with success at reproducing. These traits would be different by gender.

For a woman, the path to success seems to have been fairly straight. There was little reason to take chances or strike out on her own. There was no reason to try to separate herself from what everyone else was doing. At most, the ancestral woman wanted to make herself more desirable so she could choose a high-quality partner. Her concern, seen from the pitiless perspective of nature, would be about what her children will be like and how well they will be cared for. It wasn't about whether she would have children at all. The odds were generally good that she would have some.

Thus, most women who ever lived faced relatively favorable odds, and their psyches were correspondingly adapted to these favorable circumstances. Play it safe, be like everyone else, and there would be sufficient chances to become pregnant. She just had to choose a good offer, such as a man who could and would provide for her and the children.

Life has handed you a good thing; don't blow it. That's nature's message to women.

Therefore, crucially, there was no need for nature to instill particular traits in a woman to increase her chances of having a baby. Nature didn't have much need or opportunity to select among women in favor of traits that promoted having babies, because most women had babies. No extra drive, no special motivation, was needed.

In contrast, the average man was destined for reproductive oblivion. The option of playing it safe and doing like everyone else would have been a foolish one. Most of the men would fail to reproduce, and if you failed to surpass them, you would fail too.

That's why we are descended from playing-it-safe women and risk-taking men. Later in the book we shall have occasion to consider questions like, why was it so rare for fifty women to band together to build a ship and sail off into unknown seas to explore? The fact that men instead of women did this is a cause of gender differences in wealth, power, and other things, as we shall see. But remember the most underappreciated fact. From the perspective of nature and evolution, reproduction is the bottom line. Women who sailed off into unknown parts were probably less likely than others to pass on their genes. It would be foolish for women to take such chances. They might drown or be eaten by cannibals or succumb to strange new diseases. Instead, stay home and act like the rest of the women, and you will get to have your babies.

But for men the calculus was different. For the man to stay at home and play it safe was not playing it safe, because the average man was not destined to reproduce. Yes, many men who sailed off to explore unknown seas ended up drowning, or being eaten by cannibals, or dying from disease, and they lost their gamble. But gambling was still the best strategy perhaps, because staying at home for them also meant losing. Some men did come back from their travels rich enough to improve their chances of getting a wife or two and supporting a pack of youngsters.

You can argue, philosophically, which life was preferable: to stay at home, safe and reasonably comfortable, go through life, not reproduce, and die peacefully, versus go out into the world and risk much and suffer, yet, as one of the lucky ones, come home rich, take a wife or two, and have sons and daughters. But which life is preferable is not the point. People today are descended from the men who did take the gamble (and who won). The psychology of men who live today, to the extent it has any genetic or biological basis, leans toward the highly ambitious man.

To put it another way, risk-taking for women meant giving up a relatively sure thing for an uncertain chance. That is foolish. Risk-taking for men meant giving up a sure loss, exchanging definite failure for possible failure. Viewed in terms of the biological criterion of reproduction, it made sense for men to take risks and for women to avoid risks.

Crucially, today's men are descended disproportionately from those enterprising winners! The ones who took it easy and stayed home generally did not pass on their genes, and so today's male population has no trace of them.

Before we start feeling sorry for men, let's look at another implication of the most underappreciated fact, which underscores the conclusion that men were bred to risk more than women.

Losing is one side of gambling. The other is winning. There are differences between men and women in terms of what makes winners. Yes, men have less to lose by taking chances in life, but they also have more to gain. (Remember, we are speaking of winning and losing by nature's measure, namely creating offspring.)

After all, every baby ever born had a mother and a father, at least in the biological sense. If plenty of men had no babies, then plenty of other men had high numbers of babies, indeed more than the average woman. The underappreciated fact works both ways. If a man's odds of having any children were only half those of the average woman, that also means that our forefathers averaged twice as many children as our foremothers.

As usual, men go to extremes. In terms of number of children, most women have at least one, and relatively few women have more than, say, a dozen. (Indeed, if you only count the children who survive to bear grandchildren, probably few women in prehistory and ancient history had more than half a dozen.)

In contrast, there are plenty of men at the extremes. As we have seen, many men have no children. Others have far more than the most prolific women do.

Genghis Khan was one of the greatest conquerors in world history. He built an army that subdued much of the known world. He is also said to have had hundreds of children, probably well over a thousand. Great risks and exertions went into his conquests, and indeed at several points in his life it looked as if he would die young and have no children whatsoever. But he persevered and passed on his genes very effectively.

We can debate why no women have achieved what Genghis Khan did, why none have even come close. Perhaps our Imaginary Feminist will grumble that there was some kind of "glass ceiling" holding nomadic Mongol women back. But the evolutionary theorists have a more plausible answer: There is no reason for a woman to take such risks and sacrifices. Even if a woman did conquer the known world, she could still have only maybe half a dozen babies. (If she spent as much time on horseback and in battle as Genghis Khan, it would have been quite difficult to make time for even half a dozen pregnancies!) There was no payoff for trying for more. It is simply impossible for a woman to have a hundred babies. It is possible for a man, and some men have done it.

Thus, the most underappreciated fact—that we are descended from twice as many women as men—means two things. Men have been the big losers AND big winners, in ways that women generally were not. To the extent that the human mind and its pack of wants and needs was shaped by evolution based on reproduction, men are less likely to play it safe. Nature pushed men to play big games for big stakes.

The Impulse to Do Better

Picture two boys bicycling down the same deserted lane, or skiing down the same slope, or swimming next to each other in the same pool. Just by chance, they end up next to each other, going in the same direction at about the same speed. What happens? Each one quickens his pace a little. Both of them wonder whether the other is seeing this as competition, for in the past, sometimes when someone caught up to you, he yelled something as he passed you, signifying that he thought he had triumphed over you. So you were alert to it.

Two girls, not so much, I think.

During the writing of this book, I spent a few weeks at an obscure resort in Aruba, where I have gone for many years. When I became a windsurfer, I learned that Aruba has among the most reliable winds in the Western Hemisphere. I spent three weeks there, mostly writing my books and papers, but taking an intense two- to three-hour break every afternoon to head out on the water for some high-speed, delicately balanced, physically exhausting but exhilarating sailing.

Mostly people just go back and forth on the water. Every so often, however, one finds oneself next to another windsurfer who is going in the same direction (directions are constrained by the wind) and at about the same speed. This happened to me several times. Invariably, both I and the other guy (it was never a woman) would notice each other and start to tighten up our sailing, engaging in an impromptu race. We would turn at some spot toward the end of the general area, often waiting for the other to turn also, and then race back the other way. The other fellows were usually more skilled sailors than I was, at least in the sense that they had mastered the fancy turns that I never learned. Still, for just going straight ahead, you don't need turns, and I do fairly well when I get going.

It felt juvenile, and it was. The challenge brought out the boy in us, even though all of us were men over forty and in some cases, we were both closer to sixty. There was a difference. When I was young, I would have mainly wanted to surge ahead and win, but in adulthood I enjoyed it most if we were fairly evenly matched. The fun was in trying to coax every ounce of speed out of your board and sail, and in feeling the thrill of hurtling across the water with only nature's power and your own strength and skill, with another surfer doing the same a few yards away. The wind has gusts and lulls, there are waves and other things to cope with, yet you try to maintain a speed comparable to a fast bicycle on land.

Later on, we stopped to chat good-naturedly about the unofficial racing, about who had had the advantage under which circumstances and so forth. We had indeed both known we were racing against each other.

That evening, back at the resort, I asked the women windsurfers whether they did impromptu racing. They said no. They thought it was some kind of silly male competitiveness thing. They just wanted to enjoy the feeling of movement.

I suspect they are typical. Can you imagine two fifty-year-old women out on the water, noticing each other, and automatically trying to speed up, to outdo each other? Can you imagine that as one spots the other, she pulls in harder on the sail, yanks the mast back, leans out farther backwards over the water, straining her body harder in the attempt to make her board fly over the water faster than the other woman?

Let us suspend value judgments for a moment. This impulse to compete, to try to best the other at some physical task, seems to come more naturally to the male than to the female of the species. Assuming both men and women have sound reasons for feeling the ways they do, why might that difference exist?

These days, the natural impulse to want to outdo one's rivals is usually described as another sign of why men are inferior, this silly automatic competitiveness about little things, like which boy can skip a flat stone over the water with the most skips.

But that is what it means to be male. It has its roots in the most underappreciated fact. Most men who ever lived have been genetically erased from the human population. The men who didn't care about outdoing other men, who were content to take it easy and go along easily and let others push ahead (the way many women are content)—those guys did not reproduce. The men who pushed ahead were more likely to reproduce, and today's men are descended from them. To leave offspring, you had to outdo other men.

Women did not face those long odds. To the extent that women competed with each other, they competed to get a better versus less desirable mate. And they did this not by besting other women at physical tasks, but by being more beautiful and sweet and lovable than the others.

The relentless competitive urge is one difference we notice about the sexes, and I certainly concur with the general impression that the relentless male competitiveness can be downright annoying. Women seek to make friends and make others feel good and get along. All that is much nicer than trying to outdo each other on every little task that comes along.

But men are descended from men who did manage to outperform other men. The sad fact, as we have seen, is that the nice guys often did not pass on their genes. The men who competed ruthlessly managed to get to the top of the hierarchy, where they could have their pick of the females (and maybe have several). They produced sons (and daughters). The nice guys who were pleasant and easygoing and who didn't care so much about out-doing the other men achieved less, attracted fewer females, and left behind fewer descendants.

We saw in the first chapter that pretty much everybody likes women more than men. My theory is that women really are more lovable than men.

Men can be lovable too. After all, most men do persuade women to love them. It's just they don't always want to be lovable. For women, being liked and loved is a top priority most of the time. Men would like to be liked and loved, but they have other goals too, and sometimes those other goals take priority. Men want to fight their way to the top.

Don't get me wrong. Women would like to be at the top of the hierar-chy also. It's just that when there is a choice between being nice and lovable as opposed to battling one's way to the top, women are more likely to choose being nice and lovable, whereas more men would opt for fight-ing to the top.

All of this, I suggest, is rooted in our evolutionary history, especially the most underappreciated fact. Women had babies whether they fought their way to the top or not. Being lovable is what enabled women to have better quality babies. In contrast, men had more babies and better quality ones if they fought their way to the top. Being lovable may have mattered for men too, but not as much.

Striving for Greatness

Humans are not wild horses, but then again they are not completely different either. The female horses all had their babies, and the more nurturing and loving they were, the better their babies flourished. For the male horses, being loving and nurturing led nowhere. Being rough, aggres-sive, and ambitious mattered. The male horses that had those traits, along with physical prowess, were the only ones who sired offspring.

The next generation inherited the traits that made for reproductive success. For the females, being attractive, healthy, and, yes, loving and lovable were the traits that were passed along to the offspring. For the males, the vital traits were strength, aggressiveness, and ambition.

Earlier we mentioned Genghis Khan. By some estimates, the majority of babies born in central Asia today have in their veins some of the blood of this one remarkable man. Imagine that: the majority of those millions of people are descended from one individual. No woman of his era could possibly have achieved that.[1] But a man could do it, if he fathered enough children who had a sufficiently good start in life to reach the point of having their own children.

For a man to achieve that much of a biological impact on a large population many centuries after his life, what traits did he require? He had to be immensely ambitious, talented, and successful. He had to be willing to take tremendous risks and undergo severe hardships while pursuing them.

Also, obviously, he had to like having sex with many different women. Had he been content with monogamy, his offspring would have numbered no more than his wife's. To produce a giant brood, he needed to copulate with hundreds of women. And to have the opportunity to do that, he had to be immensely successful in social, political, and economic terms. Such success, in turn, required considerable talents and powerful motivations. (And no small measure of luck. But there is no gene for luck.)

What, then, do today's baby boys in central Asia get from their genetic link to Khan? Perhaps they inherit some talent and ability. But as I have said, the ability differences between men and women are small.

Instead, let me emphasize that what they inherit from their world-beating ancestor is a pattern of motivation. Genghis Khan strove for greatness. Even after he had achieved enough wealth and power to live comfortably, he continued to pursue conquests. He led his armies on further marches. They roved out of Asia into Europe and the Middle East. The historical time of his life coincided with the Crusades. The European Christians had battled the Arab Muslim forces of the Middle East to an approximate standstill, where the capabilities of the two sides were fairly evenly matched, producing a delicate peace. The Mongols rollicked through this and so far outclassed both sides that neither could begin to compete with them.

---

1 At least not by her own efforts. I do realize that everyone descended from Genghis Khan is also descended from his mother. Exploring the implications of this peculiar loophole will lead to considerations that are even more politically incorrect than the rest of this discussion.

Being nominally Christian, the Mongols sized up the opportunities and made the Pope an offer that they would conquer and subdue the entire Holy Land—something Christians had tried and failed to do for generations—and turn it over to the Roman Christians to administer, provided they acknowledge Mongol supremacy and pay a nominal tribute. The Pope's men debated the offer but could not accept Mongol Christianity because it deviated in various minor ways from their own current theological opinions. They also did not quite want to admit that the Mongols were a superior power. So they refused.

The Mongols sent a raiding party into Georgia, south of Russia, just to explore what was up there. The Georgians responded by mobilizing their entire nation's power, their greatest knights and warriors, led by their king, all of whom came out to defend their nation's sacred honor and faith and home turf against these barbarian raiders. The Georgian nation's finest knights were obliterated in a single battle. Genghis Khan wasn't even there, although his troops fought the way he had taught them. His military tactics so far surpassed that of the Westerners that a raiding party with no particular objectives could easily dominate the best that the Europeans could produce.

My point with all of this is that natural selection has imbued human males with one motivation that is stronger in them than in the females of the species. Striving for greatness is one way to describe it. Perhaps that is one small but important part of what today's central Asian boy babies inherit from Genghis Khan and many others like him.

In each man, in some small way, there is has a hankering to be great. When you are young and formulating your life's ambitions, you perhaps dream of exceptional greatness. As a boy you may seek to outdo others at little games and races. In adulthood, a man seeks to find something he can do better than the others who are nearby. He dreams, perhaps, of outdoing them all, of scoring a touchdown in the Super Bowl or of winning grand awards or of producing an invention or founding an organization that earns him millions of dollars. He may settle for circumscribed greatness, such as finding something he can do better than his colleagues at work.

Some day, he thinks, there will be applause for him. People will speak of him with respect and appreciation. They will recognize that he attained something unusual, extraordinary, remarkable, and they will look up to him. If reproduction drives the unconscious hankerings, then perhaps at some level he imagines that when he reaches his pinnacle of greatness, women will flock to him and smile and take him to bed. For his ancestors, that was the difference between fathering a bumper crop of babies versus ending life as a mostly celibate dead end. For today's man, the link to reproduction has been severed. Monogamy and other factors ensure that less successful men can have children, while even the most successful men, because of the monogamy laws, may have only one or two. Perhaps ironically, or as a spiteful victory of culture over nature, today's downtrodden, unproductive, and feckless men often produce more children than sophisticated, wealthy, well-educated, successful men.

Of course, individual men don't regard making babies as their overriding goal, even if evolution has molded them to do things that happen to produce more children. Biology has not made men want children as much as they want sex. Biology managed to get men to participate in reproducing the species by making them desire sex, regardless of babies. Acting on that inclination, men have invented ways of having sex without making babies (another victory of culture over nature!). Successful men do not necessarily want to have a hundred babies, but they often do want to have sex with a hundred women. And the culture they have created cooperates. Today's highly successful men have multiple sex partners (perhaps not a hundred, though some do), but often they carefully avoid having a bumper crop of babies. Indeed, the norms and laws that promote monogamy mean that successful men must conceal their sexual dalliances, and toward that end preventing pregnancy is vital.

So natural selection and the tough reproductive odds have ensured that modern men are descended, not necessarily from men who wanted to have dozens of babies, but from men who wanted to achieve greatness and rise above other men. The men who lacked the impulse to seek greatness did not pass on their genes very successfully. As a result, the passion to seek greatness flows in the blood of today's men.

Women reproduced regardless of whether they strove for greatness. The women who did not strive for greatness had just as many babies as those who did. If anything, striving for greatness has often demanded (and still demands) a dedication to work and career that is difficult to reconcile with having a large brood of children. Hence, that passion for greatness may not be as deeply ingrained in the psychology of today's women.

The motivational difference in terms of striving for greatness is the main point of this chapter. The final sections develop various implications of it.

Traded-off Traits

Many different motivations can be understood on the basis of the most underappreciated fact. Risk taking has already been mentioned. Men have less to lose and more to gain, and so nature favored risk-taking men more than women. The riskier the career, the greater the preponderance of males. You see relatively few women going into high-risk careers such as politics, racing cars, professional gambling, and investment banking. It is quite difficult to think of a high-risk career that attracts substantially more women than men.

Creativity is another approach. Men need to find ways to stand out. Following along the standard path may lead to biological failure, and we are descended from more of the men who sought a new angle, a different approach, a novel strategy.

In the last chapter, we pondered the difference in creativity. Men and women seem to have equal creative abilities and creative potential, at least when they are tested. Yet somehow, throughout history and all over the world, men seem much more passionately driven to create than women are. My best guess is that this reflects the result of the most underappreciated fact. Something deep inside a man, the product of centuries of evolution, nudges him along to try to create something new and different—and not only to create it, but to use that creation to make his mark in the broader society, to set him apart from and possibly above other men. After all, he is mainly descended from the men who did succeed in rising above others. The men who, like women, may have had creative ability but did not feel any deep passionate urge to make something different were less likely to pass on their genes. Actually being creative, as in producing something new and remarkable and wonderful, enabled the men to gain respect and status and to attract the interest of women, and so being creative improved their success at reproducing.

Competition and ambition are also important, as is aggression in the broader sense of being aggressive in pursuit of goals. Women may compete for the best mates, but they are not really competing against each other as to whether they will be able to have any babies at all. Every man faces extinction. He competes against other men to get to the top, where wealth and status are to be had. Nature instilled that drive in him, because wealth and status attract women. Irrespective of procreation, gay men and men who do not want children still may have plenty of ambition to rise to the top.

And it never really ends. A man can always get richer and more powerful. Usually, at least in principle, he can have more babies too. The men who were content to reach a certain moderate level of success and to have a child or two may have kept their line of descendants alive, but the men who kept striving and became ever richer and more powerful—and fathered ever more babies—were generally much more prolific at attracting women and leaving offspring. Today's population is descended disproportionately from that sort of man.

So ambition is likely to be more pronounced in men than in women. Women didn't need ambition in order to reproduce. Men did. Or at least, all else being equal, men with ambition left behind more children than men who lacked ambition. More of today's men are descended from the forefathers with ambition.

The sex drive is another likely consequence of the most underappreciated fact. Nature built men to live with the reality that they very well might not reproduce at all. Hence, it became crucial to capitalize on every opportunity. A young man who refused an offer of intercourse on a chance meeting with a comely lass in the woods might have passed up his only chance to have a child.

Those concerns don't apply to women. Mostly, women throughout our history could expect to have many more opportunities for sex than they needed to produce babies. (This is still true today, for those who may not have noticed.) For a woman, the game is about finding the best quality mate, someone with good genetic quality and who will stick around to support her and the children.

She doesn't need to be biologically wired to leap at every opportunity for sex. He does. Or at least, having that sexual eagerness would likely pay off in terms of more offspring. It might help him beat the odds and avoid extinction. Or it might give him an additional child or two on top of his legitimate heirs. Either way, being easily aroused would be a biologically rewarded strategy for men much more than for women.

Why Men Go to Extremes

The most underappreciated fact may have something to say about the pattern discussed in the opening chapters, namely that men go to extremes more than women. Nature plays the dice more with men than women. Men are nature's playthings, nature's guinea pigs.

This argument is speculative. I have discussed this with various experts and mostly they think it is likely somewhat true, though it is far from a proven fact (and genuine experts tend to be quite cautious about making statements beyond what is definitively known).

Here's one reason men may be more likely to be genetically extreme than women. Think of a mutation, that is, a novel and unusual combination of genes, as an experiment: trying out a new trait to see how it fares. That's what drives evolution. Inevitably, most of these experiments are failures. Unlike human experiments, which are carefully planned and thought out, nature's experiments are designed at random, just producing a new genetic combination to see what happens. Evolution is very much about hit-or-miss trial and error, and there are many more errors than successes, more misses than hits.

The optimal vehicle for a genetic experiment would have two characteristics. If the experiment is a failure, it should be quickly eliminated from the gene pool, so that the bad mutation doesn't contaminate the species for many future generations. On the other side, if the experiment is a success, ideally it should spread quickly through the gene pool.

Put more bluntly, if the mutant is a loser, it should have no babies, and if it is a winner, it should have lots of babies, who in turn should have lots more babies. I say "should" in terms of what will yield the best results for the species and gene pool. (There is no moral "should" here.)

Males are much better suited for this role of nature's guinea pig than females. Remember, a woman can give birth only about once a year, whereas a man can father many different children in the same year. Meanwhile, many males have no offspring, while most females do have at least one child and usually more than that.

Consider the wild horses again. The dominant male that summer has sex with all the females. The females have one foal each. He has a whole crop of them. The other males in the herd have none, or almost none. A few years in the future, when that summer's crop of foals is grown to adulthood, that stallion's sons compete for the top position, and the winning son gets to have sex with all the stallion's daughters. His other sons are again left out.

To make the point extra clear, suppose there were four mutants in that crop of newborn horses: two sons and two daughters. One of each is superior to all the others, maybe stronger or faster, more good-looking, and with better hearing. The other two mutants are biologically inferior specimens to all the others: weak, sickly, stupid, unattractive, partly deaf.

The superior son, boosted by his advantage, has a better-than-average chance to win the competition to become the alpha male. As a result, he will have sex with all the females. Hence the next generation in that herd will all have his traits, including those that made him a superior specimen. The loser son will most likely not have sex at all. His mutation will die with him. In this way, the next crop of foals will be superior to the previous one. Due to nature's experiments with the males, the genetic quality of the herd will have improved.

Now consider the two mutant daughters. The superior daughter will have one foal that summer. But so will the inferior one. The genetic quality of the herd will not change much.

Put in terms of nature trying out experiments, the experiment with the sons brought about significant progress in the species: the superior trait quickly spread through the group, while the inferior trait was flushed out of its gene pool within one generation. But the experiment on the females failed to produce change. Both the superior and the inferior trait survived into next generation.

Maybe, over many generations, the female experiment would work out too. At some point, the superior female might have more babies than the inferior female. But the results are far more powerful and immediate with the male. For that reason, perhaps, nature prefers to experiment on males.

This difference could explain the male extremity pattern. Nature rolls the dice more aggressively with males than females, because it is easier to capitalize on wins and cut the losses.

CHAPTER 5

Are Women More Social?

I LIKE WOMEN. To be blunt and undiplomatic, I like women better than men. Somehow women are more fun to talk to than men, more satisfying to have long-term friendships and relationships with, and nicer to live with.

In this, I'm not alone. On average, most people (both men and women) like women better than men. We have already seen that people hold more favorable stereotypes of women than men (the "WAW" effect), but there's more than that. There have been research studies showing that people who have at least a ten-minute conversation with a woman at any point during the day end up happier that day, on average, as compared to people who don't speak to a woman that day. Talking to a man provides no such boost to mood and well-being. This is not to say that talking to men is bad. And some men are no doubt inspiring. Still, on average, speaking with women is good for body and soul in a way that isn't matched by the indifferent effects of speaking with men.

Chapter 4 concluded that women are generally more lovable than men, and that the difference lies in what people want most. Men would like to be lovable, but they have other priorities, like competing against other men and striving for greatness.

As mentioned previously, men can be lovable when they want to be. Most men manage it well enough to persuade somebody to love them and marry them. But then other concerns surface. In Flaubert's famous novel, *Madame Bovary*, the young Charles Bovary was at first consumed by his love for Emma. His world revolved around her. He devoted plenty of time and energy to thinking of ways to win her heart. He succeeded. When she married him, he was ecstatic for a while. Then he turned his attention back to his work and other pursuits, more or less taking her for granted.

True, people will sometimes gravitate toward powerful men, but this is more about the power than the man himself. Over years of attending professional conferences, I have noticed that when the top journal editors—these are probably the most powerful people in a scientific field, able to do significant good or harm to young careers, and they are mostly men—walk through a meeting, they typically have a big entourage of smiling people accompanying them and talking rapidly to them. Once they stop being editors, however, these same guys wander alone through the social hours, drink in hand, hoping to latch on to somebody else's conversational group. In other words, at one of these conferences, it's difficult to get a word with a current editor, but you can chat with an ex-editor for an hour. Once the man's power is gone, so is his entourage. No wonder some men become depressed and lonely when they retire.

One common way of understanding these patterns is to say that women are simply more social than men. Women have better interpersonal skills, are better at understanding people, better at communicating with them, and better at understanding them.

This common view is wrong. But it takes a bit of looking to discern the tradeoffs and complications.

You'd Hardly Notice

Here are two recent news stories that appeared while I was starting to write this book. They could be replaced by any number of similar others.

One appeared in *USA Today*, under the headline, "More women of color take lead on path to entrepreneurship." The other, on Yahoo! News, had the headline "Researchers identify 'male warrior effect'." If you read both stories carefully, they suggest important tradeoffs and point to some good things about men, but these are well concealed. From the headlines and opening paragraphs, you'd conclude that these stories show women out-performing men in business and being more peacefully inclined. Both suggest that women will function better in a modern, peaceful society. Again, women seem more socially adept than men.

The *USA Today* story was about how African American women now own more companies than their male counterparts. Similar patterns are found across other racial and ethnic categories. Women start more small businesses than men do. The thrust of the article was that women are doing great while men, well, aren't.

But if you read the whole long article, toward the end there is mention that women still "lag behind" on some measures, such as owning a business that employs anyone except the owner, or starting a business that makes enough of a profit to support a family. Apparently this tsunami of women's businesses consists mostly of part-time, one-person operations, whereas the men start and run bigger outfits that earn more money. I shall soon propose that this is a very typical difference and holds important clues as to some things men might be good for.

The Yahoo! News story started off depicting men as violent warmongers but in the very last paragraph noted that this could be a double-edged sword (yes, they used precisely that violent metaphor) because it could have positive consequences. If you read the full story, the research behind the "male warrior effect" actually had no hint of violent behavior in it. The men in the study cooperated to invest their money in a collective venture that would benefit them all. Men did this more when they knew their group was competing against other groups, whereas the women failed to respond to the group competition aspect of the study. The last paragraph conceded that this pattern of cooperative investment could be useful for building social institutions and governments, as well as for war.

To me, the least interesting aspect of these stories is the anti-male bias. The headlines and opening paragraphs, which are all that many people read, depict women as energetic, constructive, and peace-loving creatures while men are lazy losers and violent warmakers. The research on which they are based actually showed positive male behavior too, but this is quite far hidden toward the back of the story. All journalists learn to write so as to put the important information up front and bury other details away in the back, on the assumption that most readers start at the beginning and stop reading at some point, so the first paragraphs of any story are more widely read than the last ones.

Unfortunately, this style of coverage makes it harder for us to appreciate the genuine tradeoffs that exist. My theory is that men and women are genuinely different in ways that are built on tradeoffs. Anything good about women is likely balanced against something that is good about men.

More bluntly, I agree with much of what you hear. Men do have some serious drawbacks and bad traits. But mostly these are linked to some very positive traits that at least are useful for the society—for the cultural system that might be competing against other tribes or other countries.

Hints of some of the neglected virtues of men can be found in these two stories. The media are sensitive to avoid any charges of anti-female bias, and so they are reluctant to report anything that suggests men would be better than women in any respect, but I think these stories do point toward some very important realities. In both stories, men were working together with other men to build groups that can perform and create value. In the lab "warrior effect" experiments, the men were pooling their money to form cooperative groups. In the *USA Today* report on entrepreneurship, they were creating large businesses.

It is a fact that women start more small businesses than men do. But it is also a fact that men create and run more large businesses than women do. I think these findings reflect the basic differences and point toward some things that are good about men, as well as some things that are good about women. There are tradeoffs underlying all these.

The specific finding in the "male warrior effect" was that men worked together more when in competition with another group, whereas women pooled and invested the same amount regardless of competition. Thus, men compete in groups, against other groups of men.

Agreeing with our Imaginary Feminist, today's conventional wisdom in academia depicts culture and history as revolving around conspiracies among men to oppress women. Men are against women, in this view. My reading of the facts is somewhat different. I think men compete mainly against other men. That has been the basic fact and driving force in the historical progress of human culture. The actual data in the "Male warrior effect" work fit that view. It isn't about men against women: It's about men against men. In historical fact, men have always competed against other men. It is still happening. Often men competed for women, thus regarding women as the prize for victory, an attitude that probably goes back quite far through our evolutionary history, into other species where the alpha male (who got to the top by besting other males) was the only one that was allowed to have sex. But seeing women as the prize is quite different from seeing them as the enemy. I don't think men see women as the enemy.

If anything, I suspect most men like women more than they like each other. I do, as I already said. If this is true, the idea that men in general conspire together against women is dubious.

This point will be worth bringing up again, when we consider the history of culture and ponder why women ended up in an inferior, "oppressed" position in society. The standard view is that men banded together against women. I suggest, instead, that it is because men banded together against other men, though there is obviously more to the story than that. For now, just notice that in this research, like in other studies, men readily and perhaps instinctively band together to compete against other groups of men.

The Case for Women Being More Social

The idea that women are more social than men has a long history. It is one major theme in the female superiority literature: one of the big things that most people agree women are better at. Women are considered to be the experts on relationships. They show their feelings and understand those of others better than men do. (Actually this is not so well documented in fact. Women say they are better at these things, compared to what men say about themselves, but objective tests often find small or no differences.)

Brain research has strengthened the stereotype that women are more interpersonally oriented than men, at least in some respects. Indeed, Simon Baron-Cohen has concluded that the disorder of autism represents an extreme form of the typical male brain. Autistic individuals may be quite intelligent and capable of remarkable mental feats in terms of mastering systems of information, but they are not good at understanding *people*. According to Baron-Cohen, the brain has a tradeoff between empathizing and systematizing. The female brain tends to be geared toward empathy, which includes emotional sensitivity to other people and deep interest in understanding them and their feelings. In contrast, the male brain is oriented toward understanding systems, which means figuring out general principles of how things operate and function together, and this applies to inanimate objects as much as social systems. Male brains are fascinated by abstractions and the interrelationships of multiple parts of things. Female brains are fascinated by human emotions and the unique properties of individual persons.

The idea that women are more social than men was articulated beautifully in a major review article in 1997 by Drs. Susan Cross and Laura Madsen. They amassed an impressive set of research findings to make their point about women being the more interpersonally adept and successful gender. For example, plenty of evidence shows that men are more aggressive than women. Why? Aggression can destroy relationships. If you hit a lover or a friend, the relationship could come to a quick end. Cross and Madsen said that men are willing to hit because they don't care about relationships. To women, it's not worth the risk. So that's why men hit people and women don't: Women are more social than men.

The two scholars had other arguments. They pointed out that in self-concepts, men tend to emphasize how they are different, unique, and independent. Meanwhile, women focus their self-concepts on how they are related to others. Ask a man to say something about himself, and he's likely to bring up some special skill or accomplishment that sets him apart from others. Ask a woman, and she's more likely to mention her relationships—she is so-and-so's mother or wife. Thus again, said Cross and Madsen, women want to connect, and men want to separate.

They had to struggle a bit with a few facts that didn't' fit the picture they were painting. Cross and Madsen noted that much research had shown that men are more likely to help people than women are. Helping is a way to connect with others, so that ought to have disturbed those authors who were eagerly painting men as less social than women. It did bother them, a little. But they managed to shrug it off. They said, maybe women haven't been socialized to help.

The picture that emerged from this review was that women are concerned with connecting with other people—with forming and maintaining close interpersonal relationships. Men aren't. Men seem content to break bonds, push people away, and strike out on their own.

Cross and Madsen made a good case. In fact, their article was published in one of the most prestigious and competitive journals in all of psychology. As one of the experts who helped evaluate it, I voted for publication—even though I realized that someone might draw a different conclusion from all their evidence.

The Need to Belong

There was something wrong all along with the conclusion that women are more social than men.

In the first place, men need other people just as much as women need other people. No humans are designed by nature to go it alone. All over the world, people live in small social groups, usually embedded in larger social groups. And men have mostly formed and run those groups, especially the large ones. Hello? How does that square with the idea that men aren't social?

The "need to belong" is one of the most basic and influential human needs. That was the gist of a major review article the internationally acclaimed scholar Professor Mark Leary and I published in 1995. Doing the research for that article took several years and changed the way he and I thought about the world. Probably most psychologists had had some idea that people are driven to connect with others, but few had anticipated how much that need is behind seemingly every corner of the psyche and all manner of behavior. (I know neither Dr. Leary nor I had realized how powerful that was when we started the project.) In the dozen years after that article was published, it was listed in the bibliographies of more than a thousand other journal articles, plus many books. That is an indication that plenty of experts were influenced by it.

Just to give you an idea: the need to belong drives both thinking and feeling. In fact, most increases in belongingness bring positive emotion, and most decreases bring negative emotion, which is a clue that the whole emotion system is geared to make you connect with others. That may not be the only function of emotions, but it is obviously a major one.

Even physical health is strongly tied to belongingness. People who are alone in the world are more likely to die, and at an earlier age, from just about every known cause of death, as compared to people who are connected to others. When loners get sick, they are less likely to recover, and if they do, it takes them longer. This is true for everything from a cut on their finger to tuberculosis and heart attacks. And it isn't just physical health: mental health shows the same pattern. People who are alone in the world (and even those who just feel more alone) suffer from a broad range of mental illnesses, more than people who are socially connected.

The picture of the human being that emerges from that work is that humans are strongly, deeply, basically programmed to connect with others. Everything about the human psyche—its wants, its needs, its preferences, its capabilities—pushes it to belong.

The need to belong is not limited to women. Men have it too. If belongingness were mainly a female goal, the data would have been much weaker overall. But all those facts apply to men. Men who are alone in the world get sicker and die younger than men who have strong social networks, just like women. The conclusion that "men don't care about relationships" is at odds with a large mass of research findings.

That article was the reason the editor contacted me for an opinion on whether the Cross and Madsen paper should be published. Their opinion, that men aren't very social, seemed to pose a direct contradiction to the conclusion Leary and I had reached, which is that everybody needs to belong (and which likewise had just come out in that same journal). The editor wanted to know my opinion as to whether to publish their paper, and if not, why not. Their paper, and Leary's and my paper, couldn't both be right.

I generally try to go out of my way to support publishing research that goes against my views. I regard that as a helpful process for reaching the best conclusions. I try not to get ego-invested with particular ideas, and I very much prefer to change my views when new findings bring new insights. So I voted in favor of publishing the Cross and Madsen paper. But I had some doubts, and so, along with an energetic young researcher named Kristin Sommer who had just finished her PhD, I started looking into the research on gender differences in being social.

Why, then, did Cross and Madsen think that it's mainly just women who are social? One resolution, which they seem to have favored, is the by now common view that men are an inferior copy of women. In that view, both men and women might want relationships and might benefit from them, but women are better designed to succeed at this. Men blunder around, seeking independence, getting into fights, doing other things that sabotage their relationships, at cost to themselves. Essentially, men are just poorly designed human beings. There are actually plenty of experts around who think that is precisely true.

But it's wrong.

No, They Aren't

You could make a case for women being the more social gender. In fact, that's just what Cross and Madsen did. It misses a key point.

Women are indeed more social if you define "social" only in terms of one-to-one close, intimate relationships. But if you look at bigger groups, then *men* are more social than women.

Thus, the simple ideas that men are poorly designed humans, or that they somehow lack the need to belong, are silly. To understand the difference between men and women, it is necessary to recognize two different spheres of social interaction and two different ways of being social. Women are designed for the small, intimate sphere of close relationships in which people connect one to one. Men are better designed for the large sphere in which there are more connections to more people. These connections aren't as close or as intense, by and large, as the intimate relationships at which women specialize. But they are important in other ways.

Let's return to the arguments that Cross and Madsen used to make the case that women are more social than men. Start with aggression. They said, quite reasonably, that women avoid aggression because aggression can damage close social bonds. The greater aggressiveness of men seems to indicate that men don't care about breaking social bonds.

It's a clever explanation, but it doesn't fit all the facts. If you look specifically at what happens in close relationships, it turns out women are plenty aggressive in them—if anything, more violent than men. It isn't politically correct to point it out, but the data are quite solid on this. Women are more likely than men to attack their romantic partners physically—everything from a slap on the face to assault with a deadly weapon. Women's violence doesn't get the media attention that men's violence does, for several reasons. First, men are less willing than women to report the incidents. Second, when both spouses are violent, the police usually blame the man and take the woman's side. Third, perhaps, women are better at playing the victim role. Fourth, and by far the most important, men are bigger and stronger than women, so the same amount of aggression produces much more harm when perpetrated by a man than by a woman. In other words, if husband and wife start hitting each other, she's likely to come out second best. It's why most men don't pick a fight with a guy who's eight inches taller and eighty pounds heavier than they are.

Women also commit more child abuse than men, although this is hard to untangle from the fact that they spend much more time with children than men do. But in terms of violence toward all relationship partners, women initiate slightly more aggression than men do. Even if you regard the difference as small and call it even, this finding is completely incompatible with the theory that women refrain from violence because they are afraid of damaging relationships. Women don't mind perpetrating violent acts against intimate partners, or at least they don't mind it any more than men do.

The difference lies elsewhere. Men engage in acts of violence in the broader social sphere. Boys fight other boys in their school or neighborhood. Men get into fights with distant acquaintances and total strangers. A man may go to a bar, take offense at what someone else says, and end up in a nasty fight, sometimes even a deadly one. Women generally don't do such things. Imagine a woman going shopping at the mall and getting into a knife fight with a woman she never met before. By and large, this kind of thing just doesn't happen.

Women don't hit strangers. That's where the big gender difference in aggression is to be found.

Thus, the difference between male and female aggression has nothing to do with close relationships, contrary to what Cross and Madsen mistakenly thought. The difference lies in distant or stranger relationships. And so the difference in aggression is not based on women's reluctance to risk a close relationship. It's because of a difference in the kind of relationship that people care about. Women care about what intimate partners think, and so they will fight there. Men will too. Women don't care as much about what strangers or distant acquaintances think, and so they won't fight them. Men care, and men will fight them.

Helping is in some ways the opposite of aggression, so it is a useful counterpoint. Hurting is bad; helping is good. So when helping and hurting show the same conclusion, we have broad agreement and can be confident we're on to something.

Helping shows the same pattern as aggression. As mentioned earlier, research has shown repeatedly that men help more than women. Cross and Madsen had to dodge and duck this fact to maintain their thesis that women are more social than men. They eventually fell back on the standard sort of argument that the reason women don't help must be that women are oppressed: patriarchal socialization doesn't encourage women to be helpful. The Imaginary Feminist nodded approvingly.

The real reason most research finds men to be more helpful than women is that most research looks at interactions between strangers, usually unacquainted members of a large group (like fellow students at the same university). A typical lab experiment will stage-manage a fake emergency and see whether the research participant (who doesn't know it's staged) takes action to help the apparent victim. In these settings, men help more than women. But that's helping a stranger. Meanwhile, though, if you look at helping within close relationships, the difference vanishes or reverses (just as with aggression). Who cares for the sick, comforts the upset, sacrifices one's own career prospects in order to take care of someone else? Yes, some men do, but women probably do it more. Within close relationships, women are as helpful if not more helpful than men.

Thus, the same pattern is found with both helping and aggression. People help and hurt more in the relationships they care about. Both men and women do these things in close, intimate relationships, but women do them a bit more. In the broader sphere of weaker social relationships among a larger group, men do these things more than women.

Hence, we concluded that women are more social than men only if you focus exclusively on intimacy and family. In the larger social sphere, men are, if anything, more social than women.

A great deal of other information points to the same conclusion. For example, researchers who observe children on the playground find that girls will typically pair off and stay together for a full hour. In the same time frame, boys either play one-on-one with a revolving series of partners or play in large groups. Experimental studies have also been done in which two children are allowed to get settled into playing together and then a third child is brought in. Girls usually reject the third girl, but boys welcome the third boy into their game. This doesn't mean that boys are "more social" any more than the greater pair-bonding signals greater sociality among girls. Girls want the one-on-one connection, and so having a third person spoils the event. Boys are more oriented toward larger groups, and so adding a third boy doesn't spoil their game.

When the article by Cross and Madsen was published along with my and Sommer's counterpoint, it caught the interest of other researchers, some of whom started conducting experiments to test these competing theories. Between then and now, plenty of others have pitted them against each other. The data overwhelmingly backed our view, and Cross and Madsen have graciously changed their opinion to come round to ours.[1] Men are not less social than women. Rather, men and women are social in different ways.

Two Ways of Being Social

What all this points to is that there are two very different ways of being social that correspond to two different types of relationships. The genders differ as to which one they specialize in.

The one sphere involves close, intimate interactions. The main type of relationship is made up of two persons, who interact on a one-to-one basis. The technical term for this kind of interpersonal structure is the "dyad," which is based on the Latin and Greek words for "two." Another common term is the "pair bond."

The other sphere involves less intimacy but more people. Its main type of relationship is made up of larger groups, which can range from three to millions of people. Most commonly, think of groups ranging from half a dozen to a couple thousand people.

Psychology, and surprisingly even my own field of social psychology, tends to focus mainly on the first kind. Research articles and books about interpersonal relationships are about intimate interactions, indeed mainly romantic relationships.

Close, one-to-one relationships are important. Probably they are in fact the most important relationships that people have. They certainly are the most satisfying and have the clearest effects on mental and physical health. But other relationships matter too. The loose network of acquaintances, colleagues, and other associates is an important dimension of human social life.

---

1 This, incidentally, is how science is supposed to work, with teams of researchers building on each other's work. Sommer and I never would have started our project had we not read Cross and Madsen's paper.

How Big Is Your Unit?

Once the social world is sorted into different kinds of relationships, then, it is possible to revisit the question of which gender is more social. The answer depends on which size of social unit you are talking about. If you take the usual, somewhat myopic focus of most psychologists, you emphasize the one-to-one pattern of intimate relationships: the pair bond. In that milieu, yes, women seem more social than men.

But if you emphasize the larger social group, then men begin to seem more social. Try this thought experiment: List as many large group activities as you can think of. Then ask yourself which gender tends to gravitate toward those activities. In general, the answer is men. Your list might include politics, team sports, large corporations, military groups, economic systems, maybe even fields that work by the accumulation of knowledge from many different sources, as in science and technology. These are things that attract both genders—but men more than women. It is very difficult to come up with any kind of large group activity that appeals to women more than men.

Now let's return to the view that sees women as more social than men, and the stacked-deck evidence it claimed. Viewed in the proper light, it doesn't show that women are more social overall. Rather, it shows that women are more oriented toward the intimate form of social relating, whereas men are more oriented toward the larger group.

Traded-off Traits

Now we come to the heart of the question of how men and women are different. Let's consider how a variety of traits make crucial tradeoffs between being better at intimacy versus more effective in large groups. If women's interests and desires are oriented more toward the intimate relationship, while men orient more toward the large group, then men and women will differ along these dimensions.

Which is better? Again, I wish we could stop thinking this way, because these comparisons, dripping with value judgments, have poisoned the atmosphere for studying gender. Neither is better. They are different. Each style of interacting is better suited for one kind of relationship and correspondingly less well suited for the other. That's what a tradeoff is all about.

The female style builds a few strong, close social bonds. The male style builds many weaker ones. Do you want a loving marriage with strong family ties? Then you need the female style. Do you want a work group, like a ship's crew or a hunting group or a soccer team? Then the male style will work better.

The crucial point is that these require tradeoffs. You might say that the ideal human being would be good at both intimate relationships and large group interactions. I agree! But perhaps that is not so easy for nature to arrange. Perhaps being good at one means being less good at the other. After all, when the kids have only one hour on the playground, they have to choose between spending the whole hour playing with the same one best-friend playmate or instead playing with lots of different kids.

Once we get past the poisonous question of which gender is better, we can start to see the tradeoffs. And these may extend far beyond than how to pass an hour on the playground. They go deep into the human mind. The same traits that make someone better at close relationships may make one less well suited for large groups, and vice versa. Because both are important, nature preserved differences. In a nutshell, that's a major reason why there are some average personality differences between men and women.

Sharing Your Feelings

Women show their feelings more than men. This is a standard, well-documented difference between the sexes. On this, the stereotypes are correct. Men are more likely than women to hold their feelings inside and even to deny having them.

Being highly expressive with your feelings is great for intimacy. Two people who show their feelings right away can understand each other better and, as a result, can give each other the love, warmth, and other things they need. They can spot problems early and can anticipate what will make the other happy or sad. Intimate relationships are designed for supporting one another, and expressing your feelings freely will help this process.

But in large groups, emotional expression can make you vulnerable to rivals, who can spot and exploit your weaknesses. In economic transactions, like haggling over the price of a shirt or a used car, showing your feelings can weaken your bargaining position. And in many other ways, wearing your heart on your sleeve is not the most effective strategy for working your way up to the top. To function effectively in a large group, it is probably more useful to be somewhat reserved about showing your feelings, and likewise it may be prudent not to leap to the conclusions about others, who may likewise be playing close to the vest.

Crying is a good example. Crying is a vivid expression of a person's current emotional state. Someone who can express herself by crying probably will make a better relationship partner than someone who never cries. Crying may be very effective with someone who loves you, because it gets that person's attention and elicits concern and motivates that person to help you. (That's why babies cry!) But crying also reveals one's weakness. Crying in the presence of rivals or enemies may encourage them to pounce on you, to take advantage. As we move men and women into ever more similar, intermixed lives, men have begun to cry more, but before about the 1960s American men knew not to cry, and I believe this was the standard male role for thousands of years. And for good reason.

Similar arguments apply to other emotions. Expressing fear may be useful in close relationships, especially for someone who is not very powerful and needs help from others. In a large group, however, expressing fear has multiple drawbacks. It reveals your weakness to rivals and enemies. Even among friends, it can be seen as damaging to the group. When soldiers prepare to go into battle, what good does it do to show fear? Each man is struggling to overcome his own fear, in order to do what has to be done. Another man expressing his fear makes it harder for everyone else. It lowers the group's morale. If one guy is crying, it is harder for all the others to get themselves set for battle, to do what needs to be done. And not being ready will increase their risk of losing the battle and being hurt or killed.

Even with happy, positive feelings, there are reasons to keep them hidden from the group. Showing joy, excitement, pleasure, and even interest can weaken your bargaining position. (Never tell the owner of the used car you like that you simply must have it!)

Anger is the most likely exception, and on this, men are probably just as willing as women to express their feelings. Anger has advantages even in dealing with strangers. Recent studies suggest that showing anger during negotiation can make the other side more willing to make a deal, or to accept an offer that is less favorable to them and more favorable to the angry person. So men do show feelings when doing so is helpful to social life in groups.

Expressing Other Things

Feelings aren't the only things people talk about of course—nor are they the only topic on which men and women express themselves differently. In recent years, there has been much discussion of differences in speech styles. Deborah Tannen's book *You Just Don't Understand*, based on work by the linguist Robin Lakoff, detailed how men tend to use clear, strong, forceful language, whereas women use more gentle, indirect styles of expressing themselves. In a restaurant, a woman might say to the waiter, "Could I please maybe have some water when you get a chance? I'm really thirsty. I'm sorry. Thank you." A man might find it sufficient to say, "Could we get some water over here?"

The stock explanation for these has been that men have more power than women and hence use powerful forms of expression. But the idea that all men think of themselves as powerful beings is one of the most absurd and unfounded assertions in the gender studies arena. The Imaginary Feminist often starts her analyses by thinking of the male role as one of power. Few actual men think that way. Most men know there is a hierarchy of power and that they are far from the top.

Instead of power, one can see the difference in expressive styles as another manifestation of the different spheres. The gentle, asking, indirect style of speech favored by many women is suitable for an interaction among equals or near-equals in an intimate relationship. The questioning, apologetic style of talking to the waiter in my example would be a fine way to ask a favor of a relationship partner. It assumes the other person cares about you and would like to provide for you, so merely hinting at what you need is enough. And you don't want to impose, because you care about the person, so you justify your request and leave ample room for the person to decline.

The male style is probably better suited to operating in a large group. In such a group, you don't assume the other cares greatly about you or is attending closely to what you want and need. You have to say very plainly and directly what you want. Imagine a football coach saying, "Do you think maybe we could please try a screen pass here? If you think it's a good idea.

We don't have to do it if anybody doesn't feel good about it. I just thought it was something we maybe could consider. I'm sorry. Thanks." Or, likewise, imagine an officer in the middle of a battle speaking in such terms about advancing on the enemy's flank.

Two Versions of Fairness

Fairness is important in all human social relations, whether large or small. But there are two different kinds of fairness. Experts call these equity and equality. Equality means treating everyone the same (obviously). Equity means giving out rewards in proportion to what each person contributed. Under equity, the person who contributes more or better work gets a proportionately bigger share of the reward.

Suppose you were to see an ad offering $400 to paint somebody's garage, and you team up with three other people to do it. Everyone agrees to get started at 9 A.M. on Sunday and stay till it's done. You're there at 8:45 and you start setting up. When two of the others arrive at 9:30, you're already painting. The fourth person gets there at 11, helps a little, takes frequent breaks to talk on the cell phone, disappears for an hour at lunch time, and then has to leave early. One of the others also leaves early, so you and the last other person finish the job. Should the money be divided equally ($100 each), or should you get a bigger share while the slacker gets a smaller one? Both outcomes can be considered fair, but one is fair based on equality, while the other is based on equity.

Researchers have developed laboratory methods to test for these differences. Typically, a group of research participants will be set to work on some task. At the end, the experimenter will tell one participant that the group has earned a certain amount of money and it is up to that person to divide it up. You can keep it all for yourself or spread it around in any way you think best. What would you do?

The typical finding is that men and women react differently. And no, very few people decide to keep all the money for themselves. The women tend to divide the money equally, giving an identical share to each person. The men divide it up equitably, which means that those who worked harder and produced more get a bigger share of the money. Which is better? Which is fairer? Neither is inherently the better or right way. Rather, the two systems reflect different ideas of fairness.

You can't do both at once. Equity relies on unequal rewards, which is the opposite of equality. Hence, there is a tradeoff: more of one means less of the other.

Intimate relationships tend to work best with equality. There are so many forms of interaction that it is hard to keep track of who is doing more in what sphere. One earns more money, the other does more housework; one cleans the yard, the other makes dinner. Trying to decide whose contributions are worth more is divisive. If the other people in the garage-painting example were your brothers and sisters, probably you would lean toward an equal division of the money, though there might be some grumbling about the slacker.

But in large groups, equity works better. If the people in the garage painting example were distant acquaintances, and if they insisted on dividing up the money with equal $100 shares for everybody, that would probably be the end of the group: You would not be likely to sign up for another job with that same bunch.

The motto of communism was, "from each according to his ability; to each according to his need." We say that communism has been discredited, but in fact most families today operate as small communes, pretty much along the lines of that motto. Nobody says the six-year-old can't have good food or quality medical care because of not having contributed enough to the family income. Communism works fine in the intimate sphere. But not for big groups. It's no accident that every large organization today pays people different amounts. Equality—giving everybody exactly the same salary, from the janitor to the CEO—won't produce good results.

Thus, the men favor equity, which works best in large groups. Women favor equality, which is ideal for one-to-one intimate relationships.

Hierarchy versus Equality

Any group, from two to two million people, can be organized in different ways. Equality puts everyone at the same level of status and authority. Hierarchy arranges them in order from high to low. With hierarchy, the ones at the top have various advantages over the ones at the bottom: possibly more power for making decisions about what the group should do, bigger shares of the rewards, even just enjoying the feelings of superiority.

Which is better? Again, it depends. In intimate relationships, equality may work best, though certainly sometimes a parent has to tell a child not to play with knives. Still, between adults, equality can improve intimacy, insofar as the two may interact more freely and may have more mutual respect and feeling for each other. It is perhaps not surprising that modern marriage has evolved toward ever greater emphasis on equality.

In larger groups and working groups, however, hierarchy is probably more effective if not essential. Modern families can move toward equality because their function is now mainly just to provide intimate relationships, with love and support, to each other. In the past, the family was first and foremost an economic unit, typically working together to operate a farm or sometimes a shop. In other words, the main purpose of the family was to work together to produce something. In those days, there was less of a push toward equality and more hierarchy, typically with a mature adult man in the role of the boss or CEO.

As for larger groups, hierarchy is the norm. Can you imagine an army or even a platoon operating effectively with everyone being equal, nobody in command at all? The same for a corporation with nobody as a boss? Or a football team? In large groups that have to get things done, hierarchy is almost a necessity.

Status hierarchies are not entirely the product of human culture and in fact are found in nature. Pecking orders, alphas, and other terms refer to the dominance hierarchy that typically evolves in many animal groups. But as a general rule, these are more common and more pronounced among males. Remember the wild horses we talked about in the previous chapter: There are big rewards for the male who makes it to the top spot. He gets to have sex, and lots of it, as well as various other pleasures like first pick of the food. The other males fare worse than he does. For the females, there is much less at stake. Under those circumstances, the males who care most about hierarchies will be the ones who pass along their genes, and so modern men are descended from the most status-conscious ancestors. The females, meanwhile, were able to reproduce at about the same rate regardless of their position in any hierarchy. As a result, the females who were content to stay quietly near the bottom of the heap—the less ambitious ones, we might say—still kept their genes in the gene pool.

Indeed, genuine equality is probably a cultural invention. Hierarchy is natural. But hierarchy is more effective for large groups that need to accomplish things. Equality appeals because it feels better and probably makes for healthier close relationships.

Competition versus Cooperation

Cooperation is useful in all social groups, large and small. But in some cases one has to choose between cooperating, as in helping others to achieve their goals, and competing against them. Then one must trade off cooperation versus competition.

The larger the group, the more competition matters and pays. What is the point of trying to outdo your spouse, of trying to show that you are better, smarter, faster, or stronger than she is at something? Competitions like that are not likely to change the relationship for the better. But in a large group, proving your worth does pay off. This follows directly from two of the differences we've already covered, namely equity and hierarchy. Large groups tend to bestow rewards unequally, giving bigger rewards to those who are better and do better. There are major advantages to being high in the hierarchy. You get up there by competing. You have to best your rivals, who want the same spot you do up near the top.

And so people who are designed to function in large groups are likely to lean toward being competitive.

Male competitiveness is much mocked and maligned. Sometimes it is frivolous, as when the boys on the beach try to skip the stone more times than each other. But it probably has a sound basis in biology. In our evolutionary past, the males who didn't compete hard enough to make it to the top didn't get to have sex and therefore didn't pass on their genes, so their descendants are not among us today. Meanwhile, the ones who cared passionately about competing, even the ones who were unpleasantly competitive, were more likely than others to make it to the top, and their descendants are everywhere today. We inherited their genes—and the urge to make it to the top along with them.

Agency and Communion

Probably the most widely accepted gender difference in personality is invoked by the clunky terms *agency* and *communion*. The terms were introduced by a philosopher named Bakan back in the 1960s, and several leading researchers on gender adopted them. *Communion* refers to merging with others, caring about them, being closely linked to them, and other related desires and behaviors. The term *agency* comes from being agentic, as in being someone who acts. In personality terms, it denotes initiative, autonomy, and generally regarding oneself as responsible for getting things done.

When researchers first began to survey the results of all the different trait and behavior patterns they found between men and women, many turned to this distinction as the best way of summing things up. Men were more agentic than women, while women were more communal than men. This distinction has stood the test of time reasonably well.

Why do the genders differ in that way? Again, it seems that those traits would be differentially suited to the different social spheres. In a close relationship, it is fair to assume that others care about you, and for you to care about them would be good for the relationship. To devote oneself to taking care of them, to identify strongly with them, to share everything with them—all of that seems a fine recipe for building a strong relationship, especially if others act the same.

In a large group, however, you cannot assume that others care about you. In fact, we shall return to this crucial fact later when we consider how expendable the members of male groups are. Ultimately, everyone is replaced in such a group, whether we are talking about the San Francisco Giants, the U.S. Marines, or the Milwaukee Fire Department. To make your way in such a group, it is vital to look out actively for your interests. You have to decide what role you want to play in the group. Possibly you have to best several rivals for that job—and the more desirable your spot is, the more competition there is likely to be.

Assertiveness is one important form of agency. It means being willing to stand up for yourself and what you think is right, and to take charge of situations. It too seems much more needed in a large group, where meek and silent types can get shoved aside, than in a pair bond in which both people seek to take care of each other. Men are on average more assertive than women. Again, the male personality pattern thus fits what is best for large groups.

Nurturance is an important form of communion. It means wanting to take care of others and being sensitive to their needs. Women are more nurturing than men, in general.

Self-Concept

Another familiar and well-documented difference concerns how people think about and describe themselves. The classic Ingmar Bergmann film *Scenes from a Marriage* dramatized this. Early in the film, the interviewer asks them to tell a bit about themselves. The man rattles off a list of his traits, focusing on what his special qualities are. The woman seems unsure of how to respond and simply reiterates her love for her husband and their children.

Although men and women are in some ways becoming more similar to each other with the passing decades, there are still differences in what is emphasized in their self-concepts. Women are more likely to view themselves and describe themselves in terms of what are called relational traits, that is, traits that focus on being related to other people. Their identities are bound up in their social connections.

Men, meanwhile, emphasize traits that make them stand out from others, and they think of themselves more than women do as separate units. In fact, this difference was cited by Cross and Madsen (the researchers we discussed earlier) as another sign that women were more social than men. In their view, men's self-concepts focused on themselves as independent and unique and thus apart from others, whereas women's self-concepts were based on connections to others.

Again, though, it would be a mistake to see the independence and uniqueness in men's self-concepts as a sign that men are not social. Rather, these traits reflect men's way of being social. Men's social groups thrive on having different men specialize in different roles. In this sense, human groups are rather different from animal groups, and in fact this is one of the things that distinguishes human culture from the way most animals are social. If you look at some of the most successful groups in the world today, such as large corporations, they are full of a great many people, each of which performs a different job. The corporation is thus a giant system with many roles that specialize in different tasks, all of which are coordinated to enable the group to achieve its goals.

Having each person perform a different task, rather than having everyone do the same thing, enables each person to become expert at what he (or she) does. Nature has capitalized on this to some extent in having males and females specialize in different roles, but those roles are relatively inflexible and the unit (the pair) isn't large enough to yield huge gains. For a contrast, look at the assembly line, in which each worker specializes in one task and knows how to do it perfectly. Assembly lines took over the automobile industry precisely because they worked so well: They enabled the quality and quantity of manufacturing to be vastly improved. Companies could make more and better cars for less money using the assembly line than with other methods.

To succeed in such a group, a person needs to become different from others by cultivating some special ability or skill. The assembly line is made up of specialists, so anyone who wants to do well there has to be able to specialize. The large groups favored by men have this feature, and therefore men have selves that cultivate and emphasize ways of being different. The intimate pair relationships favored by women often involve mutuality, and so both people need to be the same in crucial ways. But to make your way in a large group, you need to be different. That's why men's self-concepts emphasize differences while women's self-concepts focus on social connections.

Consider a brass band. To succeed, the band needs an assortment of instruments. Twelve French horns won't make a very successful group. It's better to have a trumpet, a trombone, a sax, a tuba, and so forth, including one French horn. A man living in a small village with such a band may aspire to belong to it, and to succeed he needs to develop one of those skills. His chances are best if he learns an instrument that the band needs but nobody else can play.

This was the crucial mistake made by Cross and Madsen in their interpretation of male self-concepts. They thought that being different from others meant being separate from others. But for men, being different is a way to belong to others, a way to cement your place in the group. If you're the only one who can play the bass guitar, or throw a curve ball, or find water, or catch fish, or program a computer, they can't afford to get rid of you.

A mother doesn't have to learn the trombone to win her baby's love. Her child will love her regardless. (If anything, the baby might prefer that she not play the trombone!) Her husband will also love her without her being a trombone virtuoso. And so developing specialized skills and unique attributes is much less relevant for the kind of social life that women favor. But it is an important and valuable basis for connecting with others in the large social groups favored by men.

Earlier in this chapter, I said men weren't as lovable as women. Developing special skills is part of the explanation. If you're the only one who can play the trombone, the brass band will keep you regardless of how lovable or unlovable you are (although maybe not if you are completely impossible to get along with). Forced to choose between someone who is likable but with no musical aptitude and someone else who's rather aloof and grumpy but can make the trombone sing and soar, the band will usually choose the better musician rather than the boon companion. If it doesn't, the band will likely pay a high price in quality and hence in success. Other bands with better musicians will outperform it.

In short, for the kind of social relations men create, it is often more important to be capable than to be lovable. It's especially important to be capable at something relatively rare and valuable. That takes agency.

Morality and What's Right

Do men and women have different styles of moral thinking? This has been a controversial question in psychology.

The psychology of how people think about moral issues, about good and bad and right and wrong, was greatly influenced by the early thinker Lawrence Kohlberg. He developed a series of stages by which he claimed people matured into more advanced and sophisticated levels of moral understanding. Children might start out by judging good and bad based on how things turn out, but at more advanced levels they learn to judge by intentions. To the small child, spilled milk is bad, period, but the more mature thinker can distinguish between intentional and accidental spilling, and only the former is morally objectionable. At the highest levels, one moves on to judging things according to abstract principles.

Kohlberg proposed rather airily that the sequence he identified was universal. In 1983, a sharp rebuke came in an influential book by Carol Gilligan called *In a Different Voice*. She argued that Kohlberg's sequence might apply to men but that women used a different style of moral reasoning. She called this latter style the "ethic of care." Essentially she said women favor a kind of cronyism, favoring people to whom they have close relationships and seeking what is best for them.

Gilligan's analysis started from interviews she conducted with women going through abortion procedures. Although she avoided any sort of systematic or statistical analysis (some women scholars reject such approaches as masculine, though most women scientists are horrified by that attitude and affirm the value of rigorous scientific methods), she did make a strong case that some women sometimes think differently. She applied her theories to a great many phenomena, such as the fact that boys' games last longer than girls' games, because when there is a dispute, boys avoid personal feelings and appeal to abstract rules, and in the extreme case they settle for a do-over. In contrast, when a conflict develops in a girls' game, each side is concerned more for the feelings of one's partners than for abstract principles, and the game is likely to come to an abrupt end.

Gilligan's theory has remained oddly popular in some circles. It has its detractors. Janet Shibley Hyde, whom I quoted in a previous chapter as a leading exponent of the view that gender differences are small and trivial, has done a systematic analysis of research results. She used a statistical technique called meta-analysis, which combines the results from many different studies and is regarded by scientists everywhere as one of the most decisive ways to evaluate a theory. Her conclusion was that Gilligan's theory is wrong.

There is, however, one way that Gilligan's theory could still be valid, despite the avalanche of data that Hyde presented. Like most gender researchers, Hyde's interest was in ability, and as I have said, the more important differences are in motivation. The research results that Hyde compiled are generally tests of ability. They give people questionnaires with hypothetical dilemmas and ask them to make a moral judgment. Sure enough, men and women reason about these dilemmas in the same ways. That was her basis for concluding that Gilligan was wrong.

It is nonetheless possible that when people confront moral dilemmas in their own lives, they think about them differently than how they respond to the imaginary ones on the questionnaires. Thus, women *can* reason according to abstract principles just like men do, and in that sense they conform to the scheme Kohlberg developed. But perhaps women choose to think differently about moral issues in their own lives.

Take an extreme case, perhaps, such as knowing that your child has performed some horrible crime. Would you report your own child to the police? It is conceivable that a man would be more likely than a woman to report it. If so, that would fit Gilligan's theory: Men are swayed more by the abstract principles and rules, whereas women come down on the side of taking care of their own.

At present, we do not know the answer. But let us assume that there was at least a shred of correctness in Gilligan's theory. Again, it seems to fit the general thrust that men and women orient toward different kinds of social relations.

Fairness in the sense of abstract rules is best suited to large groups. Indeed, countries that do not have the rule of law, as in rules that apply equally to everyone, suffer multiple disadvantages because of them. Countries in which the ruling class follows a Gilligan-style "ethic of care" are deeply troubled places. The rulers direct wealth and power to their relatives and leave the outsiders at a severe disadvantage, thus undermining public trust, entrepreneurship, and many other vital functions.

Meanwhile, though, the ethic of care, and taking care of the ones you love, seems well suited to a kind of social life that is based on intimate relationships and mutual love and support. If you committed murder and had to tell someone, I suspect you would tell your mother sooner than your father, because you would have more reason to hope that the mother's care for you would supersede any sense of obligation to report the crime. Not in all cases, of course, but more people would rather tell their mother than their father.

Ultimately, systems may favor punishing the guilty, which a male sense of justice may find appropriate even while a female sort of compassion might object. Recent brain research has shown that men and women respond differently to seeing a guilty person punished. In research by Tania Singer and her colleagues, people first played a trust game with a couple of other persons. These others pretended to be subjects in the experiment too, but in fact they were working for the researchers and followed predetermined scripts. One of them played fairly, while the other cheated and betrayed trust. Later, the real subject watched both of the others receive painful electric shocks, while brain responses were measured.

Both men and women reacted with distress to seeing the fair player get hurt. But men and women had different reactions to seeing the unfair player in pain. Women still felt the same empathic distress that they felt for the fair player. Thus, they felt sorry for human suffering, regardless of how the person had behaved. But men had much less empathy or sympathy for the unfair player's pain.

These findings suggest that men's and women's brains react differently. Women react as one would with a one-to-one pair bond, sharing the suffering of the other person. Their reaction did not change based on whether the person had violated the implicit norms of group behavior and trust. Such a reaction is well suited to dealing with a close relationship partner: You share the person's feelings and have empathy, even if that means forgiving misbehavior. Men's reactions were, again, better suited to the large group. Those who behave in ways that violate the abstract principles of proper group behavior, such as fairness and reciprocity, deserve to be punished, and apparently the men did not feel sorry for them. Men felt sorry only for the good group members who suffered after playing fairly.

Is That All?

My list of traded-off traits is hardly exhaustive, but this is not the place for a comprehensive survey of traits on which men and women differ. I certainly think there are other differences that reflect the different social spheres.

The crucial point is that men and women have a basic motivational difference in the kinds of social interactions and relationships that they cultivate. The differences we observe between men and women in personality traits can, to some extent, be understood as tradeoffs. The different kinds of social relationships require different kinds of traits, and so there are some tradeoffs.

The two ways of being social provide keys to understanding many of differences between men and women. They also provide a basis for understanding what men are good for. The next couple of chapters will ponder the value of these large networks of shallow relationships.

What is more important to you, having a few close friends or having a large number of people who know you? Most people say the few close relationships are more important. As we have seen, the bias in favor of close relationships is widely shared, and there are some valid reasons for it. Close relationships have a strong impact on mental and physical health, among other things. Close relationships are more satisfying than casual acquaintances.

But we shouldn't necessarily regard men as second-class humans just because they specialize in the less favored type of relationships. There are benefits to the large networks of weak ties. Ultimately, such networks are what culture is built upon and what it emerges from.

CHAPTER 6

How Culture Works

S occer, or football as it is known in most of the world, is a useful point of departure for thinking about culture. Team sports with scores and referees are unknown in nature. Culture invented soccer, lavishes abundant resources on it, and continues to refine it.

Imagine two full teams with players who are about equally matched in all the relevant inputs: strength, skill, talent, stamina, experience, and motivation. The only difference is that one group of players has just met each other for the first time five minutes before the game starts, while the other has been working together with a coach for two years. It's quite obvious the second team has a definite advantage and is likely to win the game. But why, exactly? The difference is not in the individual players. Rather, it's in the group. The team that has been working together is more than the sum of its parts. It has a system, including plans, plays, and other ideas to organize it. The other team lacks that.

Having a *system* produces benefits.

Another classic example is the assembly line. When cars were first manufactured for sale, each one was built by two or three mechanics. Obviously, each mechanic needed an immense wealth of knowledge to make all the parts and put them together. To pay such highly trained experts for so much work over a long period of time made the labor cost very high, and so early cars were extremely expensive. (Remember, those same three guys were still drawing their high wages even when they were just tightening the screws or sweeping the floor.) Only a few very rich individuals could afford cars.

All that was replaced by the assembly line. Henry Ford figured out how to have a large number of workers each do a very specific task. Because nobody except the planners needed to understand how everything fit together, the workers could be trained in a few days for their specific individual tasks. This cut the labor cost drastically. The assembly line was a system, in which each person performed one job and all the jobs meshed to produce cars. The result was that the price of cars plummeted, enabling them to be bought by non-rich people. Eventually even the factory workers themselves could afford to buy the cars they helped make.

Once again, the system benefited nearly everyone. The car companies made more money, cars became more widely available, and even ordinary working people could afford to buy them.

This book is about how culture exploits men. We are nearly ready to examine some of the specific ways culture finds men most useful. But that discussion won't make sense unless it's clear what culture is, and how it works. To say that culture exploits men (and that it exploits women too, which it certainly does) is to say that it uses people for its own goals. And that suggests it has goals. So we have to understand how a culture can have goals—and what those goals are.

Before we can say anything like, "culture wants women to breed babies, and it wants men to be soldiers," we have to agree on how it can "want" anything. Technically, a system can't really "want" things. It's just a system: an abstract set of relationships. But those abstract relationships are powerful engines for making life better.

What a Culture Is for

Let's go back to nature for a minute. Think of monkeys, or apes, or wolves for that matter. These are social animals, which means they live in groups. And the groups have natural needs.

What are natural needs? Food, water, shelter, warmth, safety, social contact, and so forth. All these can be subsumed under survival and reproduction. Life survives only because living things work hard at surviving. Living things who don't care about staying alive might not search hard enough for food or run hard enough from whoever wants to kill and eat them. Death has to win only once, but life has to win every day.

And in the end death wins. Nature hasn't found a way to enable any animal to live forever. Nature wants the species to survive more or less forever, and it can't achieve that by making individuals who survive forever. So the next best thing is reproduction. Before a living creature grows old, it tries to make new copies or new versions of itself—new, young versions that can live into the future and, in turn, reproduce themselves before they get old and die. Nature has programmed living things to do that.

Survival and reproduction are the keys to success at life. Those are what drive evolution. Those are the biological goals.

Some experts might object here on a technicality. They say survival is important only insofar as it contributes to reproduction. They are right. But because survival strategies are often different from reproductive ones, and sometimes there are conflicts, it is worth talking about both. This is especially relevant to culture, because a culture does not have to die, and so it does not have to reproduce, in the sense of creating new little cultures that are copies of itself. Cultures can succeed by surviving forever. That's getting ahead of the story, though.

Social groups probably formed in the first place because they yielded benefits for survival and reproduction. Consider the difference between a monkey living alone and one living with a group of monkeys. In the group, there is much greater safety. In the group, there may be food to share. In the group, there are other monkeys to have sex with, and so it's easier to make babies if one lives in a group than if one lives alone. In these and other ways, being in the group helps the monkey survive and reproduce better than it could if it were all alone.

So far, so good. Monkeys don't have much in the way of culture. Occasionally they will have a little of it.

The "potato washing" story has become emblematic of animal culture. Monkeys on a Japanese island ate potatoes they dug from the ground. Unfortunately, these came out of the ground with dirt stuck to them. Having no choice, the monkeys ate the dirt too, which tasted bad and was hard on the teeth and bad for their digestion. Eating clean potatoes would have been a little better for survival, but they didn't have that option, so they ate the dirty ones.

One day researchers noticed that a female adult monkey made a discovery: She rinsed her potato off in the water, thereby getting the dirt off. This became her regular practice. Other monkeys in the tribe saw her and copied the potato-washing trick, which then spread throughout the tribe (except for the power elite, the oldest males). There was no sign of active teaching, but mimicry was enough, and the youngsters picked it up quickly. Years later, after that monkey and all her contemporaries had died, that tribe of monkeys was still washing its potatoes, whereas other groups of monkeys of the same species did not.

Researchers call that culture: It was a learned behavior pattern based on information shared throughout the group and passed along to subsequent generations.

Notice what their little bit of culture did for the monkeys. It made their lives better. Probably by eating less dirt they were a bit healthier, and so it may have improved their survival. At least, it made their food taste better, and for the most part tasting good is a sign that something is good for you. Setting aside ice cream and similar oddities of advanced (or, if you prefer, degenerate) culture, things taste good because they promote survival. There's a reason potatoes taste good and dirt tastes bad: potatoes promote survival and dirt doesn't. If there were ever monkeys that liked the taste of dirt better than the taste of potatoes and other nutritious food, they didn't survive long enough to reproduce.

If the monkeys had had more culture, it might have provided more benefits like this for them. Look what culture does for us. Food is there, without most of us having to grow it or kill it. Culture provides remarkably effective health care and superb quality shelter. (Even low-rent apartments are nicer than living in trees or caves.) With its laws and police, culture makes sure nobody is too mean to anybody else.

That's one key to culture. It's a system to provide for material needs. It manages the large group of people.

To appreciate what culture does, it helps to try to imagine what life would be like if culture were immediately canceled. Suppose, suddenly, by magic, our culture ceased to exist. All the people would be there, and you'd wake up in your same bed, but what would you do? There would be no job for you. In fact, there would be no laws telling you what to do and what not to do—as well as no laws protecting you from what others might do to you. Money would cease to exist. There would not even be language. Your supply of food from stores and restaurants would stop, so one priority would be to figure out how to get something to eat. Also all the utilities would stop, so you might not have access to heat, or clean water, or electricity.

Thus, a big part of what culture does is to provide these things.

Now introduce one more wrinkle. Let's say a tribe of apes has a nice life in their little corner of the jungle. There were some fruit trees to feed them, shaded places to rest, and a pretty waterfall to give fresh, tasty drinks. But then another group of apes moved into the area and wanted all of those same things. What happens? Do they share? Do they fight? Do they just annoy one another until one group leaves? And which one ends up the winner?

With apes, probably the bigger group is going to be the winner. The relative number of bodies is also one crucial factor when human groups come into conflict, also. But with humans, there are additional factors.

Monkeys don't have much culture, so culture isn't likely to make much difference in their conflicts over territory. But suppose one group of monkeys did have culture. Suppose they had a system for working together, sharing information, dividing up tasks, and making decisions collectively for the best of the group. And suppose the other group didn't have anything like that.

In that case, the tribe with culture probably would prevail over the other, even if the group sizes were similar. In human history, small groups with more advanced and powerful culture have sometimes prevailed over much larger groups. A couple of hundred Spanish soldiers overthrew the vast and mighty Inca empire. The soccer game example that began this chapter was intended to make a similar point.

We should resist calling one culture better than another. But one culture can be more effective, especially at winning a conflict against a rival culture. One culture can be stronger than another. One culture can take over another and replace it.

What Culture Is

We are now ready to articulate what culture is. The difference can be seen by comparing the group of apes (or people) who have culture against the group who doesn't.

Culture is a system. It coordinates multiple parts and helps them work together. A group with culture is more organized than a group without culture.

Culture is something a group of people has. You don't have culture by yourself. A society (organized group of people) has culture.

Culture is partly made out of information. There are at least two main types of this information. One is a set of shared beliefs and values. The other is shared knowledge of how to do things. Culture consists of both.

The central importance of information is a vital reason that all human cultures have language. Anthropologists, who study different cultures, love to discover ways that make each culture different, special, unique. But they've never found a culture that doesn't have language. It would be quite a feather in someone's cap to discover a human culture without language, and the anthropologist who made such a discovery would probably win prizes and promotions. But don't count on finding such a culture. Language is the best all-purpose tool ever discovered, and it enormously expands what culture can do in terms of storing, analyzing, communicating, and manipulating information. Without language, information (the lifeblood of culture) is very difficult to use. There will probably never be a human culture that doesn't use language.

Culture is a system with several purposes. The primary ones are to provide for the material needs of the people. A culture that fails to provide food and water, safety, and an opportunity to raise children will not survive. Nor will a culture survive if it cannot defend itself against its enemies, whether these be found in nature (illness, cold) or in other cultures (and their invading armies).

Another purpose of culture is to enable people to live together. Social life isn't easy. Conflict is inevitable, if only because two creatures both want the last or best piece of food or the more comfortable place to sleep. In most animal societies, conflict comes down to "might makes right." Human culture has far more elaborate systems to settle conflicts: property rights, courts of law, patents, traditions. In fact, most law and morality can be understood as rules for settling the inevitable conflicts of social life by some means other than letting the bigger, stronger person do and have whatever he wants.

Culture isn't made of a single piece, either. It is more like a variety of big structures that are loosely interconnected. Society typically organizes a culture into multiple large structures. Look at the social world you live in. It doesn't connect every person to every other person equally. Each person is closely connected to some, moderately connected with others, and only remotely connected to others. Sometimes the connections fluctuate, like when a contractor is at your house every day for two months redoing your kitchen and then vanishes from your life forever. There are families, corporations, universities, government agencies, military units, and so forth. Even the military consists of small groups loosely connected to other small groups inside larger groups (troops, regiments, divisions, armies). The same is true for government bodies (different agencies, committees, offices) and universities (departments). Of course, these organizations didn't start out being that elaborate and complex. Complexity increased over time, because complex organization can accomplish things that can't be accomplished by simpler structures. If you consider the problems facing the world today (e.g., global warming, terrorism, pandemics), you can see that they are not likely to be handled by single persons—more likely by large and complex networks of organizations.

These large and complex networks of organizations (*institutions* is the preferred term in sociology) will be important in our understanding of how culture exploits men, because the daily work of most men in most modern cultures occurs in these institutions.

That's what culture is. But let me add two more observations, which put things in perspective.

First, at a basic level, culture is a biological strategy. In other words, ultimately culture exists because it is a way to promote survival and reproduction. All living things have natural impulses to survive and reproduce, and the ones that achieve those more effectively are the ones that continue to exist across the generations. Culture came to exist on the planet because it improved the odds of survival and reproduction. (Indeed, increasingly humans survive and reproduce at the expense of most of the other animals!)

One reason our human species has dominated the planet instead of the Neanderthals (who were here before us and were doing quite well) is that our culture was better than theirs. The Neanderthals actually had bigger brains and bigger bodies than we did, so in one-to-one combat they would likely have prevailed. But we were better at culture, and so when our ancestors moved into areas where Neanderthals lived, the Neanderthals lost out. We had a better system than they did for survival and reproduction. We took their lands and ate their lunch. Today they are extinct while we own the planet.

The second point is that that human evolution probably centered on developing the traits needed for culture. After all, if culture makes life better, why don't wolves and monkeys and squirrels have extensive cultures? But you need a pretty smart and flexible mind in order to be capable of culture. If we were to give a wolf or gorilla or squirrel an apartment, a car, and a job at the bank, it still wouldn't be able to function effectively in culture. Its mind is too primitive. What makes us human—the evolved psychological traits that set us apart from the rest of the animal kingdom— is our competence for culture.

Culture is thus the key to human nature. It starts with being capable of language (hearing, speaking, understanding, storing the meanings of words, plus combining words via grammar so as to express complex ideas). It includes recognizing that other people have minds like our own. It includes something that people call free will, namely a more complicated way of making decisions and controlling behavior, especially for following rules. It includes self-control and self-awareness and a variety of other things.

What's in It for Me?

Cultures can have plenty of complex, even strange aspects and details. Certainly, there are peculiar customs, like sending all the children out on one agreed-upon autumn evening dressed in costumes to ask for candy.

But boiled down their essentials, cultures are systems to enable people to get what they need. They enable people to live and work together and, crucially, to prepare the next generation. Cultures are systems to help people get food and shelter, and care for the sick, and important things like that.

Why do people need culture, then? After all, animals have little or no culture, and they manage to get food and water and all the rest.

That's an important challenge. The answer is that culture enables groups of people to get those things *better*. As in, better than they would otherwise. And perhaps better than other, rival groups of people. Remember, forward progress in both nature and culture is driven by competition among members of the species.

Let us return to the differences among three options: living alone in the forest, living in a group of other people without culture, and living in a group with culture.

Take yourself (or any other human being), for example. No doubt you have a variety of natural abilities: strength, endurance, intelligence. If you abruptly found yourself alone on the distant island, with no chance of seeing any other humans for a year, you might be able to get by. Life would be tough, but perhaps you could manage to take care of yourself. Your natural abilities would allow you to eke out a meager existence. Maybe you can learn to trap squirrels to eat and possibly find some fruits or vegetables. You can build yourself a little shelter with branches and leaves, to keep the rain off and maybe reduce the cold at night.

Alone, we can barely get by. But as part of a culture, we can live much better. We can have great food, much better than squirrel meat and dug-up roots. We can sleep in fine beds in warm houses.

Culture is a multiplier. It makes your physical and mental abilities go much farther. That is, your same physical and mental capabilities allow you to make a much better life for yourself working within a culture than working without one. That's what culture is good for, and why it is good for you.

Even critics who complain most bitterly about American (or other) culture benefit from it. Even they who see it is as a plot by men to exploit women don't really want to get rid of culture per se. That's because they live much better in culture than without. Maybe they have legitimate complaints, about not being respected or paid enough, or about how the women they see on television make them think they aren't as slim as they would like to be. Maybe they think some parents don't do enough to encourage their daughters to want to become nuclear physicists or combat soldiers. But they wouldn't want to give up the benefits of (yes, "patriarchal") culture, such as indoor plumbing, electricity, supermarkets, and hospitals.

Most animals would love to get their food from supermarkets and restaurants, if they could. Animals like cooked food if we cook it for them, but they can't figure out how to cook it themselves.

Cooking is a great example of the benefits of culture. If cooking had never been invented, it would be hard for one person in one lifetime to figure out how to do it. Instead, cooking was developed over many generations. Crucially, each generation passed along what it learned to the next. We are still learning: As I wrote the first draft of this chapter, New York City had just passed a law banning restaurants from cooking with *trans*-fats, because eating food cooked with them is bad for one's health. Notice that "bad" in this sense means a slight increase in the chances of getting sick many years later. When our ancestors were first figuring out how to cook, their failed experiments usually meant eating something that had them vomiting violently within the hour. We've come far since then.

And look what cooking has done. Many foods are much healthier when they are cooked. Some foods cannot be eaten without cooking. Rice, after all, is perhaps the most common food in world history, in the sense that more people have lived off of rice than any other food. But rice has to be cooked. Without cooking, those people would have not had their main food.

Benefits of Life with a System

Let's use the term "system gain" to refer to this multiplier effect of culture. Essentially, system gain means that the whole is more than the sum of its parts. It's the difference between the soccer team that is just a collection of skilled individuals and the one that knows how to play like a team. The same people, with the same mental and physical abilities, can live better with culture than without. Culture is a system and it adds something to the group—indeed, it adds something that can be measured in the ultimate yardstick of biological reality, namely, better survival and better reproduction.

Think of the earlier example of what would happen if American culture suddenly ceased to exist. We'd all be on our own. Life would be much harder and harsher.

The point is, we live much better with culture than without. That would be true even if we were exactly the same people, with the same abilities, strengths, skills, weaknesses, and insights. But culture multiplies the power of those abilities to make you healthy, happy, and comfortable. Your same physical and mental capabilities bring you a better life if you use them as part of culture rather than using them entirely on your own.

The computer has become one of psychology's favorite metaphors for the human mind, and it is helpful here. When personal computers first came out, they sat on desks, plugged in only to an electricity source. Now they are connected to the Internet.

The difference between a computer by itself and a computer connected to the Internet is revealing. It is the same machine but it can accomplish a great deal more when it is online. This corresponds to what happens with brains and culture. The human brain can accomplish quite a bit on its own. Yet that same brain can accomplish a great deal more when it is connected to culture.

That is system gain. The parts are good by themselves, but they are better when they are part of the system.

Sometimes an abrupt change of system can provide a shocking difference. The Zulus were a small, third-rate, sleepy vassal tribe in southern Africa. When the visionary leader Shaka took over, he promptly overhauled their culture. In particular, he trained all the men in new military tactics that he had invented, increased the power of the king over all subjects (including instant execution for displeasing him in any way), and organized their resources for conquest. In a couple of decades, he built it into one of the greatest empires ever known in southwestern Africa, indeed one whose effects and legacies are still influential today. When he took over, it was exactly the same group of people over which his predecessor had presided, but his new system enabled it to accomplish things that had been undreamt of in its entire history.

So how does system gain arise? Just precisely how does a culture manage to make the whole more than the sum of its parts?

How Culture Succeeds, Part One: Information

Thus far we have seen that culture makes life better for people. Also, it does this by means of system gain. The whole is more than the sum of its parts because of what is gained by virtue of the system. (The system is what makes the whole be the whole. It is what the whole has in addition to its parts.) System gain is the key to explaining why people are better off being part of the system than being alone.

Now we turn to the crucial question of how system gain operates. Just what happens in a culture that enables the whole to be more than the sum of its parts?

First consider information. Humans are an information-using species. Cultures are based partly on information. Information is the lifeblood of culture.

A first and huge advantage of culture is the pooling and accumulating of information. When an animal reaches the end of its life, its brain contains mainly the knowledge it got from its own experiences. It knows what it found out and figured out during its life. Humans, in contrast, can know far more than what they learned from their own direct experience. They can learn what countless other humans have figured out.

Language enables humans to share information far more and far better than any other creature on earth. People can find out different things and tell each other.

A big advantage of this is that information is not just stored in an individual mind but in the group. The group has a collection of knowledge.

What happens when a new generation is born? Here the advantages of culture are even bigger. Humans tell their youngsters plenty of what they learned. Animals mostly cannot do this. Young animals learn by copying their elders and so forth, but most experts doubt that animals do anything at all in the form of intentional teaching. And certainly no animal species has anything like formal schools—unlike every country in human civilization.

Remember the monkey who figured out how to wash potatoes? Her story is a small version of what culture is all about. She solved a problem for herself. The other monkeys copied it, and so that information was shared across the group. (This was true even though she did not clearly engage in any deliberate effort to share her solution or to teach others how to wash potatoes.) And the next generation copied it. That tribe of monkeys enjoyed one small benefit of culture.

Imagine that kind of process done over and over, with many aspects of life, and you can begin to appreciate why human life has improved so much over the centuries, even while other species mostly live in the same way they always have.

The monkey example leaves out one even bigger advantage of this: progressive accumulation. Each human generation can learn what its parents knew. Therefore it can start from there and add to it. Its creative efforts can take things even another step or two farther.

In general, each new generation of animals starts over, facing the same problems and trying to solve them, just as its parents and great-great-grandparents did. Each new human generation, in contrast, can take up where its parents left off.

Only one person has to invent a car, or a light bulb, or a computer, for example. Then that person's invention is owned by the group. The knowledge resides there in the culture. The next generation doesn't have to invent it again. The next generation can start with what that person did and maybe make it better—a safer car, a brighter light bulb, a more powerful computer.

It is possible to view culture as a continuation of biological evolution by other means. Evolution slowly made life better by changing the physical makeup of animals. It made for progress, but it was very slow. Culture vastly reduced the time needed for improvements, thus greatly speeding up the pace of progress.

Put another way, a group of humans doesn't have to wait hundreds of thousands of years for genetic change in order for them to be able to live better lives. These days, the pace of improvement in human life is measured in decades, not millennia.

How Culture Succeeds: Specialized Jobs

A second advantage of culture involves the division of labor. Instead of each person doing everything, each person does a different task.

Early factories did not use division of labor. They were simply buildings where men got together to make things. (The word "factory" is short for "manufactory," and it just meant a place where stuff was manufactured.) Each man made the whole product, working mostly by himself. This was difficult and expensive. Take a car, as a powerful example. How much does one person have to know to build a car? A car is a very complicated structure with many parts that have to work and interact properly. Obviously he would not figure it all out by himself. Rather, he would learn what other men had figured out. Even so, the amount of information he would have to master in order to build a car himself would be immense. Likewise, he would have to have a great many skills, including being able to make many different parts and put them together, using many different tools.

It is no accident that such "manufactories" soon gave way to division of labor. With cars, the assembly line eventually triumphed. The assembly line was mentioned at the start of this chapter as a classic example of the benefits of culture. On the assembly line, each person does just one specific job. No extensive training is needed, no years of study to master a wealth of information. One man, one tool, one quick job, done over and over. Many men (and later, women), working together with a system, were able to make cars faster and better—and cheaper—than what those experts could do.

The mechanic who built the entire car himself had spent years of learning and training. The workers on the assembly line could be trained very quickly, in some cases even just a day or two.

 Ironically, assembly line cars end up better made than hand-crafted ones, despite being made by people who knew much less and had received much briefer training. (Because of that, assembly-line cars were cheaper too.) That is because division of labor produces specialists. Everyone does one task and becomes expert at it.

There is so much information to master in building a car that one person cannot be an expert at every task. Maybe the lone worker is very good at several things but not all of them—say, wiring the window wipers, or installing the air conditioning system. The solitary builder's car therefore has window wipers that do not work so well, or an air conditioning system that frequently breaks down. With the modern system, however, the window wipers are made by people who are specialists at making them and installed by other specialists who are expert at installing them. The specialists are expert at their very narrow, specific tasks.

Even though the solitary mechanic knows far more than the assembly line worker, the assembly line car is built more expertly. Each assembly line worker is an expert at his specific task. As a result, every part of the job is done expertly. Not so for the solitary mechanic, despite his vastly greater knowledge. There were some things he wasn't so great at, and those things got done less well.

The trend toward division of labor and specialization is one of the most universal and one-way trends in history. People specialize more and more narrowly. The reason is that it produces better and better results. You can see this everywhere.

Look at medicine: General practitioners once served entire communities, but now medicine is administered by ever larger networks of specialists. There is too much information for one general practitioner to know. You're better off having your kidney operated on by a kidney specialist, your hormones treated by a hormone specialist, your X-ray films checked by a radiology specialist.

I remember the first time I had a wisdom tooth removed. It was stuck at a bad angle inside my gums. My family dentist said he could probably do the job. But he said, why don't you have it done by somebody who per-forms these operations every day? It will be a struggle for me, but routine for him. He was right. Division of labor makes specialists, and specialists do what they do better than generalists.

To go from life-and-death to mere entertainment, the same evolution can be seen in sports. Football (the American version this time) was once played by two teams of eleven men, and the same men played the entire game. But the pressure of competition soon led to the discovery that specialists play better than generalists, and so after a few decades all major teams had entirely separate rosters for offense and for defense. Soon there was yet another group for the kicking plays. And not long afterward, they started developing even more narrow specialties: short yardage specialists, running backs who do not run (they block or catch instead), nickel defenders. Specialization will proceed as far as the rules allow, because teams that use specialists will generally defeat the teams that don't.

How Culture Succeeds: Trade

Exchange is another key to culture—another source of system gain.

When I first began reading economists, I was baffled by their claim that trade increases wealth. How could this be? If Joe and Bob trade their shirts, there still aren't any more shirts. Swapping doesn't make more.

But of course the economists are correct. Swapping shirts is a mislead-ing example. A better example would be this: Suppose I have a garden full of tomato plants, and suddenly in August I find myself up to my ears in tomatoes. I eat all I can and freeze some for the winter, but I still have more than I can use. Meanwhile, Jeremy goes fishing and comes home with a truckload of fish, indeed more than he could use.

If we don't trade, I eat only tomatoes and the rest go to rot, while Jeremy eats only fish and lets the rest of them spoil. But if we swap some of our surplus, both of us eat both tomatoes and fish. Both of us are better off—effectively richer.

Trade works even better in combination with the cultural benefit covered in the preceding section, namely specialization and division of labor. Different people specialize in making different things. If they put in the time and effort to learn to make them really well, the products can be better, but because they need many different things to survive, they have to trade them. The expert at hunting rabbits, the expert at making pots, and the expert at building roofs will all be best off if they trade their handiwork for each other's.

Where Systems Gain the Most

Culture exists in groups. And large groups are better than small groups for this. Hence culture will thrive most effectively in a large group.

The preceding sections made several points about the huge advantages culture can offer. Accumulation of knowledge, division of labor, and trade are all vital means by which culture can make life better. But all of these advantages will operate more effectively in larger groups.

Consider the accumulation of knowledge. The more people there are who solve problems and share them with others, the faster the group's knowledge base will build up. The group's stockpile of information will grow faster if fifty people share what they learn than if only three people share what they learn.

Likewise, specialization and division of labor can be most effective in a larger group, because people can specialize more narrowly.

And trade, too, will improve life to a greater degree if the trading network is larger. More people with more different products can create a more efficient market, which means that all the individuals have a better chance of trading what they have to give to get what they most need and want.

That's why globalization is coming, whether we like it or not. Some people will suffer from globalization, but more people will benefit. If you have something that a woman in China wants, and she has something you want, you're both better off if you can make the deal than if you can't. These mutual benefits will prove irresistible in the long run.

Why this Matters for Men and Women

The value of larger groups of people for sharing information and so forth may seem obvious. It is, however, highly relevant to the issues of gender politics. As we have seen, men and women specialize in different kinds of social relationships. Women are better designed by nature to create and sustain close, intimate, caring, one-to-one relationships. Men are more designed to function in larger groups and systems.

Therefore, culture is more likely to emerge from groups of men than from groups of women.

Put another way, men are more likely than women to create the kind of groups that will produce culture and its gains.

The differences are probably deeply rooted in the brain. Remember the point about the female brain being made for empathy and the male brain for systems? Empathy is better for intimacy, and so women's intimate relationships will be better than men's. But culture is a system, and so the system-oriented male brains will be more congenial to culture.

Let me reiterate that I think gender differences are more about motivation than ability. Women can think quite effectively in terms of systems, and men are very capable of empathizing with intimate partners. But when left to their own preferences, the two genders will tend to create different kinds of relationships. The women will prefer to create the close, intimate, supportive ones. The men will prefer to create the large groups, along with their systems.

This will be highly relevant to the next several chapters. It offers a new basis for understanding gender inequality in culture (and hence the question with which the previous chapter ended, namely why are women victims of culture?). It also points the way to addressing the core questions about how culture exploits men. After all, culture originated as a system to get the most out of a group of men, so as to enable them to outperform and defeat other groups of men with other systems, and so culture originated as a way of exploiting men. Later, culture took a look at women and began to find ways of exploiting them too. But the origins of culture lie in the emergence of systems that could make the most out of the men in it.

There will be more about this in the next chapters. For now, let us finish our examination of how culture functions.

How Can Cultures Want Anything?

Now we turn to a nagging question. This is a book about how culture "exploits" men. It "uses" men to get the things that it "wants." But a culture is not an agent, like an animal or person. It is an abstract system made up of ideas and relationships. How can it "want" anything?

Strictly speaking, it cannot. Saying that culture "wants" this or that is a figure of speech. It is a bit like saying that the plan for a football play "wants" the receiver to run deep, catch the ball, and maybe score a touchdown. The play is an abstract idea and doesn't want in the sense that a hungry dog wants a piece of meat. But cultures will act as if they were agents who want things.

The reason for this lies in the question of survival. A culture is an abstract system and therefore technically does not care whether the people in the system get enough water, for example, to survive. But a system that fails to provide water for its people will soon disappear. Either the people who use the waterless system will die, or they will chuck that system and replace it with a different system that does get them water.

Competition between cultures intensifies the appearance that a culture wants and needs things. A culture that fails to encourage innovation or military fortitude might survive for a long time by itself with no rivals in sight, for example. But if a rival group appears with a different system that is better at promoting innovation and military success, the rival group will take over from the lackadaisical one.

One classic (and somewhat politically sensitive) question is why European culture came to dominate the globe so heavily. There are many reasons, including some geographical advantages such as the east–west dimension that Jared Diamond has explicated in his bestselling *Guns, Germs, and Steel*. But Asian cultures enjoyed exactly that same advantage. Why did Europe briefly dominate Asia as well as the rest of the world over the last couple of centuries?

One answer is that European cultures "wanted" more innovation than Asian ones—due to the close proximity of competing groups. The historian William H. McNeill has analyzed this in his classic work *The Pursuit of Power*. At some point China settled into a single empire, ruled loosely from the center. (Similar things happened in Japan and India.) Then there was no pressure for military innovation, because the country was more or less at peace and was not fighting wars. If anything, military innovation was discouraged, because it might enable local groups to resist the central authority.

Around the same time, Europe had coalesced into a set of small countries that were constantly fighting each other. Each time one lost a war it reflected on its mistakes and searched desperately for ways to make its armies, navies, and weapons stronger the next time around. It experimented with strange ideas that were utterly foreign to the entrenched ways that armies operated—ideas like drill to get all the soldiers march in step (the Dutch), like promoting non-aristocrats into the officer ranks based on soldiering merit (the French), and even like doing paperwork to plan strategies and logistics (the Prussians). They also used their science and technology to develop better weapons, including cannons that could be brought to a battlefield pulled by horses, and rifles that became more accurate and quicker to reload.

In short, the Europeans worked so hard at keeping up with each other that, as a side effect, they came to outclass the rest of the world.

It is fanciful to say that European cultures "wanted" better weapons and tactics. But they acted as if they did. European cultures raised questions and bestowed rewards in ways that stimulated individual men and women (well, mostly men) to create improvements. They also copied the innovations of their neighbors and enemies.

Saying that culture "wants" men to do certain things is not unlike saying that nature wants things. Nature does not really want anything, but animals who do not care about survival and reproduction will not survive and reproduce as well as those who do, and so eventually all animals will be descended from the ones who strove earnestly to survive and reproduce.

What Do Cultures Want?

What do cultures want? As I have said, the idea of cultures wanting anything is just a convenient figure of speech. It might be more precise to say, what do successful cultures (i.e., cultures that survive and flourish and can fend off hostile rivals) encourage their people to accomplish? But the shorthand is that cultures want things.

Here's a useful beginner list of what cultures want. It may not be exhaustive. But it is sufficient to understand the sorts of things that a culture needs in order to be successful—and on that basis to begin asking what men are good for. (Women too.)

First, a culture needs to provide for people's basic material needs. A culture is a system that belongs to a group of people, and those people have needs. They also have wants, which can increase. The line between needs and wants continues to blur. A recent survey asked people to characterize various products as either luxuries or necessities. You might think necessities would stop at food, water, and shelter, but a majority of

Americans now regard cable television as a necessity, and at least one car. Computers did not exist until after the Second World War, and no individuals owned them until the 1980s. Yet now the majority of Americans consider them a necessity. Even cell phones are rated as necessities by almost half the population.

In any case, providing for the basic needs of life is important, and this can be subsumed under the broader category of creating and increasing wealth. A culture in which people remain poor is not doing well and is in danger of being overrun by others. Rich cultures enable their people to live in peace and comfort—or, if they choose, to dominate their neighbors.

The issue of dominating the neighbors brings up the second cultural need, namely military strength. In isolation, a culture might not need much in the way of military power. But given the relentless growth of world population, the good places to live soon attracted different groups. Conflict between groups, like conflict between persons, is an almost inevitable part of human life, as long as the different ones live in the same area and compete for some of the same resources. War is one way of resolving those conflicts.

Hence a successful culture usually needs an effective military capability. A culture needs at least to be able to defend itself. This includes some soldiers and some weapons for them to use. It may include considerably more, such as spies, a weapons industry, research and development of new battlefield technology, logistics, computer networks, and planning.

The next two needs, stability and progress, seem like contradictions (staying the same versus change), but this is misleading. Most people want both stability and progress. Stability refers to internal social relations that are peaceful, predictable, and harmonious. Human life is change but yearns for stability. People are happier and healthier if they know where they will sleep tonight and where their next meal is coming from. Stability also requires keeping internal chaos at bay, such as by resolving conflicts. As I said, conflict between individuals is part of social life, and culture has to have some way of resolving it, whether by courts of law, or police, or strong social norms and pressures. Put another way, cultures depend on people following rules, and there has to be some mechanism to make people obey the rules.

Progress means innovation. It is not really needed, unless a culture is competing against rivals who are making progress. Innovation can improve military strength, increase wealth, or just simply make life better in small ways. For example, there was no absolute need to invent the radio or the iPod, but many people are better off because of those inventions.

A final need, population increase, presents a host of issues. Let me concede right off the bat that it is not universal. Nomadic, hunter-gatherer cultures may have struggled to keep their populations from increasing so as not to exceed the carrying capacity of their environment. In other words, they lived in a niche that could support only so many people, and they had to be careful not to produce too many babies. In some cases, they had to resort to extreme measures such as infanticide to keep the population down.

But once agriculture began to provide more food, then there was less need to restrain the population. That did not immediately mean that growth was desirable, either, though most scholars agree that agriculture did allow the population to increase dramatically (albeit at the cost of periodic famines, such as when crops failed).

The most urgent need for actual increase in population comes from competition among different groups. It is not popular to point this out, but many great cultural conflicts in world history have been shaped if not decided by who had more people.

The most obvious advantage of more people is in military contests. I say "obvious" with hesitation, because it is perhaps less obvious to the modern mind than to observers of bygone eras. Modern technology can make a huge difference, and in fact we have seen relatively small numbers of American soldiers defeat large Iraqi armies by dint of superior weapons. And the adventurous wars of the nineteenth century, still sometimes depicted in popular films and books, did record instances of small modern troops with rifles defeating larger hordes of enemies fighting with bows and arrows or spears. It is true that a severe mismatch in weaponry can enable a small group to defeat a much larger one.

Through most of history, however, war meant hand-to-hand, face-to-face fighting with simple weapons like spears. In spear warfare, whoever had more soldiers usually won. This isn't how it looks in the movies, which are fond of depicting heroic fighting and brilliant tactics allowing small bands to win victory against overwhelming odds. But don't believe the movies on this score. When it's fifty guys with spears against a hundred guys with spears, you can be fairly sure how the battle will turn out.

Thus, through most of history and prehistory, group conflict on the battlefield was relatively straightforward. Might made right. And might came from numbers.

Population increase has other benefits. More people mean a bigger system and therefore, at least potentially, a more specialized and efficient one. In a democracy, more people mean more votes. With a functioning economy, more people can mean more wealth. I already pointed out that culture depends on sharing information, and having more people means more potential contributions to the common stock of knowledge.

The course of world history has been shaped in part by religious clashes, and there too numbers made a difference. At one time, Judaism was an established religion with a sizable number of people, whereas Christianity was a tiny upstart sect that split off from it. The Christians knew that their small numbers made them vulnerable, and indeed the Jewish establishment was able to dominate them in their home territory. The Christian leaders decided they would go abroad and try to gain converts. Meanwhile, the Jewish leaders, remaining true to their doctrine of being a chosen people, did not seek to convert outsiders to Judaism and in some respects actively discouraged it. Within a few centuries, and aided by some lucky breaks, the Christians outnumbered the Jews, setting the stage for them to become the dominating group—able to bully and persecute and occasionally massacre the outnumbered Jews—for centuries.

Note, again, that hardly anybody ever said that having the numbers gave them the right to persecute the other religion. The conflicts were always phrased in terms of ideas and religious doctrines and God's favor. When they had the numbers, Jews picked on Christians as a heretical and deviant set of wrongheaded believers. When the Christians had the majority, they picked on the Jews in the name of religious truth and other abstract concepts. In both cases, however, having more people enabled them to do it and get away with it.

There have been many different versions of Christianity, of course. One notable one was the Shakers. They were exceptionally peaceful and virtuous, which helped them attract converts. Their concept of virtue included abstaining completely from sex, consistent with some of the early Christian ideals and writings. (Sure enough, celibacy is still an ideal that is a required commitment for all Catholic nuns and priests.) But the Shakers gradually disappeared from the scene. Can you guess why? No sex, no children. And no religion is able to survive on continually attracting new converts.

In contrast, one of the new religious movements that has been most successful at continuing to grow is the Church of Latter Day Saints, also known as the Mormons. Unlike the Shakers, they believe in sex and are strongly pro-family and pro-child. (They even espoused polygamy for a while, though they no longer do.) A crucial reason for their success as a religious movement has been the steady increase in their numbers.

Aside from competition, there are also internal benefits from an increasing population, and these apply especially to the modern world. Young people compete for jobs, and their work generates money that can be used for social programs, including the support of old people. China's population is now declining,[1] and several European countries face similar prospects of decreasing populations. I am glad to see these trends, because I believe overpopulation by humans is the greatest threat to the future of the planet and our place in it. But economists take a dim view of population declines and point out, correctly, that these countries will have trouble supporting so many retired persons, especially now that people often retire at sixty or sixty-five and live until eighty-five or ninety. When the retirees outnumber the workers, the burden on the workers is quite heavy, and workers get to keep much less of the money they make.

For all these reasons, most cultures seek to maintain and even increase their populations. The methods are quite diverse. There are religious commandments to multiply and to refrain from using birth control. There are tax advantages given to people who have children. (When I became a parent, I was shocked to discover how the government sought to subsidize my parenthood with tax deductions, even while my usage of society's institutions and services went up significantly. Parents ought to pay extra taxes, not less!) Some countries give generous cash payments to parents and families with children. Parents of large families are often regarded with special respect and prestige. Adults who choose to remain childless are subjected to frequent subtle pressures from parents to change their minds.

---

1 There is a bit of ambiguity in those numbers. Possibly it is just that growth has leveled off.

Summing Up

Cultures are systems that groups of people use to live together. A culture is a biological strategy, which is to say a way that a group of people seeks to improve survival and reproduction. Cultures compete against other systems.

Cultures that succeed promote certain things. These include progress, based partly on accumulating knowledge, and partly on developing a more efficient and effective system (e.g., division of labor, with specialists performing important tasks expertly). Cultures succeed in competing against their neighbors to the extent that they promote innovation, the creation of wealth, military effectiveness, and increasing population.

Culture depends on a system that links together the actions of many different people. The bigger the group, the more powerful the system and hence the better job it can do at serving people's needs. Hence culture flourishes best with big groups. In principle, the members of these groups could be either men or women. Culture is gender-neutral in theory. In practice, women gravitate toward close one-to-one relationships, which offer only limited opportunities to benefit from the advantages of systems. Men are more oriented than women toward large groups. Hence culture will tend to grow from groups of men more than from groups of women.

CHAPTER 7

Women, Men, and Culture

The Roots of Inequality

I N NO SOCIETY ON EARTH today are women fully equal to men. In every country in the world, men rank higher than women. In some societies, the difference is slight and they are approaching equality. In others, women are at a severe disadvantage compared to men. But women always have an inferior place. Moreover, it has for the most part always been thus, as far back as we have evidence.

Why?

Two explanations have held sway. The standard one for a long time was that the social roles were based on the innate superiority of men. Women were considered inherently inferior beings, and so their lower status in society was to be expected. It was natural.

Feminist theory reacted against this, rejecting any notion of female inferiority. Instead, it accused men of plotting against women. Men banded together to push women down. The Imaginary Feminist has a quick answer ready for any questions about the origins of gender inequality: oppression.

The first theory, that women are inferior and incompetent, has been proven wrong. The second theory has nothing much in the way of proof. At least it doesn't have a great deal of proof against it, like the other one. But its main advantage is that it is the only alternative to the discredited theory of female inferiority.

It is time for another explanation. This chapter provides one.

How Did We Get Here?

These are the facts on which I think most scholars agree.

Prehistoric human groups were hunters and gatherers. These small groups had a simple, peaceful, but not very secure life. Typically, the men hunted animals, and the women gathered nuts, fruits, and other such food.

The men and women thus had their separate spheres of productive activity. Crucially, these were not much different in status. Status tends to depend partly on how the culture values your contribution to the group's welfare. Men's contribution was approximately equal to women's. The little foods gathered by the women were reliably there most days, and they furnished many crucial calories. The men's hunts sometimes yielded big game and hence feasts, but (many) other times the men brought home nothing. When researchers have tried to calculate the men's versus women's separate contributions to the total food, in nutritional units such as calories, they tend to conclude that the men contributed slightly more overall, but not by much, and the difference was not regarded as a big deal. The reliability of the women's contribution certainly made up for its lesser caloric content: It's important to have something to eat every day. Plus, the men seemingly ought to contribute more calories than the women since, as bigger creatures, they surely would consume more.

Thus, both genders contributed to providing for the group. Men and women were more or less equal partners. Neither had to work very hard (about three hours per day may have been typical). Gathering food enabled the women to stay near the home camp and look after the children. The men roamed farther afield.

Some nomads also kept groups of animals. The men, as hunters and ostensible animal experts, tended to be in charge of the herds. The nomads would move around so that their animals could graze.

A crucial step came when people began planting crops. The nomadic lifestyle, which meant moving around and setting up camp in different places, was replaced by staying in the same place all year. With the advent of farming, people had to work much harder—but the food supply increased dramatically, and with it the population also began to increase. Culture also progressed in various ways such as ownership of land. Nomads and hunter-gatherers did not own the land, nor did they own much else, except perhaps their herds of animals and a few portable possessions.

At this point the status difference between men and women began to increase. Men became the owners of property and the bosses of the farms. Women still made essential contributions, and indeed a successful farm without a woman was close to unthinkable in many cultures. Still, women's position was now clearly subordinate to men's.

In other words, farming societies still had separate men's and women's spheres that did separate tasks. Both tasks were essential. But the men's tasks and roles came to be regarded as higher in status than the women's.

From the dawn of agriculture across the centuries of history, men and women followed separate life paths, with the women's sphere being viewed (by both men and women) as the lesser or inferior one. Gender inequality was a basic fact of social organization. By this time there was no avoiding the truth that the men had higher status than the women. Still, there was no questioning the value of both. In colonial America or early modern Europe, each household needed a man and a woman, because men and women did separate jobs, and both were indispensable to survival.

Finally, after the Enlightenment (the 1700s, around when the American Revolution occurred), women slowly began to ask and then demand that the inequality between the genders be reduced. By this point society consisted of vast and complex social institutions: universities, factories, banks, churches, and more. Very few of these treated women the same as men. Many key positions were reserved for men only.

Various individuals, both male and female, argued that women should be treated more as equals of men by these institutions. A women's movement campaigned for this, focusing for a while on letting women vote in the elections. Gradually the men who were in charge of these institutions came to agree that women deserved access. The all-male electorate voted to extend voting rights to women. Other rights followed.

The relegation of women to an inferior position was supported in part by stereotypes. Most (though not all) intelligent men and women believed that women were not as capable as men of performing many of the difficult jobs in society, from working in coal mines to conducting scientific research to running a government. Over time, research has shown that the stereotypes about innate female incompetence are generally wrong.

In the twentieth century, women continued to campaign for better treatment. Laws were passed to ensure that women received, first, rights equal to those of men and then some preferential treatments. Whereas the first women sought only to be allowed to work and compete alongside the men, later generations of women wanted the institutions to change to accommodate them and to treat them better than men. Not all women made such demands.

Ultimately, many women wanted the separation of male and female spheres to end. They wanted to become equal partners in the institutions of the men's sphere. They also wanted the men to come into the women's sphere and take an equal share of housework and child care.

As we have moved into the twenty-first century, we have certainly seen massive movements along those lines. The merging remains incomplete but it has come far. Men do vastly more in the domestic (formerly female) sphere than they did. Women are far more widely active in the major social (formerly male) institutions than they previously were.

The Stock Explanation

It has become conventional wisdom to explain these events based on the idea that men banded together to exploit and oppress women. At some point during the prehistoric era of gender equality, supposedly, there was a conspiracy by men to seize power for themselves and push women down. There is essentially no record of such a conspiracy or historical change. The Imaginary Feminist likes to say that part of the male conspiracy included erasing it from history, so it would never be known. This seems implausible, however, not least because it would have had to happen over and over, in pretty much every tribe and society in the world, because all these groups ended up being ruled by men.

The conventional wisdom continues by saying that women eventually began to win their freedom back, while the men are supposedly still resisting with backlashes, glass ceilings, and other antifemale patriarchal dirty tricks. Again, there is actually hardly any evidence to support these plots. The Imaginary Feminist encourages people to take the outcome as evidence for the process. That is, the argument goes more or less that there are relatively few top executives who are women, and so the only possible explanation is that the men are plotting and scheming to prevent women from getting those jobs. Or that fact that women earn less money than men is supposedly a clear sign that there is unfair discrimination against women. Sometimes the existence of stereotypes of women as inferior is pointed to as a sign of the male conspiracy, on the argument that men just invented false ideas of female incompetence to justify refusing to hire or promote women.

Beyond the Gender Wars

Let's try to come up with another explanation, preferably one that isn't based on a dastardly plot by men against women. Let's also question the assumption that men and women are basically enemies. In fact, as I've said, I think that assumption is wrong and that men and women mostly like each other and help each other and get along pretty well. In particular, men don't see women as their enemy. Throughout the history of our species, when men have banded together, it was mainly against other groups of men.

The Prehistoric Starting Point

Let's go back to the starting point, namely a prehistoric pattern of hunter-gatherer life in which men and women had separate spheres but were roughly equal in status and respect. Again, the people in these separate spheres were not enemies. They were partners and allies. They took care of each other. The men provided for the women in large ways, and the women took direct care both of the men and crucially of the next generation of both males and females.

In these different spheres, men built relationships with men, and women built relationships with women. They built them differently, according to the different inclinations of men and women that we discussed in Chapter 5. The way that men and women collectively treated each other reflected those different patterns of interacting. Women took care of men by providing intimacy and love and physical care in close, intimate relationships, and they did the same with the babies. Men took care of women by participating in big group activities, which could accomplish things that lone individuals couldn't, and which therefore enabled the man to bring back big game meat or whatever. That way the women benefited from the men's group activities.

The women's sphere was built on one-to-one close, intimate, supportive relationships. The men's sphere, in contrast, was built to feature a broader collection of shallower relationships. Although one-to-one close friendships undoubtedly formed among men, the larger group was much more important and central to the male social life than the female one.

Moreover, humans are psychologically built for culture. They share information, accumulate knowledge, specialize in different tasks, and so forth. Culture exists in and emerges from the social group, not the individual person. And so culture would slowly make its progress in the groups formed by the social relationships. These relationships would start to acquire the benefits of systems.

As it happens, though, there's only so much cultural progress you can get in a two-person close relationship. A two-person group (a dyad) isn't big enough to capitalize on many of the benefits of systems. Two people may share information, but the accumulation of knowledge will be much slower than in a large group.

The upshot is that **human culture emerged mostly from the men's sphere.** The pattern of relationships in the women's sphere is profoundly important for health, welfare, and the continuation of the species across generations. For nurturance and social support, that style of relationship was and still is superior to most of what was found in the men's sphere. But the men's sphere was better suited for creating culture.

The larger groups can accumulate more information and build up more knowledge (as compared to a two-person relationship). They offered much more scope for division of labor and specialization. Competition, sometimes friendly and sometimes cruel, allowed different ideas to be tried out against each other, so that the group as a whole could benefit from what the winner came up with. The losers in these competitions suffered various costs and punishments and deprivations. More important, the losers' approaches or strategies were discarded, while the rest of the group copied the successful strategies of the winners. In this way, the male competition advanced the group. The women's sphere did not create losers in the same way, which undoubtedly made it more agreeable to live in—but without losers, there were also no clear winners, and progress was slower.

Incidentally, I suspect that that's why many women today ultimately don't "get" sports—that is, why most women don't ever really care about sports the way men do and don't really understand why the men are so interested in sports. Most women don't resonate to the fundamental importance of proving who's better at doing things, even, or especially, doing things that are pretty useless from a practical or biological standpoint, like pole vaulting or throwing a curve ball. That's what gets men interested in sports, the proving of who's better, because that's what male social life is like. That's what a large group is like. Women don't socialize in large groups, so they aren't attuned to that kind of competition, and often it strikes them as silly.

I have always thought that the biggest difference between male and female interest in sports would be found not so much in watching games or enjoying them (though there are probably differences there) but rather in whether they check the scores. How often do you make the effort to find out the final score of a game you didn't watch? I'll bet that men do this much more than women. It matters to men, because the final score is one bit of proof about which side is superior. The male psyche is attuned to competition between groups, to one group pushing ahead of another and dominating it.

The Basis for Gender Inequality

The emergence of culture from the men's sphere was the basic cause of gender inequality.

As civilization progressed, men came to have higher status than women. This was not because women had some innate inferiority to men. Neither was it because of some conspiracy by the men to defraud and oppress women.

Men gained higher status because wealth, knowledge, and power were created in the men's sphere.

The large group organization of the men's sphere gradually (and often painfully) produced progress on a variety of fronts. Men created art and literature, religion, philosophy, science, military organization, trade and economic relations, technology, political structures and government, and the rest. In general, these benefit from large groups with weak social ties. They do not depend on intimate pair bonds nearly as much.

Rising or Falling?

As society moved from prehistoric, nomadic tribes to the settled societies of the modern world, giant social structures (institutions) were created: corporations, universities, banks, hospitals, marketplaces, governments, police forces, medical services. In general, these too were created by men.

These had a further and crucial consequence. They all created and accumulated wealth, knowledge, and power. Wealth, knowledge, and power were thus created in the men's sphere by all these institutions.

The conventional wisdom emphasizes that women's status declined as culture progressed. This is one way of looking at it, but it is flawed. The decline was relative rather than absolute. I have already pointed out that women actually became better off than their ancestors: Modern women live better than primitive women did. Women fared worse only relative to men. If it's relative, then we could put it another way. Perhaps women stayed roughly where they were, while men moved ahead.

In terms of cultural progress, wealth, knowledge, and power are extremely important. Considering that these things were being created mainly in the men's sphere and not much in the women's sphere, it would be hard for the women's sphere to keep up. Instead, and inevitably, the world of women would tend to fall behind. But that does not mean that the women got worse off or were pushed into inferior positions. Rather, it means that they simply failed to keep up with the advances in the men's sphere.

Nor were they really trying to do so. The men were still quite willing to share the fruits of their cultural activities with women. But naturally the men just shared on their own terms. Controlling wealth, knowledge, and power did elevate the men and change the terms on which men and women related to each other.

To be sure, there was a bit of cultural activity in the women's sphere. We should not make all-or-nothing statements. The women accumulated and improved the stock of knowledge about some things, such as cooking, and perhaps some lore about health and herbal cures. The Imaginary Feminist reminds us that women worked collectively and creatively in making big quilts. Still, these improvements were few and limited, and in the long run they amounted to much less than the progress that was made in the men's sphere.

The creation of large social institutions was where the differences between men and women became huge and influential. The men formed armies, churches, corporations, unions, and governments. The women did not. Much later, the women did begin to form a few large groups, but mostly these were aimed at protesting against what the men did. Women's groups essentially reacted to what men had done. Men created groups that were proactive.

Discussing these issues can make people sensitive and easy to offend. It is best to set aside value judgments, but if one needs to bring them in, let me point out a couple things. Women's sphere provided necessities, whereas the men's sphere provided optionals, including culture. If we really want to say who had the more important job, it was the women, because without the loving care to bring up the next generation, neither the small tribe nor the species as a whole would continue. But the men created the culture, and so in terms of what culture recognizes and values, the men's activities would get more recognition and credit. Cultural judgments of prestige are thus somewhat unfair to traditional women, because of culture's being created by men. Nonetheless, they have consequences, and some women did start to feel like second-class citizens.

Revising Childbirth

One dramatic and revealing contrast concerns giving birth. What could be more feminine than giving birth? The birthing process has always been central to women's lives, and for the thousands of years when men and women had separate social spheres, giving birth was quite definitely in the women's sphere. Usually, men were completely excluded. They were not welcome and usually not even not permitted to be present. All the information and knowledge about the birthing process were kept to women alone.

And then something curious happened. Gradually, after a long time, men were permitted access, and by using the male methods of pooling information and letting rival theories compete, men discovered ways to make the birth process safer. Male medicine has been able to change the birthing process so that many mothers and babies survive who would otherwise have died. It was mainly men, developing their theories about medicine and germs and painkillers and how the body works, who ultimately figured out ways to make childbirth safer, less painful, and less lethal for women and their babies. Indeed, these improvements came relatively fast, when contrasted with the thousands of years during which women held a monopoly on information about birthing.

A similar point could be made about the health of young children. Again, taking care of offspring is almost always central to the women's sphere and something they have done for centuries. One sad fact was that a great many young children died. Again, it was the progress in research by men that led to extraordinary reductions in the death rate of small children. In the 1700s people routinely expected some of their babies to die before the age of 5. Women were intellectually capable of solving this problem, but they did not, whereas progress in the men's sphere eventually did. These days, at least in Western countries, a child's death is a rare and tragic event, not an everyday occurrence as it once was.

That's how things went. The type of relationships that women prefer and create are vital to the human race and are, all things considered, more satisfying than the relationships men create. But remember my point about tradeoffs. Each advantage is likely compensated elsewhere. The superior intimacy and benefits of women's relationships is based on things that make those relationships less suitable to the development of cultural progress. The men's relationships—large groups working together and against each other, competing, striving, experimenting with innovations that might help them best their rivals—gradually drove the progress of culture.

Even in colonial America the rate of death during childbirth was significant. It was customary for a woman to make two sets of preparations before she entered her confinement for giving birth. One set of preparations was for adding the baby to the household. The other was for her own death. As she prepared to give birth, she knew there was a significant chance that she would die. (The historian Edwin Shorter puts the odds at about 1.4%: That is, about one out of every seventy live births resulted in the mother's death, even by 1800. And most women would give birth several times.) Her family had to be prepared for this: Who would cook tomorrow's dinner, mend their clothes, and do all the other essential tasks for which a colonial household depended on the wife and mother?

As always, we should strive to be fair to both sides. The women had done the crucial part successfully, which is to say they had managed to get enough babies born and raised that the small groups and the species as a whole had survived. Women had managed the process so that the majority of births were successful. The men were merely improving on a process that was already successful.

Still, for the men to find ways to improve on a quintessentially female activity is impressive as well. It reveals the strengths of men and of male ways of doing things. The men had built up medical knowledge in their large groups and networks, and individual men, competing against other men to succeed in their careers, and pooling information across broad networks of weak relationships, brought this male body of knowledge to bear on the problems and solved quite a few of them. From the perspective of the species, the male improvements were not necessary, but they certainly meant a powerfully meaningful improvement to all those mothers and babies who lived instead of dying.

I like this example of birthing because it has nothing to do with the idea of men and women as enemies. Instead, it shows how men and women depended on each other and did things for each other. More important, it shows the value of the men's networks even where one might least expect it. Women had owned all the information and knowledge about childbirth for thousands of years. Yet when the men were finally allowed into the picture, they were able to make significant additions and improvements.

Again, this has nothing to do with differences in capability or intelligence or concern. It is simply a product of the different kinds of relationships that men and women create. When the women had their monopoly on information about childbirth, they passed it on via their one-to-one contacts and relationships: from mother to daughter, and sometimes from one midwife to her client or to another individual woman training to be a midwife. And as I said, this was sufficient to get the job done, and successfully in general. But the large male networks of shallow relationships, marked by competition between men with different theories and by other men paying attention to who won these competitions, were able to make progress in ways that intimate one-to-one relationships were not.

Creating Innovations for Culture

Perhaps you are not persuaded by the birthing example. Let's look for some kind of broader influence. How about checking the very things that drive the culture forward and make progress: innovations?

Innovations require creativity. We considered creativity earlier, with the discussion of jazz musicians. Based on research using psychological tests of creativity, the conclusion was that women are just as creative as men.

But based on the historical difference in creative output, I proposed that men are more interested than women to use their creative abilities to make their mark in the giant social structure and thereby to contribute to cultural progress.

The Imaginary Feminist remains unconvinced by data from the past. To her, the fact that women generated very little creative output throughout history is just a sign that they were oppressed, and part of their being oppressed meant that they weren't "allowed" to make new innovations. (She is sure to mention again all the quilts women made, as proof of their creativity.) She thinks things will be different now that women have been liberated to pursue their creative inspirations.

A clever and creative way of testing this was suggested to me by a colleague. She said to see what gender difference there might be in patents. The U.S. Patent Office is quite willing to issue patents to anyone, and in recent decades women have been working in huge numbers throughout the economy. If there is a gender difference in getting patents, it is not likely due to oppression. If anything, the Patent Office, like just about every other major institution, has made extra efforts to be welcoming to women.

I contacted the U.S. Patent Office and asked for their figures. They were quite cooperative and directed me to an official report they had done a few years ago, *Buttons to Biotech: U.S. Patenting by Women, 1977 to 1996.*

The simple conclusion is that patents are overwhelmingly sought by and given to men. Thus, the major cultural innovations that reach the level of being officially recognized with legal protection are created mainly by men.

They did not actually count male versus female patents, because many patents have multiple inventors. What they counted was whether any of the inventors was a female. This was done because there were so few patents that included any female inventors that that was the only way to get a decent number.

During the 20-year period covered by the report, 94.3% of the patents went to men and all-male groups. The remaining 5.7% went to male–female teams, groups of women, and individual women. No breakdown among the latter categories was supplied, but two-thirds of those patents were held by corporations, which suggests that male–female teams would be typical.

There was an upward trend over the period. In 1996, the last year, almost 10% of the patents included at least one female inventor.

Again, it is implausible that the low rate of female patents reflects some kind of societal oppression, such as the Patent Office selectively refusing patents by women and favoring those by men, or that schools are forbidding girl students to be creative while encouraging boys.

Much more plausibly, this huge imbalance reflects the motivational differences we have seen repeatedly. Women may be just as creative as men. But men far exceed women in their desire to make a mark in a large social system. Getting a patent takes more than being creative. It means caring about registering one's innovation in a way that reserves legal rights, thereby enabling the person to use the invention to make money. Put another way, a patent reflects several things: having a good new idea, being willing to take the risks and chances (and hard work) involved in developing it, and having the drive to use that idea to advance one's position and perhaps make money in the society at large.

This is not unlike the difference in small business ownership that we also discussed earlier. Women start more small businesses than men, which argues against the Imaginary Feminist's claim that society oppresses women and prevents them from engaging in business. But women's small businesses stay very small, while the ones men start are more likely to grow.

Men and Money in the Bank

The previous section talked about innovation, in terms of making patents. Let us now go to something seemingly opposite, namely banking. Cultures and societies depend heavily on banks. When many banks were threatened with failure in 2008, economists who normally oppose government bailouts for troubled firms nonetheless supported bailing out the banks. They pointed out that banks are special cases and the entire economy depends on having banks do their work.

Banks do not simply keep your money on a shelf, of course. They invest it. Proper investments enable the money to increase and, probably more important, make investments that allow progress to happen. A company may need money to start up or expand its operations, which can lead to increased profits for the company and its investors, increased tax revenues for the government, and more goods and services available to consumers. A good investment thus benefits everyone. A poor investment is a detriment.

Investment banking is all about risk. Who goes into that field? According to the most underappreciated fact about gender, namely the difference in reproductive odds throughout evolutionary history, men are more willing than women to take risks. Hence that field should attract more men than women.

It does. Recent evidence has confirmed over and over that more men than women go into investment banking. The difference is not one of discrimination—rather, it seems to depend on individual choices and on the male hormones that influence them. A recent study measured testosterone among male and female students at a prominent business school (the University of Chicago), and then it tracked their careers after they got their MBAs. It also measured, in the lab, their willingness to take a financial risk right away by asking them how much money they would choose as a sure thing rather than participate in a lottery that had a 50–50 chance of getting nothing or a big ($200) prize.

The men were more willing than the women to take the risk on the lottery. For the women, even a very low sure thing was preferable to taking a chance. The men were more willing to take their chances on the lottery. Testosterone levels also predicted willingness to take a risk, with higher testosterone associated with more risk. Likewise, the willingness to choose a career in the risky field of finance (e.g., investment banking) was higher among men and among women who had high testosterone levels.

Thus, men are more willing than women to take the kinds of chances on which financial progress depends. This does not mean that their decisions are correct. Plenty of investments yield mediocre or even poor results. But someone has to take the chances by making those investments, if the economy is to function properly and gradually bring the progress that makes a society strong and rich.

Who Against Whom?

Crucially, all this production of culture in the men's sphere was not produced by an alliance of all men against all women, as the Imaginary Feminist is fond of asserting. Instead, it was produced by alliances of some men working with each other and, crucially, against other groups of men.

I pointed out that the Imaginary Feminist has emphasized a plot by all men against all women—and that there is very little evidence of such a plot. In place of that plot, my theory says culture emerged from groups of men competing against other groups of men. It's fair to turn the tables on me. I have reproached the standard theory for its lack of evidence. Is there any evidence for my theory?

Frankly, I think there is abundant of evidence, even something of an embarrassment of riches. History is full of accounts of groups of men competing against other groups of men. There is an enormous amount of historical evidence of men banding together to conspire and work against other groups of men. Men competed against other groups in trade and commerce. They competed in science and technology. They competed in politics. They competed on the battlefield.

Remember what we covered in the opening chapter about male winners and losers? There is ample evidence of this in history too. The men who succeeded in these competitions sometimes enjoyed great rewards, the best of what was available at the time. And many losers paid heavy prices, including ruination and death.

Of course, not all men have played for high stakes. Many lived in a hut with a small family and farmed a small plot of ground. They lived from season to season as best they could. There were no spectacular successes, and although there were failures, they were of a small scale. Still, history and progress were driven forward by the minority of men who did band together to play at the big games.

Probably you could open almost any chapter from any major history textbook and it would be partly or even mainly concerned with groups of men working against other groups of men.

The fact that culture emerged from the men's sphere is the key reason for the increase in gender inequality. Crucially, the difference did not arise because women were pushed down, as the Imaginary Feminist argues. Rather, it arose because men went up. The sometimes brutal competition of men against men, pitting different systems and products and ideas against each other, gradually produced immense progress in the men's sphere. The women's sphere did not produce progress. It stayed pretty much the same, filled with love, care, gossip, household chores, the joys and burdens of children, and the cultivation of intimacy.

Remember, too, it is not because women were unable to engage in cultural activities like the men were doing. It was because the kind of relationships they specialized in just so happened to be less conducive to generating culture collectively.

The Toll of Time

As a result, as the centuries went by, the men's sphere became rich, powerful, and influential. The women's sphere stayed mostly where it was.

Can you name achievements by large groups of men? That is rather easy. Ships explored foreign lands. Banks financed new ventures. Armies conquered territories. Teams of scientists came up with discoveries and innovations.

And how about achievements by large groups of women? This is difficult. One has to search hard through history to find instances of, say, a large group of women building or buying a ship and sailing off to explore foreign lands, or forming a conglomerate to make and sell goods for profit.

Remember my point that gender differences are mostly in motivation, not ability? I think a group of a hundred women would have been just as capable as a group of a hundred men of building a ship and sailing off to explore. The difference is not one of ability. Women could have done it if they wanted to do so. But they did not want to do so. Women mostly do not do things in big groups.

Indeed, the main thing women have done in large groups is to protest and complain about the men and the men's activities. On this, women have been useful and successful in collective work. I refer here not only to the feminist movements from the suffragists onward, but also to various campaigns to protest men's drunkenness, to reduce vice such as by getting men to stop using prostitutes, and the like. Women's groups were also active in campaigning against slavery.

In general, though, large groups of women were not an engine of cultural progress. They have functioned only as a reaction against the problems and excesses of the men's activities, and that only intermittently.

The topic is sensitive, and I don't want to be misunderstood. The fact that throughout history women collectively achieved so little, measured in terms of cultural progress, could be misconstrued to argue that women are inferior in some way. I wish to be most emphatic that that is not what I am saying. Women are not inferior.

Instead, that fact derives from the social organization of women's lives, as I have said. Women were busy doing vital things for keeping the human race alive: creating and sustaining close, loving, intimate, nurturing relationships. These center on cultivating close, intimate, one-on-one relationships. It was just an unfortunate fact that progress in culture is best facilitated by larger social groups, of the sort that the men naturally favored in their sphere.

As for Stereotypes

That does, however, bring us to the issue of the stereotypes of women's inferiority. These days it is common for intellectuals to adopt a self-righteous posture of indignation or mockery at the prejudices of earlier eras. I have done this too. One hunts down some extreme statements from writers of bygone eras, such as the assertion by Reverend John Putnam in 1791 that the wonderful new American Constitution guarantees every man "is born with an equal right to be elected to the highest office ... And every woman is born with equal right to be the wife of the most eminent man."

The truth is that there were some stereotypes about women being inferior to men on many abilities. Another truth is that, now that women have moved into the men's sphere en masse, we see that those stereotypes were all or mostly wrong. Women are able to perform just fine in most of the roles in the men's sphere. Women have plenty of abilities.

But we can perhaps understand why those stereotypes arose, even while we recognize them now as wrong. The Imaginary Feminist says, for example, that when women asked to be admitted to the universities the men had created, the men trotted out (perhaps even deliberately invented) their theories of female intellectual inferiority to justify denying them access. I suggest, instead, that it was more or less an honest mistake. The men had in fact created these marvelous universities in their sphere. The women had never created anything comparable. As I noted earlier, women had not even been able to solve some of the vexing problems of childbirth until male medicine showed the way. It was understandable that men would think that women were not capable of such intellectual work.

The stereotype of female inferiority, in this view, resembles one of the classic findings in my own field of social psychology. It has several names such as correspondence bias and the fundamental attribution error. Essentially, it means interpreting someone's behavior as stemming from inner traits when in fact it is caused by external circumstances.

Women did not create intellectual achievements in their sphere, not because of any lack of intelligence, but because the social relationships in their sphere were not conducive to the competitive battle of ideas and accumulation of knowledge across generations. But people made the standard mistake of attributing the lack of intellectual achievement to a lack of intellectual ability.

And What About Oppression?

I have shown how we can understand the lower status of women as a result of how society and culture evolved. We don't have to assume it was the result of men oppressing women.

Does that mean there has been no oppression?

The answer, I think, is that there probably has been some, but probably only a fraction of what has been accused and assumed. The amount by which men have oppressed women has been grossly overestimated, but it is not zero.

It is possible to interpret much of history as men oppressing women, especially if one does not look too closely and seeks only confirming evidence. But just as plausibly, one can spin a very different interpretation. Here's another possible way to tell the story. Women kept themselves conveniently apart from the brutal, risky, and often painful strife and competition. Men fought bloody battles. Other men risked their savings in commerce, with some making fortunes and others going bankrupt. Men fought, risked, struggled, sought, suffered, and triumphed. Women mostly kept out of that.

Certainly in the early years there was nothing to prevent groups of women from forming into military groups to fight battles for territory. Nor did anything prevent groups of women from engaging in manufacture and trade to create wealth. In fact a few women did, but only a very few.

Only after a long wait, when the men had built up society into magnificent social structures with large corporations and other institutions, then only did the women come forward and demand to be given a place at the table they had not helped to build. Only after most of the risks and costs had been greatly tamed and everything was fairly safe did women venture forth. And even then they were not satisfied with getting an equal place: They demanded that the social structures the men built must be revised to make them more hospitable to women. Women insisted on affirmative action, special centers and support groups, and the changing of rules to suit their needs. These demands continue today and seem likely to go on forever, as women insist that there be special offices and accommodations and oversight bodies to take care of their special needs and demands and feelings. Women have played on men's natural love for women and protectiveness toward women, exploiting men's concern to convince men to switch things around for the betterment of women.

I am not saying this latter view is correct. I bring it up just to show how easily one can spin the historical record either way. Our society has accepted the story of men oppressing women, but it is a weak story. If it were held up to the same critical standards as other stories, it would be exposed as mostly (not completely) a fake.

Let me put this another way. Feminists have honed their skills at showing that all manner of behavior can be interpreted as men oppressing women. But often these interpretations are stretched to the point of absurdity, and many are false. In a court of law, a defendant cannot be convicted simply because someone says that one could possibly interpret the facts to be consistent with the man's guilt. Rather, clear evidence has to be found, which means that guilt is not just one possible interpretation but the *only* possible interpretation. By that rule, there is not much evidence against men as oppressors. How many broad facts can you find that cannot be interpreted in any way other than as male oppression of women?

The oppression argument has been politically useful for the women's movement. Whenever certain views are politically useful, they will tend to get used—and often overused. No doubt some people, friends of the Imaginary Feminist, have overstated the degree of oppression. Daphne Patai and Noretta Koertge, two feminist scholars who became disenchanted with life as professors of Women's Studies and who wrote a book about the problems and excesses in that field, have documented this carefully. For example, they reported how occasionally a student would object to the classroom discussions that always had the same explanation for every problem: men, men, men. In many classrooms, all women's problems are blamed on men. Students who said they liked men or thought some men were OK would be attacked by other students and sometimes by the feminist professor.

In their account, Women's Studies classes are devoted to teaching young women to become feminist activists. This involves helping them interpret all manner of behaviors as evidence of oppression. The female students learn to become "grievance collectors," that is, people who are constantly searching for things to be angry at men about. The classes find ambiguous behaviors, even sometimes innocent ones, and they interpret these as evidence that men oppress women. One gets the impression that almost every meeting of every class in Women's Studies involves hunting for grievances: Finding more reasons to think that women have been oppressed by men.

A feminist professor in Patai and Koertge's book described one of her classroom exercises. She would tell the students to go out and observe couples holding hands. Whose hand is in front? It turns out that the man's hand is nearly always in front of the woman's. Now, says the professor, look at adults holding hands with children. The grownup's hand is again usually in front, the child's hand hidden behind it and following. Thus, the professor tells the class, you can see how even the way couples express their love for each other symbolically puts the woman in the inferior position, like a child, dependent on the powerful man.

Thus is oppression seen once again. The way lovers hold hands oppresses women.

Yet there is a major flaw in that analysis. Try holding hands with anybody whose height differs from yours—and try it both ways. The taller person has the higher elbow, and so when the tall person's hand is in back, the arm near the wrist constantly bangs into the other person's arm at every step. This is uncomfortable for both people. Reverse the hands, and no banging. People will make the adjustment to stop banging their arms. They aren't even aware of doing it, and it has no symbolic meaning. It comes just from the discomfort of banging your arm into the other person's. The banging spoils most of the pleasure from hand-holding, so people find a way to hold hands that preserves the pleasure. That means the taller person's hand goes in front.

It's not oppression. In Women's Studies university classes, some feminist professors say it is. But it isn't.

Or recall the example I touched on in Chapter 1, in which some feminists insisted that urinals be removed from public institutions because men are lording it over women when they stand up to urinate. This complaint was meant seriously and was taken seriously by various institutions that complied with the demand to remove urinals in the attempt to force men to sit while they peed, like women. Did this actually reduce oppression of women? Were men oppressing women by standing up? Certainly one can come up with plenty of alternative explanations. It is simply easier, faster, and possibly more effective to pee standing up. No court of law would convict men of oppressing women based on urinating from a standing position.

The more commonly cited evidence is ambiguous too. The fact that most world leaders and CEOs of large corporations are men does not prove that men oppressed women. Women start plenty of small businesses, indeed more than men do, but they do not build them up into large ones. They could. It is hard to imagine consumers refusing to buy an item simply because the CEO of the company that manufactured it was a woman. How many shoppers even know who made the products on the shelves? As for government leaders, well, men lose far more elections than women, so you could just as easily argue that the electorate is biased against men. The plain fact is that running for high political office is a risky career choice that has always attracted more men than women and probably always will. When both candidates are men, the winner is going to be a man, and this does not indicate bias in the electorate.

Again, one can just as easily make contrary interpretations. In his book, *The Myth of Male Power*, Warren Farrell offered telling examples relevant to the story of oppression. The standard line goes that men are the masters and women are their servants or slaves. OK, says Farrell. When a master and slave are ready to go out for the evening, who holds the coat for whom, and who assists whom in putting it on? Who, master or servant, opens the door for whom and lets the other walk through it first? Who is served first at dinner, while the other waits? Who, master or slave, toils to make the money to support the other's protected life inside the comfortable home? If danger arises, who, master or slave, must face the risk and possible sacrifice of life and limb to protect the other?

Thus, over and over, the male and female roles can be analyzed in ways that indicate the man is equivalent to the slave, while the woman is equivalent to the master. No doubt one can generate some contrary examples. Nonetheless, painting a picture of human social life that feature man as master and woman as servant or slave is a highly selective, one-sided, biased interpretation.

Status Quo Bias

Once society evolved with men in a position superior to women, individual women who protested may have found themselves punished and their options blocked. Men made universities, and women did not, and so when the first women wanted to attend the men's universities, the men there said no.

People often try to preserve the status quo, especially when it is reasonably good for them and they see no need for change. When some women wanted change, some men resisted. This is not surprising. To the women, this would seem to be oppression. To the men it probably did not seem like oppression.

So let me return to the original question about oppression. Yes, there probably was some oppression, and almost certainly far less than we have been told. The idea of oppression cannot be evaluated without an open-minded, disciplined evaluation of evidence, which is what good science requires. I doubt it will get that any time soon, because it is a highly emotional and politicized concept, and because insisting on oppression is politically useful to some who seek to advance their own interests by asserting that it can be found everywhere.

Most important, though, if there was oppression, it was secondary. The real cause of women's inferior status in all societies in world history was not the oppressive conspiracies by evil men. The real cause was that the types of social groups created by men and not women gave rise to wealth, knowledge, and power. Groups of men competing against other groups of men pushed cultural progress forward. The men who lost these competitions suffered, but the ones who did well in them reaped benefits. Women did not compete in these ways. They did not suffer all the bad consequences (though the women married to the male losers certainly suffered some, just as the women who married the male winners benefited some). Crucially, women did not create the rising tides of wealth, knowledge, and power that were found in the men's sphere.

What This Means About Culture

Now we can begin to understand what sorts of things culture will find men useful for. These start with the fact that men carry much of the responsibility for creating culture in the first place. Again, this is not because women aren't capable. They are. But women's inclinations tend toward close, intimate relationships, and women are less inclined than men to think and work and strive in large systems. System-building and empire-building appeal to the male mind, with its fascination with systems and large groups, more than to the female mind, in general. Culture arises from large social systems, and men tend to create these.

According to recent neuroscience research, this is in the brain. The female brain is for empathizing (understanding and relating to individual other persons). The male brain is for systematizing. And culture is a system.

In general, the world's cultures were created by men. And as I have sought to emphasize, culture was not created because of men working together against women, as the Imaginary Feminist likes to claim. Instead, it was groups of men working together and against other groups of men.

Women had several roles in the process. Women helped men in many ways. Women were often the prize that inspired men to take the chances of creating new institutions in their quest for wealth, power, and greatness, because women prefer men who have those things. Much of what men do is ultimately aimed at appealing to women.

Still, the fact that culture and institutions are male-created explains why they have been male-dominated and male-oriented. They were made for men, not as a deliberate ploy to exclude or oppress women, but simply because women were not involved in making them. They were made to function as well as possible so as to compete against rival groups and systems. Because the groups and systems were full of men, they were made in ways that worked well with groups of men.

Regardless of whether you agree with feminists or not, one thing they have done extensively is criticize nearly every type institution in Western culture as biased against women. Corporations, universities, the mass media, the church, the police and legal system, and many more have been thus criticized. Can you think of any type of organization that has not been criticized, other than the few that have been set up expressly to articulate feminist protests and help women?

As one reads these critiques, it is difficult to avoid the impression that many women, and especially women who claim to speak for all women, regard everything in the culture as built in ways that are unfriendly to women. Why do these women think the whole culture is built in such ways?

We now are ready to answer that question. Women find culture is biased against them, in large or mostly small ways, because it was made by men for men.

Things have changed considerably now. Most institutions now recognize the need to make changes to accommodate women. Changes have been made. Yet things never seem to be satisfactory, and the demand for more changes shows no sign of coming to an end. Perhaps it will never end: Women will never feel quite at home in large organizations.

But part of the reason for this is that the female brain excels in a close, intimate, empathic interaction with another human being, more than by becoming a single cog or part in a giant system. Moreover, large organizations will continue to be built mostly by men. Large international ventures, large corporations, new global networks: These are mostly going to be initiated and built up by men, though women are perfectly competent to play any role in them.

Let's Be Fair to Both

Let's be fair to the women. They do need affirmative action, preferences, and other special programs. Culture is against them, as the great lesson of feminism taught.

But let's be fair to the men too. The reason culture is biased against women is not that men conspired to make culture as a way of oppressing women. It's because women didn't make culture or its big institutions. The men built these. Eventually the women showed up and asked, or demanded, to be allowed to participate.

Let's be fair to women. It's not that men are noble in some way, altruistically making culture for the good of all. Men made culture to compete with each other, partly to win the hearts and spread the legs of women. They made it so their own group could live well, preferably better than rival groups of men.

And once more let's be fair to women. It isn't because they aren't capable of it. Women have performed superbly on the grand stages of culture.

It's just that women collectively were more devoted to building the crucial intimate spheres of love and support, individual by individual, and were never really to accept the brutal competition and human suffering that go into creating large social structures.

Women are fully capable of performing well in high-powered jobs in large corporations. And men are fully capable of changing diapers. It's just that most of them aren't really passionate enough about those things to be willing to make the sacrifices required for that kind of life.

And once more let's be fair to men. Whatever their many faults and countless sins, great and small, they did create culture. They built up the big institutions that define the broad context of our social life, even while letting women take the lead in creating the vital small social spheres of intimacy.

It is a sad irony that today we look upon men as being collectively guilty for their roles in creating culture, because it is not sufficiently welcoming to women. Yet women failed to create culture themselves, needing instead access to what was built by the men, and in some cases ending up resenting them for it.

CHAPTER 8

Expendable Beings, Disposable Lives

P ROGRESS DOES HAVE its ugly side. Chapter 7 focused on the positive side of culture, including how progress gradually makes life better for one and all. People got healthier, happier, richer, as the march of culture brought one innovation after another. But there have certainly been negative aspects.

The Industrial Revolution started in Great Britain and helped propel it to a position as one of the world's greatest powers. But the factories that were essential for manufacturing, as well as people's homes, needed energy, and coal was the primary source. Hence the coal mines became crucial to the nation's success.

Coal mines were dirty, dangerous places back then. They are undoubtedly better now, but they are still much dirtier and more dangerous than most workplaces.

Complaints and problems about conditions in the mines attracted some attention in England early in the 1800s. A leading statesman, Lord Shaftesbury, was active in trying to make work everywhere more humane, and at his urging Parliament sponsored an investigation into working conditions in the mines. The report was published in 1842. It shocked the public. Hours were long. Accidents were common. Brutal treatment of miners, including small children who pushed the carts and performed other menial services deep in the mines for long hours every day, was found. Lung diseases were linked with working in mines. Immoral behavior was seen also.

Driven by public outrage, the British government, like many others, decided that something needed to be done. And that something was to try to reduce the human toll of suffering, injury, and death. The ideal might have been to prevent anyone from doing such dangerous work. But that wasn't feasible: The nation needed coal. And so a partial measure was needed. Somehow the country had to balance the need to save valuable lives against the demands of the workplace. The work was risky, but somebody had to do it. The only solution was to leave the work to the most expendable beings in the society.

Men.

The Mines Act of 1842 stipulated that henceforth no children below the age of 10 would be sent to work in the mines. Also no girls or women of any age. That meant that henceforth this dirty, dangerous work would be done exclusively by men, loosely defined as males past the age of 10. (Later they raised this to 12.)

In this case, it also meant relatively poor men. Very few rich men would spend much time down in the coal mines. That case is not unusual. The culture values men's lives quite differently, some far more than others. Rich men's lives are valued more than poor men's lives. Right now U.S. society is struggling with this in terms of race: If you kill a white person, your prison time tends to be longer than if you kill a black person. This violates the American sense of fair play, which means that all lives should be valued equally. It is deeply troubling that in any sense black lives are valued less than white lives (though much of that difference comes from the fact that people mainly kill members of their own race, and so if we are lenient toward black defendants, we end up being lenient to the killers of black people). Yet we don't mind the fact that men's lives are valued much less than women's. America's Declaration of Independence asserted that "all men are created equal"—and we still resonate with that phrase. Today it means that all men should be equal to all other men but less valuable than women.

As usual, with the male extremity pattern, there will be more men than women at both extremes. Probably a few male lives get more elaborate protection than any woman's. But plenty of men are valued far less. And most men know that in an emergency they would be expected to die willingly so that a woman could be saved.

This is one case where the male and female averages aren't equal. Men's lives are valued much less than women's. This lesser valuation is one key to understanding how culture uses men.

Who's Precious?

In the preface to her eye-opening and remarkable book *Who Stole Feminism?*, Christina Hoff Sommers quoted a recent book by feminist icon Gloria Steinem, in which Ms. Steinem stirred outrage over the tragic deaths of 150,000 women and girls every year from anorexia. Naomi Wolf repeated that number in her book *The Beauty Myth*, along with a choice rhetorical flourish: "How would America react to the mass self-immolation by hunger of its favorite sons?" She went on to blame men.

Her question is worth pondering: Would our society be as seemingly indifferent to the deaths of its young men as it is to the deaths of its young women?

Being a skeptic, Professor Sommers checked the numbers. The figure of 150,000 annual deaths was found in many places, in the mass media and advice columns, even in college textbooks. But its original source proved elusive. When she finally tracked it down, it turned out to have been a case of misquotation. The National Center for Health Statistics gave the official figure of 70 deaths in the most recent year, which had been about typical. Apparently someone had estimated that there were 150,000 *cases* of anorexia, not deaths.

Nonetheless, we can still consider whether the culture is equally indifferent to the deaths of men vs. women. In actual fact, the culture allows and even asks more young men than women to give up their lives. We already saw some signs of this in an earlier chapter. Far more men than women do dangerous jobs and are killed in the line of work and duty. Far more men than women are executed as criminals. And, like every other society in the history of the world, when someone's life has to be put in danger on the battlefield to protect the culture from its enemies, our society calls mainly on its young men to make this sacrifice.

The Imaginary Feminist is quick to claim that our culture values men more than women. It will therefore seem surprising to hear that the reverse is correct. Some men, perhaps, are treated as highly valuable, though we shall stop to ask whether even they get precedence over women in having their lives saved in an emergency. But for the majority of men, there is little question, and they know it. Their culture considers them expendable. Men are more expendable than women.

"Even Women and Children"

When the news media report some disaster, they sometimes use the phrase "even women and children" if such are among the victims. What exactly does that mean?

The phrase expresses the point that men's lives are valued less. "Even women and children' is short for, "it's kind of bad that grown men get killed, but it is much worse for a woman or a child to be killed. It would have been better if only men had been killed." Every time you read that phrase, it reminds you that your culture places less value on the life of a full-grown man than on anyone else's life.

A man who reads the newspapers will see that phrase probably once or twice a month, and each time it subtly tells him that his own life is worth less than the lives of other, more precious beings. Life in general may be cheap or dear, but men's lives are cheaper than women's.

This is more than just disrespect. It helps remind each man that, in a desperate situation, he is expected to give up his life quickly and readily and without complaint if doing so will save a woman or child. This message is reinforced in the other mass media, as well. Think back on movies you have watched. How many scenes can you remember in which women sacrificed their lives to save a man's life? Can you even think of one? In contrast, films in which men die protecting or saving women are so common as to have ceased to be remarkable.

In real life, men are required to follow that script and accept their lesser value. One of the most famous disasters of the twentieth century was the sinking of the *Titanic*, a giant new ship making its maiden voyage across the Atlantic and thought to have been designed to be unsinkable. The overconfidence of the designers and the rush to sail on schedule despite last-minute problems combined with the lax regulations of the era to result in too few lifeboats for the number of passengers. The unexpected collision with the iceberg ripped a vertical opening that bypassed the safeguards, and the unsinkable ship started to sink.

And so the seats were given to the women, while the men stayed on board to drown.

Class also made a difference on the *Titanic*. Rich people were more likely to survive than poor people. But the richest men had a lower survival rate (34%) than the poorest women (46%).

That fact is extraordinary. It should give serious pause to anyone who hews to the conventional wisdom (or feminist critique) that society is set up to favor the rich and powerful men at the expense of everyone else. The gentlemen traveling in first class on the *Titanic* were precisely the sort of men who are assumed to benefit from society and to get the advantages denied to everyone else. The idea of "patriarchy," even despite its fallacy of ignoring all the men at the bottom of society, entails that surely these privileged members of the male power elite are regarded by the culture as more valuable than anyone else.

Those guys *were* the patriarchs. Yet their lives were not worth as much as the lives of the lower-class women down in steerage, women who weren't even considered ladies. Those women had hardly any money or power or status, but yet simply by virtue of being female, they were privileged to get some of the too-few seats in the lifeboats while the well-dressed gentlemen stood on the deck and silently watched them leave.

It is said that the men on the deck turned their backs so as not to watch the women rowing away. Whether the women looked back at their doomed sons, husbands, and fathers is not known, but it is known that most of them refused to circle back after the ship had gone down, even though they might have been able to pull a few freezing men out of the water. (Some of the lifeboats had empty seats, and there was no place to row toward; they were just waiting out on the wide-open sea for somebody to come rescue them.) One wonders what either group might have been thinking about gender politics and the relative value of different human lives.

Modern culture has taught us to say that each life is precious and equally valuable. But some of that is mere lip service. Ideology and praxis don't always mesh. Ideology may assert that men are as valuable as women, but the facts indicate otherwise. A man who believes the official story is headed for disappointment and surprise if it is put to the test.

What Daddy Did in the War

What determines the course of your life? In America we like to believe that anyone can make anything out of his or her life. Others believe accidents of birth make a huge difference. Jared Diamond, author of *Guns, Germs, and Steel*, remarked once that geography has a huge impact on your life: It matters overwhelmingly where you are born. Gender is, of course, another accident of birth. The two are not independent. Certainly being born female in certain times and places has amounted to being dealt a poor hand. But being born male at the wrong time and place can also get you into some rather difficult situations, through no fault of your own, and requiring your own most desperate efforts even to go on living.

One phrase one no longer hears much was "What did you do in the war, Daddy?" but it was a common phrase when I was a child. Most of our fathers had been involved in the Second World War ("the war," almost as if others were also-rans) in one way or another. The question, which sometimes was used in films or shows to set up jokes, implied a certain test of manhood: Was your father a hero who had braved enemy fire to save democracy and freedom, or had he just shuffled papers and peeled potatoes?

My father, a moody man with strict discipline (for himself and others) and a fierce temper, never showed much inclination to talk about his wartime experience. He was not an easygoing father, and for many years he and I did not speak to each other at all, and in between he had similar feuds with my sister and his other relatives. But finally one day when we were sort of getting along, my wife and I shared a bottle of wine with him and started asking seriously about the war. He did open up and tell his war story.

He was just a kid in 1939 when his country invaded Poland. His own father, my grandfather, had been badly wounded in the First World War and had no enthusiasm for war, but all veterans of the first war were drafted to be officers in the second, and so, like it or not, he found himself back in uniform. I'm sure that at first he thought the war would be over before his boy would be caught up in it, but as things started to drag on he began scheming to keep his only son from becoming cannon fodder.

According to family lore, my grandfather thought the Germans had blown their best chance already at Dunkirk and would eventually lose the war. As things ground along, the initially large gap between his son's boyish age and the minimum draft age dwindled, and indeed by the end of the war the Germans were drafting all males from 13 to 70. When young Rudy, my father, reached a draft-eligible age, grandfather decided to play for time, signing the boy up for pilot training, because this contained the longest wait until the trainee was ready for combat. Grandfather was hoping his country would have lost the war before my father was old enough to fly a plane into combat. My father did learn to fly. But by 1944 the Luftwaffe had lost the air war, and its remaining planes were bombed on the ground, along with the factories that could make them. There was no more point in training pilots.

And so one morning at roll call at the training school, the commander announced that there was a change of plans. He said the young men would have the honor of joining their infantry comrades on the Russian front, which by this point was not in Russia nor even Poland but inside of Germany itself. There was one day of infantry basic training, and one day of liberty, which my father said half the boys used to write a letter home, and the rest used to visit prostitutes. (He said he wrote, though I'd hardly blame him if he did both. Very likely it was the one and only sex act some of those boys ever experienced before they died.)

The march to the front was quite demoralizing for the nervous teenagers. They had known, certainly, that war was happening and that things were going somewhat badly, though the only news source, state propaganda, remained officially optimistic. In marching to the front they saw the signs of a collapsing army being held together with severe discipline. All armies occasionally execute soldiers for disobedience, cowardice, and other mis-deeds, but researchers have established that the Germans executed their own troops in the Second World War at a rate a thousand (!) times higher than they had done in the First World War—itself hardly an inspiring, glorious triumph. The young fellows had been taught to sing while marching, but they fell silent as they walked past the uniformed corpses hanging by the neck from trees and lampposts with the signs "Coward" and "Deserter" around their necks. This was in fact happening all over, but no news of this had penetrated outside so no one knew about it, and it was a shock to see. The images still bothered my father four decades later.

They marched up to the front, crossed a river on the bridge, marched down along the river, and were told, unceremoniously but ominously, to dig in. Essentially the culture was telling these teenage boys, dig a trench here, and over the next couple days we expect you to shoot your gun at the enemy until they kill you.

Here, in a sense, my story could end. I have selected this story to illus-trate some points about how culture uses men. In effect, this was the end of the line for how my father's culture intended to use him. He had dug a little hole in the dirt. In front of him were the masses of Russian soldiers, by now well-equipped and battle-hardened. Helping him on his side was a group of teenage boys who had never even fired a shot at the enemy. He said some of them didn't know what to do when they heard that horrible metallic screaming sound that was one of the hallmarks of the Russian front. (It was the deadly Russian "Katya" rocket, and the best hope was to dive for cover.) Behind him was the river, which made retreat impossible. This was a complete death trap. After the war, only seven of the 150 boys were ever heard from.

My father was of course one of the seven lucky ones. (Lucky in this case is admittedly relative.) After the first day's firefight, when casualties were already piling up, several of the guys held a midnight conversation and decided to desert their position. This would be a tricky business. They knew of the standing orders to execute deserters on the spot, and they'd seen plenty of hanged ones on their march. You might claim to have become separated from your group in the heat of battle, but this excuse was acceptable only if you still had your gun and were within ten kilometers (about six miles) of the front. Otherwise no excuse would save you. Still, a small chance was better than staying there. My father swam the river at night, in full uniform and with his gun slung on his back, catching a bad cold in the process.

He was with several other boys. Their woebegone plan was to work their way south, staying within ten kilometers of the front (no easy chore, because it moved often and unpredictably), all the way past the Russian attack to where the Americans were advancing, and then surrender to the American forces. According to scuttlebutt, the Americans treated their prisoners better than the Russians, so it was preferable to surrender to them. Plus the Yanks were more willing to take prisoners in the first place as opposed to shooting captives on the spot. (At least that's what the boys believed—reliable information about these things would be very hard to get.) Sticking together and keeping their weapons, they managed to convince the German officers they encountered that they were not deserters but merely had gotten separated from their unit in the heat of battle. Unfortunately each officer then insisted that the boys stay with his group and fight, so they had to re-desert each night.

Ultimately, and not surprisingly, the plan failed. They woke one morning in a barn to find the Russians outside. They surrendered and were told to line up. They heard the guns clicking to get ready. My father was seventeen years old, which the United Nations today officially classifies as a child soldier. Leaning forward with his hands against the side of the barn, he thought he was going to be shot dead in the next minute. At the same age of seventeen, I was merely worried about starting college and how to talk to girls. I had scarcely ever missed a meal.

Another Russian ran up, and there was some incomprehensible discussion, and as an apparent result the young German soldiers were taken into captivity instead of shot. My father was marched with other prisoners across an entire country (Poland) and imprisoned in a Russian prison camp. Eventually he came down with typhus, and, the war now being over by some months (though German prisoners were kept for many years), the Russian policy was to release these men into the countryside so they would not die on site. Young Rudy managed to walk back across Poland (itself a tricky business, because the Poles were understandably quite pissed at all Germans and would readily kill a sickly German soldier boy). Back in Germany, he crossed the border on foot into the American occupied sector: a dash and scramble, while a machine gun sprayed at him.

He still had a long way to go. He wandered forlornly into a train station. An older woman took pity on him and bought him a ticket to ride the train for one stop. She told him she hoped somebody somewhere might do the same kindness for her son, if he was still alive. Once aboard the train, Rudy kept his seat. No conductor was going to look too closely at whether a very skinny, beat-looking young fellow in a badly trashed army uniform had failed to disembark at the station indicated on his ticket.

Eventually he made it to his family's home. This was another disappointment. The entire block of buildings was in total rubble from the firebombing, and he could find no one who knew where his family was or whether anyone was alive. But eventually he did find them. Even my grandfather made it home, much the worse for wear. Prison camp for him had meant spending a winter of sleeping outdoors on the ground, not something a fifty-year-old man can easily recover from. Still, it must have been quite a moment to have the small family of four alive and all together again.

Actually, there was a curious postscript with another narrow escape. He married a foreign exchange student and emigrated to her country, America. Soon after his U.S. citizenship was approved, he received notice of being drafted for the Korean War. Family lore has it that by fortunate coincidence my mother discovered her maternal instincts at this juncture and I was conceived, and in his new country, unlike his former one, fatherhood precluded being drafted for combat.

So that's what my father did in the Great War. It's not surprising that he was not much for telling those stories or reliving them. (In the 1960s he did watch many of the television shows devoted to the Second World War, including the prison camp comedy *Hogan's Heroes*, though he never said much.) He became quite fond of America, though he was quick to criticize the politicians and sought every legal trick to reduce the amount he paid in taxes. I think he had decided long ago that you may love your country but it doesn't love you back and will sacrifice you in a heartbeat for its projects, even if these are completely senseless.

Meanwhile, Across the Front

Growing up in America, we've seen the war movies and shows that depict the heroic American soldiers defeating the Nazi hordes and making the world safe for democracy. Expert historians say, however, that the Second World War was mainly decided on the Russian front. The American and British invasion was a sideshow, and many think its main function was to divert some of the German resources from the real battle in the east. The Germans put their best troops and resources on the Russian front, as long as they had them.

More Russians were killed in the war than all the other Allies combined, and by a wide margin. Part of this is because of the tremendous magnitude and intensity of that conflict. Part of it is because of the cavalier way the Russian high command treated its own people. Any book about how culture exploits men can profitably devote a page to recalling the Red Army's tribulations in the Second World War and what this meant for the millions of men (and a few women) who were involved. These were the people who were trying to kill my father and whom he was supposed to kill. Their story was partly hidden by the information restrictions of the Soviet Union, but in recent years more documents have come to light. The story of these soldiers is well told in works such as Catherine Merridale's *Ivan's War*.

The Russians had a much larger army than the Germans even when the war started. The Germans were counting on their superior organization and equipment to prevail, a calculation that in the end proved wrong, to be sure, but only because Stalin and his top brass were willing to expend millions of lives. Stalin had in fact just finished purging the officers and generals of his army. His slow rise of bloodthirsty paranoia showed itself in those purges, which led to the execution of many fine veteran leaders and fighters—anybody whom Stalin imagined might pose any slight threat to his hold on power. Those purges are another terrible story, but the tragic irony is worth noting: Countless men were killed precisely because they had served their country so very well that they made the rulers nervous. The mass killings of the officers had thrown the army into chaos, which was revealed in Russia's brief war with tiny Finland in the 1930s. The abysmal performance of the Russian army in that war was probably what encouraged the German high command to think that, if we are ever going to fight the Russians, now is the best time.

Communist theory had proclaimed that the cause of world socialist revolution would always be on the advance and would move steadily forward toward its inevitable triumph. Though it seems absurd, the way this theory was put into practice by the Red Army entailed making no plans or preparations whatsoever for defense or retreat. It only practiced how to attack. During the horrific first weeks of the war, when the German forces were sweeping into Russia, the Russian army should have dug in and defended its positions, but it did not know how. Instead, it attacked the Germans every day, and when each attack failed, it prepared to attack again from farther back the next day.

Attacking is costlier than defending, because attackers are out running in the open, while defenders hide in ditches or behind trees and shoot at them. This style of fighting just brought on colossal slaughter of the Russian lads, and it accomplished essentially nothing.

Another problem was the lack of equipment. The Russians had more soldiers than the Germans, but not enough guns. And so, even in the modern twentieth century, some unlucky young men were sent into combat essentially unarmed, going up against machine guns and tanks. The culture needed bodies to make waves of attackers, even though it could not equip them with the tools of the trade.

The Russians had such a very limited supply of machine guns that they decided they could not afford to issue them to their front-line soldiers at all. This is a terrible waste, because a machine gun is precisely what a defender ought to have, to mow down the attacking German soldiers.

Germany was invading, so the Russians should have been defending: hiding in ditches or behind walls and shooting their machine guns at the advancing Krauts. But because of the silly Communist dogma, the Russian soldiers were attacking, not defending. Ignoring the human suffering and just looking at it in terms of the cold facts of equipment, this meant not giving them any guns. If soldiers ran toward the German lines with machine guns and then died, the machine guns would be lost because the Germans then advanced. So the commanders decided, no machine guns for the front lines.

Instead, the Russians issued all their machine guns to their military police, who followed along behind the attacking troops to enforce the advance. Any soldier who turned around to run back from each hapless attack would be shot immediately by his comrades in the military police. This is quite revealing. The Russians used their best guns against their own people. Mostly these soldiers were simple young men, sons of peasant farmers, who had volunteered to serve their country by fighting for it. Their upstanding act of patriotism got them into a hopeless spot, worse than the proverbial rock and hard place: poorly armed and trained, running toward the German tanks and guns, with their own army's machine guns aimed at their backs. Merridale estimates that during the worst times, the average soldier lasted about three weeks before being killed or seriously crippled. (Most of the wounded were sent back into action if they could walk and shoot, so the three weeks might include being wounded once or twice before the really nasty bullet hit.) Combat duty was close to a death sentence.

After Stalingrad, things went better for the Russians, but they were never good. The general strategy was still to overpower the Germans with masses of humanity. One-third of all the soldiers in Russian military service were killed, according to Merridale. One-third! The Russian losses during *many* a single campaign, such as the defense of Kiev, exceeded the total of American and British combat deaths for the entire war, including the Pacific war.

Even apart from the horrors of combat, life was very hard. My father said that the food in prison camp was shockingly bad, seemingly inedible to the German prisoners, but they felt they could not really complain because the Russian guards had to eat the same awful stuff. At some level the state knew how bad life at the front was: Russian combat soldiers were strictly prohibited from keeping diaries. The culture sought to keep them going with vodka rations. Merridale said the ration wasn't enough to get drunk, so sometimes small groups of soldiers would take turns. The group would give all its vodka to one man, who could get properly drunk. The next night, it would be another's turn. Bad luck meant being killed just before it was your turn to get everybody's vodka. Naturally there were often tendencies to delay reporting combat deaths, so that the dead guys' vodka could be obtained and shared by the others.

Toward Gender Equality?

In the 1970s, and again in the 1990s, the United States debated whether to draft women and/or send them into combat. I followed these debates with interest, having narrowly escaped the Vietnam draft myself. The arguments were sometimes about whether women were up to the physical demands of combat, but more often they were phrased in terms of whether is it bad for women to be sent into battle. (Trench warfare can give women yeast infections, that sort of thing.) Well, point taken, it *is* bad for them. Then again, and somehow unremarked, was that being sent to war is bad for young men too. Why did this not strike anyone as odd?

But we all assume that young men are expendable. The question up for debate is whether a strong country with a nominal commitment to gender equality can expend some of its young women in the same way. The expendability of the young men is taken for granted, without question.

And thus has it ever been. To be sure, some parameters change. The battles of Rome or, indeed, of prehistory had less deadly weapons, but then again the medical care was poorer also. And it was always uglier than what you see in the movies. In films, for example, soldiers who are shot by arrows typically fall down and die right away or else they manage to recover nicely, but in reality arrow wounds typically bring a slow, painful death. Either you bleed to death over the course of several hours, or, possibly worse, the wound becomes infected (it is almost impossible to get the arrowhead out of your body) and you die miserably from the infection. Your best option after being shot with an arrow was to have someone cut off the arm or leg that was hit. This operation would generally have been done without anesthesia, using some kind of metal blade chopping or sawing through your skin and muscle and the bone.

The famous British hero Horatio Nelson was shot during a naval battle and had to have one of his arms cut off right away. He was an admiral and therefore had a bit more influence than most casualties. After the operation, which of course was performed with a metal saw and no painkiller whatsoever, he reflected that his suffering had been made slightly worse because the blade that had sawed through his living flesh had been very cold. He issued an order that henceforth the surgical tools should be warmed up a bit before they cut off the arms and legs of injured young men.

In such small ways does a culture make progress, even as it uses its male population to best its rivals.

Why Men Are More Expendable

Why do cultures regard men as more expendable than women? In this line of questioning, it is helpful to keep value judgments to a minimum. Yes, culture has been hard on many men, and hard on many women too, and for various moral or other reasons one might wish things could be different, but that is not the point. We want to understand how and why culture exploits men in particular ways. A culture is not a moral agent but an unfeeling system that is fundamentally pragmatic. With issues such as capital punishment, it is fine for humans, as moral beings, to debate whether it is right and proper to put people to death under particular circumstances, but that is not the approach here. Instead, we would ask whether it is pragmatically useful: Will the culture be more successful if it executes certain members? In the Second World War, multiple cultures and systems clashed, and they needed to sacrifice the lives of many of their people in order to achieve their goals. All sorts of people were killed, but young men were sent to death more than any others.

All the societies involved in the war lost many lives, though only some of the systems survived and prevailed. The victorious societies can remember their war dead with honor and gratitude, because the young men who died helped save the culture. The losers have a harder time making sense of it. Many mothers who painfully gave birth to baby boys and lovingly nurtured them into young manhood had to accept that their sons' deaths in a losing cause accomplished nothing.

From our perspective in our modern, supposedly enlightened culture, each new baby boy or girl is a precious life full of promising possibilities and endowed already with rights and entitlements. From the perspective of the culture as an abstract system, however, things may seem different.

By the culture's perspective, I do not mean what the ruling elite officially proclaims that it values and believes. Rather, I refer to what will enable the culture to succeed at continuing to exist, which often means making various forms of progress to outpace its rivals.

In that view, each crop of babies is less a collection of precious individualities than a collective set of opportunities—and it would probably be more accurate to say two sets. To the system, the baby girls represent first and foremost the wombs that will produce the subsequent generation. Reproduction is the key to collective success in most cases of rivalry against other systems, and so the system needs the next generation to be bigger than the present one. That means it would prefer every girl to grow up and have babies. Each woman can raise only a few successful babies, probably around a dozen at the very maximum, more commonly about half that as an upper bound. The culture can't afford to lose very many of its women, if it wants to sustain the population and ideally increase it.

The baby boys are a different matter entirely. There is much less need to preserve every one. If war is likely, then it may need to produce as many sons as possible and grow them to maturity, but mainly for the sake of feeding them to the slaughter of battle (or, more precisely, for being able to overwhelm the enemy with superior numbers). In more peaceful times, even that is not necessary.

Again, reproduction is the key. A man can reproduce over and over. Or, to put it in the most relevant terms, a few men and a great many women will produce more babies than a few women and a great many men. So the cultures that maximize the number of women will be most successful at the population contest.

From the culture's ruthlessly pragmatic perspective, therefore, it needs all its girl babies but only some of its boy babies to lead long, healthy, safe lives that contain a prolific reproductive career. To the culture trying to compete against rivals, every woman's primary job is to make babies, but only a few men are needed for stud service. The other males are expendable. Most cultures are in a chronic state of penile surplus. They have more penises than they need in order to produce the next bumper crop of babies.

Admittedly, there are exceptions. In primitive nomadic societies, especially those that relied on hunting and gathering and lived in regions where food was not abundant, it sometimes became necessary to limit the number of females in order to keep the population down. When rivals are scarce and the carrying capacity is limited, when food, for example, is scarce too, then society needs to keep the female population low. Each new womb represents a threat, not an opportunity.

In low-population societies, living at the mercy of nature and just eking out a fragile life, overpopulation is a threat, and cultures want to limit their number of females. Men may be assets, because when the population is low but some rivals exist, then one wants the soldiers. Girl babies are sometimes put to death, to keep the population from rising beyond the numbers that can be fed.

But once agriculture produces more food, and the population starts to fill in, a culture starts to bump up against rival groups. Outnumbering them is a key to success. From then on, it becomes important to produce females. That's when the penile surplus starts.

The penile surplus is not just some abstract possibility. Recall the most underappreciated fact about gender, from Chapter 4: Today's world human population is descended from twice as many women as men. That is, throughout most of our history, a minority of penises did most of the work (or had most of the fun, depending on how you look at it). World history, made of both nature and culture, has in fact discarded far more men than women, in the sense that they ended up left out of the reproductive game and were biological dead ends.

Polygamy has been practiced in most cultures in the history of the world, and the current enforcement of monogamy can be seen as relatively unusual. There is a feminist protest against polygamy, as if polygamy puts women at a disadvantage. The objection seems purely symbolic, however. It is hard to see how women are worse off under polygamy than under monogamy, if all else is equal. Many women might prefer to be the second or third wife of a rich, successful man rather than being the only wife of an unskilled laborer or even of an assistant manager of a convenience store. She and her children might live much better being supported by the wealthy man.

Even a woman who wants, for whatever personal reasons, to have a husband all to herself is better off under polygamy. Polygamy creates a shortage of wives and a surplus of potential husbands, and so the woman who wants a monogamous husband has far more men to choose from under polygamy. To illustrate, imagine a village with a hundred men and a hundred women. If ten of the men each marry nine wives, that leaves ninety single men and ten single women. Those are very nice odds for those women, even if they want monogamy.

The main legal safeguard for women under polygamy would be to forbid the man to take new wives without the consent of his current ones. This could easily be required. And I suspect many women would prefer to let their husband bring in a new wife without his having to divorce them first, which is the practical upshot of the current system and enforced monogamy. After all, many men today do marry multiple wives—they just have to divorce each one before marrying the next one. Are we sure the previous wife is always better off by virtue of laws that require him to divorce her? Polygamy gives women more options and more choices.

Why, then, has polygamy mostly been banned? The real losers under polygamy are the multitude of men. This isn't immediately obvious, but that is because of the same kind of focusing mistake we saw in Chapter 1. The error that time was in thinking society was set up to benefit men, and it came from looking only at the top, at the lucky and successful men. Critics of polygamy make the same error. The minority of rich, successful men may do well and have multiple wives and large families. But that means that most men get none. Remember the village example I just gave, in which the ten polygamous marriages took care of ninety of the women, thus leaving ninety single men and ten single women? I said that was a good situation for those women, but it is a sad one for the ninety men. Most will never marry. Many will probably never even have sex.

Monogamy thus spreads marriage around equally, to benefit men. It prevents the few men from hogging all the women. That way, every man can have a wife.

The point was, polygamy is based on male expendability. It is a way the culture can reward the most successful men, thereby pushing men to compete and strive for greatness so as to earn (and then maintain!) that enviable household. But it entails that many men will get no wife at all. Those guys are just the losers of the system. Too bad for them: they are expendable.

Explaining Male Extremity

The expendability of males in nature (complementing and underlying the cultural version of male expendability) may well be linked to a pattern we saw in the early chapters, namely the tendency of males to be more extreme than females. Nature rolls the dice with men more than with women. It produces more male geniuses and more retarded men than women. It produces wider variation in intelligence, in height, in some aspects of personality, and other factors.

You can think of extreme traits as experiments. Nature combines the genes in novel ways, experimenting randomly as to what might create a new, improved version of a human being. Most experiments will be failures, in that the random combination of genes (the mutation) will turn out to be less, rather than more, suited to success in that environment. Hence experimenting will mean more bad cases that, for reasons of biological selection and species survival, will have to suffer and die, preferably without reproducing.

Consider the example of intelligence. For human intelligence to evolve, nature had to produce changing combinations of genes to try out different versions of the brain. Some, probably most, of these would not work and would in fact produce inferior brains. Ideally, if the species is to adapt and improve, these individuals should not pass on to future generations their inferior brains. Remember, though, most human females reproduce (like most females in the species from whom we are descended). A retarded woman is likely to have some babies, and these have an above-average risk of being retarded babies themselves. It's hard to weed out bad traits in the females, because most of the women reproduce.

Meanwhile, most men do not reproduce. Only the most successful men do, and the retarded fellows are unlikely to make it into that elite group. So the experiment ends right away if it is done on the male. The unfortunate male's genes are flushed out of the gene pool, whereas the unfortunate female's genes may persist for many generations.

Thus, already, nature gets a better result by experimenting on males than on females. The experiments that turn out badly are quickly erased from the gene pool.

The other side of the coin is what happens with successful experiments, or in this example, baby geniuses. Here too the logic of male expendability promotes using men to experiment with. A genius baby boy is probably more likely than other boys born the same year to become a big success in his life. Because successful men can have multiple wives and many children, his genes will spread rapidly in the gene pool. In contrast, a baby female genius will still probably have only a few children, and so even though her genes are terrific, they can spread only slowly through the gene pool. (If the species is especially lucky, the female genius will have several sons, and they will go on to have a great many children.)

In short, nature can experiment more effectively with men than with women precisely because men are more expendable. Men are nature's guinea pigs, and that's why there are more extreme males than females.

Big Groups Are Made of Replaceable People

There is another important reason that culture regards men as more expendable than women (as many people also do). It harks back to the different social spheres. Men favor larger social groups. Unlike small groups and intimate relationships, these large groups make individual members expendable.

In the small sphere of an intimate relationship, each person is precious. When two people are in love, they do not regard each other as replaceable, and in an important sense they are not. In fact, studies show that this is one of the common mistakes and illusions that make romantic breakups so distressing—as I learned when I spent several years studying heartbreak, as described in my book (with Sara Wotman), *Breaking Hearts: The Two Sides of Unrequited Love*. The heartbroken lover thinks that he or she will never be able to find anyone to replace the lost love. In reality, people do go on to find someone else.

But even that isn't really replacing the person. The new person is seen as part of a new relationship, as opposed to continuing the same relationship with a new partner. The lost love is really and truly lost. When you deeply love one person, that person cannot be replaced.

Because women specialize in the sphere of intimate relationships, they are accustomed to being valued and in a sense indispensable. No one could replace a mother to her children. Even a woman's husband can't fully replace her. He might get a new wife, but all he has shared with her and created together would be lost, and he'd be starting over. She is accustomed to the kind of relationship in which people would sacrifice much, perhaps even their lives, for each other.

In contrast, in large groups, individuals can be replaced, and in time they are. If you look at the sorts of large organizations that men create, you will find that they routinely replace individuals. Consider the United States Navy, or IBM, or the Texas state legislature, or the Cleveland Orchestra, or the Oakland Raiders. Every single person in each of those organizations has been replaced at one time or another. Every single current member eventually will be replaced also, and the organizations will continue to exist.

Moreover, and even more to the point, large organizations typically make it clear that each individual can be replaced at almost any time. True, some people manage to make themselves quite valuable to organizations. But this is one of the benefits of expendability: It motivates people to try their best to make valuable contributions to the group effort, so that the group will retain them instead of replacing them. The threat of being replaced is often there in large groups, and it serves a useful function. It drives people to work harder to make themselves valuable to the organization, so that will keep them rather than replace them.

The male sense of being expendable may therefore be associated with the kinds of social relationships that men create. The male groups, in which people who don't love each other and sometimes don't even much like each other can still work together to achieve common goals and tasks, bring expendability with them. This is in sharp contrast to the close, intimate relationships of the women's sphere.

Some Misunderstandings

Expendability is a central but underappreciated aspect of the male role. It contributes more than we realize to misunderstandings between men and women.

It may be difficult for women to appreciate this aspect of the male role. It undoubtedly contributed to some of the negative reactions women had when they moved into men's roles and the men's world. They were shocked to find themselves treated as expendable, not valued and respected automatically.

Norah Vincent, the lesbian feminist who disguised herself to live as a man for months, acknowledged the problem. She had expected it would be great to be a man. Her plan was to sneak into the male world, enjoy the privileges of being a man, and then write an exposé to let women know what they were missing. Her book turned out very differently. Instead of male privilege, she found herself in a rough world where you have to justify your own presence and existence by your achievements. When you are in trouble, people don't automatically come forward to lend a hand or take care of you. Sink or swim. Instead of glorying in her life as a male and writing a tell-all exposé, she cut short her life as a man and returned with happy relief to her life as a woman.

The movement of women into the male world of work and giant institutions was accompanied by demands for extensive changes to those institutions. These were presented as necessary to counteract widespread discrimination and prejudice against women. Maybe there was some prejudice or discrimination, but probably few men would be surprised to hear that much of it was trumped up. Essentially, feminists demanded that women should not be treated the way men had long been treated, as expendable beings who got no respect unless they earned it. Nowadays, modern organizations often officially express their belief that everyone is entitled to respect. Such pronouncements represent a change from how they used to be. When they were filled with only men, everyone was expendable and only those who made it to the top were entitled to respect. Women found that intolerable.

Men probably also have not understood women's reactions. They thought women wanted to take their places next to men, on the same basis, which they unthinkingly assumed included the expendability aspect that men have always faced. Perhaps men also relished seeing women suffer a bit too, finding out what men had had to endure all along. *You demanded a place in the organizations we created; now let's see how you like it.* No one realized that expendability, to which men were accustomed from early on, would be shocking and unacceptable to women, who had long been accustomed to being precious and special.

Feminism certainly aggravated this misunderstanding. Feminist analysis presented culture and society as a giant conspiracy among men, which implied that men were all taking care of each other, working against women. So women assumed that men were pretty much being looked after. They even thought that as women moved into institutions, the men were conspiring against them and each woman was on her own. I assume that's why the institutions were required to change as they have: Most now have women's organizations to build network and support among women, but any such organizations for men are outlawed. Ironic!

So now the women actually have such networks and organizations. The men never did. The current state of affairs is because of the false assumption that the men did. In reality the men had many informal groups who were working against each other. These groups actually welcomed women into the fold, if they could be useful. The men didn't see women as the enemy; they saw other men, especially other groups of men, as the enemy, and so they welcomed women as allies.

It's going to be rough for young men in the future. The organizations favor women, based on the fake belief that these are needed to counteract male conspiracies, backlashes, and the like. Women are looked after and are given support networks. Men are on their own, just as they always were, except now they are at a systematic disadvantage against women too. The only thing men still have going for them is their own resources: the agentic self and the male ego. Plus the strong, almost desperate drive of the hardworking guy who knows he is expendable and will be dumped unless he produces.

The Value of a Life

Intellectual discipline requires taking note of other kinds of evidence about how society values men and women. You might look at life insurance as one index of how much lives are valued. On this, at first glance, it certainly seems that men's lives have more value. For example, one recent study of a large sample of life insurance in marriage couples found that the men's lives were valued at about three times as much as the women's lives. Many of the women's lives were not insured at all.

But does that really signify that society values men's lives more than women's? Life insurance policies are taken out by individuals. They also are not a comment on the value of the person's whole life but, instead, reflect how much money seems needed to compensate the family if that person dies. Take the fact that many women have no life insurance at all. It is hardly fair to infer from that that those women's lives have no value, or that society thinks they have no value, or that their families think that.

The higher insurance on men's lives probably reflects the fact that men earn more money. In some families, the man's income is the only income, and in others it is the main source of money. Hence the family takes out plenty of insurance to keep it going in case the man dies. If such a man dies, his wife has little or no income and, in many cases such as among the elderly, she probably has little chance of even getting a job to keep up the standard of living he has paid for. In contrast, if a wife dies, the husband can usually support himself.

The higher cash value put on a man's life thus mainly reflects what society and family consider to be one of his main purposes: to provide money for those who depend on him. The unexpected death of a man creates a financial crisis for his family, and so insurance payouts have to deal with this. A woman provides many things to her family, but it is harder to put a cash value on these. Moreover, precisely because men tend to die long before their wives, there is a highly unequal sex ratio among older people. Widowers can remarry and thus can replace what they got from their wives, at least in the view of insurance planners. Widows cannot remarry so easily and therefore need the dead husbands to continue providing for them.

Usefulness of Throwaway Persons

Let us turn now to consider how the culture benefits from male expendability.

All else being equal, one culture will prevail if its people will make more sacrifices for it, as compared to its rivals. Being able to use people as expendable can help the system flourish.

Remember, the goal of culture is to survive. It doesn't have to care about every individual. It may be better off without some of its members. That at least was the sentiment behind purges in the Nazi and Soviet regimes, before going to war. The ruling group thought their hold on power would be stronger if they killed dissidents. It didn't actually turn out that way: The Nazi "Thousand Year Empire" was overrun and bombed into unconditional surrender in barely over a decade, and the Soviet empire, supposedly the vanguard of world revolution, rotted from within and fell apart after about seven decades, followed quickly by the demise of its communist ideas in most other countries.

Nonetheless, a culture will be successful if it can use people according to its needs, up to and including taking their lives, and certainly including having them devote most of their lives (including years of hard toil) for its purposes. Let's look at some of the ways a culture can gain an advantage on its rivals by treating many of its men as expendable.

Uses of Death

First off, and most obviously, cultures benefit from having people whose lives can be sacrificed in battle. Obviously, people are not usually asked directly to die for their country or cause (though suicide missions are not unknown, and they have always been assigned more to men than women). People are asked to take the risk, however.

Some thinkers imagine that the goal in war or battle is to kill all the enemy. That is wrong, as the philosopher Elaine Scarry explained in her thoughtful book, *The Body in Pain*. War stems from incompatible ideas. Two countries have different ideas about where the border should be drawn, or how they should be treated by each other, or which one has the best political or economic or religious system. Faced with disagreement, they are willing to put some of their people's lives and limbs, and some of their wealth, in jeopardy so as to force the other to agree. The opponents like-wise think they'd rather risk some of their people and their stuff in order to win the argument. During the battles, both sides lose people and other resources (blood and treasure, in the usual phrase) in service of the ideas they favor. Almost no battles or wars are pursued until one side is totally wiped out. Rather, at some point, one side decides that it would rather give up on some of its ideas rather than lose any more of its lives and wealth. It yields.

War is thus a mixture of the material and the symbolic. The symbolic ideas of territorial or economic claims, religious beliefs, or whatever, are tied to the physical quantities of blood and money. Both sides lose blood and money until one side agrees to relinquish its symbolic claims.

The culture is invested in certain ideas, such as those regarding its rights, its land, and its system. When these ideas are challenged by an enemy, the culture needs to fight battles and wars. These involve sacrificing blood and money. Most cultures in world history have relied on their men to furnish that blood and money. Thus, the culture maintains its ideas by virtue of the sacrifices of men, including those who risk their lives in battle. Again, the culture does not usually have to ask specific men to give their lives. Rather, it asks a large number of men to take a chance by going into combat, where some of them will die.

Warfare is not an isolated case. The most persuasive and relevant figure, I think, is the one on dying on the job, which I have already mentioned in this book. In the United States, only slightly more men than women work, but thirteen men die in the line of work for every woman who does. The dangerous jobs go to men. Again, death is almost never an explicit part of the job description or a formal obligation, but the culture needs many people to take jobs that carry a slight risk of being killed. Over time, those accumulated risks take their toll, and a small percentage of the people in those jobs do end up dead. In America, as in nearly every other country, those people are mostly men.

In both work and battle, then, the culture needs to request not a specific death per se, but a willingness to put one's life on the line in a way that is likely to bring death to a few who take the chance but, it is hoped, not to most. The culture has a job to do, and it will take a certain number of deaths. The job may be a battle to be fought and preferably won. Or it could involve a fire department to be maintained that will put out fires throughout the city. Or it's a police department to control crime and occasionally engage in shooting matches with criminals. There is a price to be paid in lives in order for the culture to get these jobs done. Cultures are systems and hence pragmatic, and so getting these jobs done is the goal. If the culture has to pay the price, generally it will pay it with men's lives, not women's. This is the practical thing for almost any culture to do.

Willing to Risk

The risk and dispensability aspect is crucial to masculinity. We have seen its most obvious application, namely in terms of the chance of being abruptly killed. Risk applies in many other domains, however. In this section, we examine its relevance to achievement.

In science or business, the optimal way for the culture to provide its benefits is often not immediately obvious. It is necessary to try out different options to see which works best. This is as true for different ways of providing services (e.g., medical care, trash collection, food delivery) as goods (the best way to make a spear or sports utility vehicle), or the best scientific theory. To be most effective, the culture needs to find out which is the best. Toward that end, each option, each pathway, each opportunity, must to explored to the utmost. Some will pan out; others will not. Some will pan out only if some individuals take on severe risk and exertion.

By definition, risks have downsides, and in some cases these are large. So the agents who explore and pursue them must be expendable. The society has to accept the outcome that plenty of individuals will exhaust themselves chasing down dead ends, and end up with broken, failed lives. The manufacturers and sellers whose products are inferior will go bankrupt. The scientists who have chosen the wrong theory to test will languish in ignominious failure and possibly lose their jobs.

For reasons of maintaining the population, the culture cannot afford to lose its women down rat-holes. It can, however, afford to waste and lose men, or at least some of them. The penile surplus entails that the culture can sustain its population as long as some of the penises survive.

Suppose there is some kind of big question, and five possible answers can be put forward at that time. Cultures benefit from right answers. If several individuals pursue each of those answers, then each possible answer will get its best fair hearing. Let us assume there is some way (scientific method, or electoral vote) to pick one of them as the winner. That is how the culture gets a winner. But notice that the agents who worked for the other four possible answers, who staked their efforts and reputations and prospects for achieving wealth and respect—all those ended up in the dungheap.

For a culture to be able to get the best answer, it has to have some fairly numerous groups of individuals who are willing and able to gamble not their very lives but big parts of their lives on an idea that in many cases will turn out to be a partial or total failure. There was simply no way to know. Some hands simply don't contain winning cards, and no matter how skillfully those hands are played, the result will be failure.

Expendability and Inequality

The reference to competition brings up a broad and vital point. Many cultures treat and reward people unequally. And this can be pragmatically useful for the culture, though it can be destructive also.

Expendability contributes powerfully to the pattern of unequal rewarding. Many men know that their chances for success are tenuous and that they are utterly expendable. As the most underappreciated fact showed, in the biological competition to reproduce—which underlies almost everything else, being the key to natural selection—most men have been doomed to failure. Moreover, their failure meant more and bigger success for some-one else. The culture has rewards to give, and instead of spreading them around equally (the way a woman would do among her children), it offers a big share to those who accomplish useful things and a small or negligible share to the losers.

Not all cultures have done this, of course. Anthropologists can point to many early cultures that encourage everyone to share everything. Personal property is kept to a minimum, or status comes from giving things away, or life is simply communal. Unfortunately, however, these cultures mostly are and remain primitive. That's no accident or mere coincidence. Cultures make progress by giving unequal rewards. The cultures that don't make use of this don't bring about progress.

Ultimately, a culture will succeed best (again, in comparison with rival cultures) if it can enlarge the pie—that is, if it can increase the total rewards it has to offer. More rewards mean more to spread around and hence more well-taken-care-of members. Increasing the pie may, however, require innovation, testing, and indeed risky ventures. Hence the most pragmatic thing is for the culture to encourage people to take those risks by offering big rewards to those who manage to succeed at contributing something that will enrich or strengthen the culture as a whole.

Men are well suited to that sort of task. Men differ from each other more than women do, having more extreme versions on various traits, and so if the requirements for success are unknown but unusual, the odds are good that a man will be the best suited for whatever it is (by virtue of having extreme traits). Men are also expendable, so it is pragmatically acceptable for the culture to throw or lure a variety of men into undertaking risky ventures, without knowing which ones will turn out to have the requisite traits for success. Some will find themselves hopelessly out of their element. Others may stumble and fail due to simple bad luck. Too bad for them. The system can get what it needs without having to make sure that every individual man gets a fair shake.

From the culture's perspective, what matters is only that someone comes back with the treasure. A culture can afford to reward that man handsomely. Just as he has enriched the culture, it can enrich him, and both are better off. Rewarding him publicly and lavishly is also a good way to encourage other young men to take similar chances in the future, for other possible ways of achieving something that will benefit the culture.

Seeing him get his prizes and rewards will inspire some of them, no doubt, to take chances and ultimately waste all or part of their lives in future similar strivings. But those strivings occur amid other competitions in which someone else will again achieve something that will benefit and enrich the culture.

The economist Arthur Okun wrote an influential book entitled *Equality and Efficiency: The Big Tradeoff*. It is couched in economic jargon and full of formulas, but the key point can be translated into plain speech by saying that inequality has its benefits. In large groups in which everyone is equal, the system does not work as effectively and hence the total wealth and other benefits produced by the system are relatively small. In contrast, inequality can lead to greater productivity. In a sense, the Communist experience showed that pushing for equality essentially made everyone equally poor.

To be sure, inequality can be abused, and inequality itself is not a good or beneficial thing. Rather, inequality can be used to stimulate creativity, innovation, competition, and other behaviors that bring benefits and progress. There are countries in the world—long-suffering Africa has had more than its share of them—where a small powerful elite hoards power amid extraordinary wealth, while the rest of the population suffers in shocking poverty. Such societies are not moving forward and do not benefit from inequality. But open societies with fair opportunities for many and competitive economies can encourage people (mostly men) to take big chances. The prospect of securing huge rewards makes the big risks palatable, even appealing.

So by administering rewards unequally, the culture can promote competition and striving and all that, much of which yields dividends. Basically it can set up systems with big winners and big losers. If you aren't willing to have big losers, you can't have big winners. Remember that every woman is precious to a culture, and so consigning large numbers of them to be losers is unacceptable. But with men, it's fine, even helpful. This is part of the male role, and it includes what is best and worst about it.

CHAPTER 9

Earning Manhood, and the Male Ego

O NE OF THE MORE POPULAR SHOWS in recent years was *The Apprentice*, in which business tycoon Donald Trump put a group of aspiring young people through various competitive exercises week after week, firing one of them at the end of each episode. The last person remaining then was given a six-figure salary for a job working closely under Trump for a year.

In one episode, two members of one team were shown arguing about a difficult aspect of the upcoming task. Somebody had to take on the responsibility for doing what could be an unpromising chore that was needed for the team but carried some risk and unpleasantness. The argument became heated, as each person thought the other should do it. The woman goaded the man with the phrase "C'mon, be a man!"

Indignant, he shot back, "You be a woman!" Immediately and almost shouting, she replied "I *am* a woman!" and went on to say more things. The man sat there in silence, unable to think of what else to say.

We can understand his confusion. He did not know why he had abruptly lost that argument. She had said something to him, and he had said essentially the same thing back to her, but his reply had somehow failed utterly. He probably thought that in this age of gender equality and fair treatment for all and so forth, "Be a man" and "Be a woman" would be equal, parallel things to say. Yet they weren't. She was a woman already, and she knew it, and he did too, and she did not have to prove it. But once his manhood was questioned, he would have to do more to prove it than simply say "I *am* a man!" in a loud voice.

This brief exchange between two would-be apprentices reveals a basic asymmetry between the genders that is the focus of this chapter. Manhood must be earned. Every adult female human being is a woman, but not every adult male is a man. Most likely the recent softening and sensitizing of discourse to avoid offending anyone has muted this distinction, which means it was probably even starker in the past. Boys had to prove something in order to become men.

At issue is respect. Our culture has a long tradition of treating women as automatically worthy of respect. To be sure, the respect may have been different from and in some ways less than the respect afforded the topmost men. Nonetheless, the general assumption has long been that women automatically deserve respect. At worst, a woman could lose respect by doing something that the culture agreed was disgraceful. Up until that point, however, she was entitled to respect.

Not so for men. Men had to earn respect. In fact, as we shall see, the sorts of social groups men create by themselves are often strategically, almost intentionally, made with a shortage of respect. Whether it is a matter of demeaning titles, verbal putdowns, or other signals, men in many organizations have put up with daily doses of disrespect until and unless they proved themselves worthy of respect. The lack of respect reminds them of the importance of proving themselves as men and of earning the respect of others so as not to have to suffer the major and minor indignities that are commonplace in many such groups.

Put simply, a woman is entitled to respect until and unless she does something to lose it. A man is not entitled to respect until and unless he does something to gain it.

This is a terrifically useful system for enabling the culture to get the most out of its men.

The Real Double Standard

The women's movement taught us to appreciate how stressful life can be for women. One source of stress is being judged by things she can scarcely control, such as her appearance. Women do their utmost to exert what control they have, with clothing and makeup and dieting. But ultimately there is no substitute for youth and beauty, and a woman who lacks them cannot really obtain them. Meanwhile, even the woman who has them knows they will not last.

Men, in contrast, are judged by things that are more under their control. In some ways this is better than the woman's lot, but in other ways it is just as difficult, if not more so. The man must repeatedly achieve: obtain, surpass, conquer.

The term "double standard" has become commonplace to refer to one perspective on sexual morality. The gist was that men and women are judged differently. In particular, the double standard is usually used to refer a belief that certain sexual behaviors are acceptable for men but immoral for women. The most common of these acts is premarital sex. Thus, in traditional societies that believe in a double standard, it is acceptable for men to engage in sex before they marry, but a virtuous woman is expected to remain a virgin until her wedding night.

Evidence that the double standard exists has been surprisingly rare, and in recent decades researchers find no sign of it—if anything, it has become the norm to condemn men more severely than women for the same sexual misdeeds, such as adultery. The belief in the double standard owes much to a tricky illusion that has fooled even some experts. In polls during the early and middle parts of the twentieth century, for example, men would say that premarital sex was morally acceptable, whereas women would say it was immoral. Researchers would look at those numbers and say, "Aha! Double standard! It's OK for men and not for women." But this was a misinterpretation. The men said premarital sex was acceptable for both men and women. The women said it was immoral for both genders. Neither opinion actually indicated a double standard. Only a small minority of respondents (fewer than 10%) would say that premarital sex was acceptable for men and not women.

Also, and contrary to the view that the double standard is a ploy by men to stifle and control female sexuality, all studies that did find any support for the double standard found that it was supported mainly by women. This is because women seek to control and restrain other women's sexuality. We shall delve into the reasons for this in Chapter 10. The Imaginary Feminist's claim that the double standard is something men use to oppress and control women is for the most part a giant mistake.

For now, however, we turn to a more fundamental and more genuine double standard. This has to do with how men and women are judged and evaluated. Men are judged by their achievements. Women are judged by their appearance. To be sure, the lines are blurring now, and our society is succeeding to some extent in putting men and women on similar footings.

Men's appearance counts for more than it used to, and the same goes for women's achievements. Still, this double standard remains active. Men have to earn respect through their achievements more than women do.

For me, this recognition hit home at a professional conference I attended in New Orleans many years ago. After a hard day of attending sessions I took a walk down the deservedly famous Bourbon Street and was struck by the atmosphere. Unlike most city streets, people were permitted, even encouraged, to walk about carrying drinks as they moved from one place to the next. The range of entertainments was impressive. There was live music of all sorts, from organized bands playing in clubs to lone musicians on the street playing for tips. There were bars serving various drinks. There was a bit of street theatre. There were striptease places. There were magic shows.

Ever the social scientist, I pondered what made the place function and what its patterns were. One conclusion was that everyone seemed to want the tourist's dollars, but what they offered was different. The men all had some kind of skill to sell: music, magic tricks, or other kinds of performance. The women simply had to take off their clothes.

Once again, let me point out that I am not arguing for change or saying that one gender has it much better than the other. The traditional judgment of women based on appearance would certainly have its costs as well as benefits. If a woman was not beautiful, there was not much she could do. Yes, women do try to improve their appearance with makeup, hairstyling, jewelry, and other methods. And the increased emphasis on female thinness in recent decades has encouraged many women to compete by dieting to lose weight. But overall, many women must have been in a largely helpless situation. They were attractive or they weren't, and society (both men and women) judged them primarily on that basis.

Regardless of how one feels about judging women on the basis of looks, the main point here is that men have long faced a different set of criteria. They are judged, both by society in general and by the women they hope to attract, according to their achievements, as well as the status and money that those bring.

Sociologists long ago distinguished two ways of getting status: achieved and ascribed. Ascribed status is what somebody assigns you without your doing anything about it, such as by virtue of being born into a certain family. Achieved status is precisely what it sounds like: you earn the status by virtue of something that you do.

In those terms, men's lives revolve around achieved status, whereas female status tends to be ascribed. Neither is inherently better, but they do place different kinds of stresses and have different implications. A woman is entitled to respect by virtue of who she is, and the amount of respect may depend on her appearance, about which there is only a limited amount she can do. A man must earn respect by working at things and outdoing other men.

Precarious Manhood

Many cultures are quite explicit about a boy needing to prove himself before he can call himself a man. In some times and places, young men must kill a large animal, whether a dangerous predator or a desired source of meat to provide for the group. In others, boys must undergo ceremonies marked by painful physical tests before they can be respected as men. Men are made, not born, and the process of making is challenging if not dangerous. The process is also subject to failure: It is possible for a boy to undergo these tests and not pass, so that he remains a boy.

Don't think such views of manhood are limited to obscure, primitive groups, either. Research with modern North American college students has found similar attitudes. Professors Joseph Vandello, Jennifer Bosson, Dov Cohen, and their colleagues documented that today's young adults still view manhood and womanhood as quite different. Asked whether they agreed with (artificially concocted) proverbs such as "All boys do not grow up to become real men" and "A boy must earn his right to be called a man," the students agreed. When given comparable versions that substituted "girl" for "boy" and "woman" for "man," they disagreed. The transition from girl to woman was seen as a biological process of growing up and undergoing bodily changes. As such, it is automatic and inevitable. The transition from boy to man was seen, in contrast, as a social event that depended on achievement and earning respect.

Even more dramatic evidence came from a further study in which people were asked how they understood someone talking about having lost gender identity. When they read that somebody said he felt he was no longer a man, people understood this to mean that the fellow had failed in some social respect, such as no longer being able to support his family. People found it much harder to interpret someone saying she felt she was no longer a woman; they thought perhaps the person must have undergone a sex change operation. Thus, again, manhood is socially defined, whereas womanhood is a biological fact.

The fact that manhood must be won and can be lost puts pressure on men. Further studies by Vandello and his research group showed this. In a revealing study, people filled out a personality test and received computer-generated feedback. It came on a scale that had three arrows. One indicated the "average man's score," another indicated the "average woman's score," and the third said "your score." What the research subjects didn't know was that these results were fake. By the flip of a coin, everyone received a "your score" that was either close to the average man's or the average woman's score.

Thus, some people were told they were fairly typical for their gender, while others supposedly found out that they scored closer to the other gender. These latter ones were the focus of the study. How would people respond to being told that they resembled the other sex more than their own gender?

The women were relatively unruffled, regardless of whether they were told they resembled the typical man or the typical woman. But the men's reactions diverged. It bothered the men to be told they were like women. They showed various negative reactions, including increases in anxiety and aggressive feelings.

This will probably not be news to anyone who has spent any time on the playgrounds or locker rooms with boys. Telling a boy he is or does something "like a girl" is a serious insult. It's not because girls are less valued; many groups are valued lower than girls, such as dogs and bugs. But telling a male that he is not masculine is a threat to his identity. Manhood must be earned, and finding out that you are more feminine than masculine is a sign that you have failed to earn it. It attacks your core self in a way that women can scarcely appreciate. After all, telling a woman that she resembles a man is not nearly so threatening, according to these studies.

You Talking to Me?

Precarious manhood brings us one way of understanding the male ego. Nobody has much good to say about the male ego. Competitive, aggressive, assertive, touchy, confident to the point of cocky—it's not the most lovable of human attributes. When male egotism stands out especially, it is often obnoxious.

The male ego may be useful, adaptive, and sometimes even necessary, however, if a young fellow is to make his way in the world of men. A girl automatically becomes a woman, just by growing up. A boy does not automatically become a man. He needs to fight for that status. This requires confidence (that he can pass the tests) and competitive striving (so that he can outdo others and persevere against those who seek to prevent him from claiming manhood).

Skeptics and male-bashers such as the Imaginary Feminist like to say that insecurity lies beneath the male ego. They are right. But this insecurity is not a personality flaw in the occasional man. Rather, insecurity is part of being a man, an essential part of the male role in society. Manhood is never secure: It must be claimed via public actions, risky things seen and validated by other people—and it can be lost. The fact that manhood can be lost even after it has been successfully claimed means that the man has to watch out for threats, pretty much forever. Plus, he must be willing to defend himself and his honor if need be.

You can never be sure when a challenge to your manhood might arise. You have to be on guard. Hence the touchiness of the male ego: "You talkin' to me?" in the famous phrase Robert DeNiro's character practiced in front of the mirror in the film *Taxi Driver*. He had armed himself and was ready to defend his manhood against potential challengers.

Sometimes manhood requires actually fighting. That brings us to dueling, which is worth a pause to consider. Dueling has many of the characteristics people deplore in the male ego: competition, wasteful violence, trying to outdo others, hypersensitivity to insults. Why did it survive so long, even as governments and concerned citizens sought to stamp it out?

The Field of Honor

In many cultures, boys have to prove themselves in the hunt or in battle in order to become men. Thus, precarious manhood has a link to aggression. That link is alive and well today, deep in the minds of today's college students, as the research on "precarious manhood" showed. When a fellow's masculinity was threatened in the laboratory, such as by telling him his test responses resembled those of a typical woman, he was likely to start feeling violent, aggressive impulses. No such aggressive tendencies were stimulated by telling the female participants that they were unlike the typical woman. Thus, threats to manhood have aggressive repercussions, unlike threats to womanhood.

In Western history, many men have fought duels to defend their manhood. The term "honor" signifies respect, which is crucial to manhood. Duels were fought on the so-called "field of honor."

Many people imagine that fighting a duel was a way to resolve a dispute, as if whoever won the duel was proven right. This is mostly mistaken. True, long ago there was a legal tradition in Europe of using trial by combat to resolve disputes, based on the assumption that the Christian God would intervene to ensure that whoever's cause was right and just would prevail in the joust. But that belief faded long before dueling ended.

Rather, the point of a duel was simply to prove one's honor and manhood by taking part. In principle, it didn't really matter whether you got the better or worse of the actual fighting.

This is why dueling scars were often marks of respect. Personally, I always wondered why men of bygone eras would be proud of their dueling scars and would show them off. After all, if you had a scar, didn't that mean that the other person cut you, so in effect you lost? But duels were not about winning or losing.

The essence of dueling was that you put yourself at risk of physical harm, as a way of showing that you were serious. By taking part in a duel, you proved that you held your honorable reputation above life and limb. It was important not to back down if you were insulted, and also not to back down if you insulted someone and he challenged you. In practice, many duels were avoided, but usually this involved having others talk the two parties out of the actual fight. Alexander Hamilton is probably the most famous victim of a duel in American history, but the fatal duel was not his first, and indeed he had already gone through ten previous "affairs of honor" involving challenges to a duel, most of which had never reached the point of actual gunplay. The point of the exercise was for the two men to prove themselves willing to fight and possibly die. If others talked them out of this before the duel took place, that would satisfy everyone, because the men had shown themselves willing to fight.

Nobody expected to kill or be killed over these affronts. Indeed, according to historian Joanne B. Freeman, the most serious insult during the early years of the American republic, leading to many challenges to duel, was one man calling another man a "puppy." Puppies are soft, weak, submissive creatures, unable to defend themselves. Yet to use such an insult to another man was not presumably intended as a death warrant. It was an expression of disrespect, and if the other man refused to accept the disrespect, then both men had to prove themselves willing to fight. The actual fighting and dying were generally regarded as a regrettable and usually avoidable outcome. It was necessary that some challenges led to actual fighting, just to prove that the whole ritual was serious and not a charade.

How to Be a Man

The fact that men have to compete to earn respect was one of the big shocks to Norah Vincent, the lesbian feminist who disguised herself to live as a man for months. She thought that once she "became" a man, she would enjoy all the privileges that society reserves for men. She was shocked to find herself in a rough, difficult role, where the stressful demands to perform and compete were relentless. Her mistake had been to believe too readily what she had been told in Women's Studies classes, namely that the privileges of success are just given to men. Instead, she discovered that these privileges have to be earned via a long, hard struggle that has no promise of success.

A wise and thoughtful book by the respected sociologist Steven L. Nock undertook to understand what men's lives revolve around and, specifically, what role marriage plays in it. I have not been able to improve on the conclusion he formulated. He said that the core achievement that defines manhood in a culture is that *a man produces more than he consumes.*

Putting it that way allows for a broad range of applications. It can refer to the hunter or peasant farmer who procures food. In modern life, it can most easily be rendered in terms of money. But regardless, it is based on the recognition that we all must consume things in order to survive, and that these things must be produced before they can be consumed. A woman is a woman no matter what she produces or consumes. To earn manhood, however, the would-be man must produce more than he will consume.

The idea of producing more than you consume has several implications. The first criterion, obviously, is to produce enough to take care of yourself. Manhood has long meant self-sufficiency. An adult male who is supported by others, who does not earn enough money or bring in enough food to take care of his own needs, is not a man. Indeed, being unable to take care of himself in any of a wide range of accepted ways renders him something less than a man.

Self-support is obviously not a criterion for being a woman. Many women throughout history have been supported by men, and this did not reduce their entitlement to respect. They were women nonetheless. But a man who lives off of others is not fully a man.

The fear of dependency is fear of being less than a man. I suspect its importance and implications for the psychology of men have yet to be fully explored. We have heard that men are sometimes reluctant to ask for help, to visit the physician, to ask a stranger for directions, or, indeed, to commit themselves to a relationship with a woman who will care for them. Why? The underlying motive may well be the sense that to depend on others is to lose one's claim on manhood. Part of being a man is to be willing and able to take care of yourself.

Self-sufficiency is not enough, however, according to Nock. A man must produce enough to support himself *and then something extra*. The extra that he produces is most often earmarked to support a woman and children, of course. That is why being a provider is so central to the way women judge men and men judge themselves. Men undoubtedly feel worse at being unable to provide for their children than they feel about being unable to provide for themselves, because in a pinch they would be willing to do without themselves (rather than be dependent on someone else), but they cannot ask their children to do without. To ask your children to do without is already to admit failure.

When a woman loses her job, she has to cope with practical issues, such as loss of income. When a man loses his job, he has the same concerns but others too. Loss of a job means he does not produce more than he consumes. He is less than a man. No wonder that erectile dysfunction sometimes comes as a result of unemployment. Men without jobs feel themselves to be less than men, and their sex organs register the loss of manhood by ceasing to perform.

A revealing moment in Norah Vincent's book involved a men's group she attended. The men were instructed to make a drawing that symbolized their life. To her surprise, most of the men independently chose to draw themselves as Atlas. This is not what her theories and her Women's Studies

classes had led her to think men's lives were about! But they said they reso-
nated to the symbolism of the guy who struggles to carry the world on his
back. The burden is heavy, but many people count on him, and so he feels
he cannot let them down. To do so would make him less than a man. He
shouldn't even complain. Therefore he silently strains to hold up the entire
world so well that others will not even notice that he has to struggle.

Supporting a family is not the only way to produce more than you
consume. One can earn manhood by producing a surplus that goes in other
socially valued directions. In most modern societies, people pay taxes.
In early societies, a man could gain prestige and status simply by bringing
home food to share with others. But one way or another, that's what it
takes to be a man.

The System Takes

Who benefits from defining manhood in terms of producing more than he
consumes? Looking beyond individuals (wives, children), one can see that
the system as a whole benefits from this. The culture is better off if its men
all produce more than they consume. Through most of history, women
have not produced enough to enable their culture to outpace its rivals.
If the culture is going to prevail in the great competitions, it needs its men
to create the surplus wealth.

Remember, the culture is just a system that is supposed to provide its
members with what they need to survive and, ideally, with some of what
they want beyond that minimum. If the culture can convince most or all of
the men to produce more than they consume, then the culture will be
rich. It will have a surplus, at least, that it can use to take care of many who
cannot care for themselves, including the children, the elderly, the sick
and injured. It can use the surplus to make favorable deals with other
cultures, thereby enriching itself. It can use the surplus to support more
children, thereby increasing the size of the next generation. It can use the
surplus to support expensive male undertakings too, like military ventures. The surplus food and money can also be used to support soldiers on
the march, so they can fend off invaders and perhaps even conquer some
rich lands to add to the culture's revenues.

We have seen that men go to extremes more than women do. This
enables culture to use men in different ways. The rank and file must earn

their manhood by producing more than they consume. If this majority of men produce a nice surplus on a regular basis, it will form a steady source of wealth that the culture can use for its projects. Heroic feats are not generally necessary—just a plodding, steady productivity.

Meanwhile, the topmost men have a special role to play in the culture. The high end of the male distribution can be milked to outpace rival cultural systems. The major innovations and achievements come from them. Progress—one of the essential advantages of culture and an engine by which cultures compete against their rivals—depends heavily on these selected individuals.

The culture is attuned by design (and by trial and error) to reserve its rewards for the men who strengthen it. To be competitive and successful, a culture must get the most talented and capable of its members to put forth huge amounts of effort, even at substantial cost to themselves, to contribute great things to the culture.

One of the great catchphrases from the late days of the Soviet Union summarized people's attitudes about their jobs: "They pretend to pay us, and we pretend to work." The ideology of communism opposed incentives for hard work and achievement. Wealth was to be shared equally. This system failed. Without rewarding people for the effort, sacrifice, and risk needed for exceptional achievements, wealth was not created, progress and innovation were lacking, and productivity was poor. The Soviet Union failed to generate enough wealth to pay people with money that had real value, and so people responded by working less hard. The downward cycle contributed mightily to the collapse of the Soviet Union. In contrast, other countries had systems that rewarded achievement, and these created wealth and progress.

The main assets of a culture are knowledge, power, land, and money, and perhaps influence stemming from other sources (e.g., diplomacy). The most capable individuals may enrich the culture by increasing these things. Because it is hard to know in advance who these talented individuals are, many effective cultures rely on competition. They induce many men to strive for these great rewards, even though only a few can win them. Too bad for the losers. Overall, the society benefits.

In a nutshell, a culture needs its most talented individuals to put forth maximum effort to contribute what they can to the cultural system. The less talented men, not so much. They should just do their dull jobs, pay taxes, occasionally show up for battle if needed, produce quality off-spring, and generally stay out of trouble. But to prevail in tough competition with other cultures, a culture must milk its elite. Talent is there in either gender (though at the top levels, because of male variability, there will be somewhat more males).

What motivates these men to put in the effort and sacrifices? Culture has to harness what the individual is born with. The innate motivational resources of the male are more useful for the culture than the female. Female motivational resources are more suited toward quality reproduction. Total population size is a basic help toward success in every cultural competition—including on the battlefield. But for innovation, which really enables a culture to move ahead of its rivals, most cultures have to depend on their elite men.

We have said that men are judged based on achievements and these judgments are essentially a matter of achieved status. Some aspects of capability are beyond the individual man's control, however. Intelligence, size, strength, and many other attributes depend substantially on your genes. The top achievements depend on a combination of innate ability and hard work. To get these achievements, the culture wants to encourage many men to work hard. Some of them will fail because of bad luck, but others will fail because they did not have the requisite ability, and no amount of hard work can overcome that. That is the core tragedy of the workaholic. Superhuman exertions combined with middling talents will not bring one to the pinnacle of success in most cases.

It's a Dirty Job, but...

Being a man means producing more than you consume. Yet that isn't all it means. When someone says, "C'mon, be a man," he or she isn't usually saying, "Hey, produce more than you consume." More often, perhaps, it means that there is a dirty or dangerous job that needs to be done. Such jobs aren't considered suitable for women and children, as we saw with the British mining laws and plenty of others.

Culture needs many of these jobs to be done, and it expects men to do them. Individual people usually also typically depend on men to do them. To be fair, there are dirty diapers and dirty dishes and plenty of other dirty things in the traditionally women's sphere, so dirt is hardly limited to men.

The strenuous and dangerous jobs are probably more unilaterally assigned to men.

Mostly, men have recognized that dangerous jobs fall to them and, more important, that to be a man they have to accept them. Whether this will continue is not entirely clear. Today's men are brought up on a rhetoric of equality, and at some point they may balk at letting women be exempted from certain unpleasant tasks.

Even more important, the psychological processes that enable men to do the dangerous jobs may be weakened. Men of past eras were famously out of touch with their feelings. Today's men are brought up to be more like women, and that includes becoming more conversant with their own emotions. But might that undermine the ability to make themselves do what needs to be done?

To do the dirty or dangerous jobs, you have to put your feelings aside. Being a man in that sense meant that you focused on the task at hand. It meant others could count on you not to let your emotions interfere with getting the job done. One reason traditional societies put those jobs on men was that women might be too fearful or squeamish or tentative to do them. Traditional men weren't supposed to admit to having such feelings. Yet nowadays we encourage young men to revel in their feelings. Having uncorked the emotional bottle, can we count on the men to stuff the feelings back inside and cork them away when we need them to do so?

The traditional male role had definite privileges, but it also had duties and obligations. Our culture has come far along in doing away with those privileges. It has been slower about equalizing the duties and obligations. (To quote Farrell once more, "Women have rights. Men have responsibilities.") As we make men more like women and remove their traditional privileges, they may begin to object more strenuously to the duties and responsibilities. The obligations of fatherhood weigh far less on today's man than on earlier generations, as indicated not least by the increasing numbers of men who abandon pregnant girlfriends or small children.

If our society does succeed in eliminating both the privileges and the obligations of manhood, it will be embarking on a remarkable social experiment. Possibly it will work out fine. But don't bet anything you can't afford to lose.

Striving for Greatness

This book is about what men are good for, as seen from the perspective of cultures that are competing against other cultures. One answer is that culture benefits disproportionately from the deeds and achievements of great men. To achieve great things, however, they mostly cannot settle for an easy, pampered life of luxury and privilege. When leaders or other elite men do settle for such lives of pleasure and ease (as has not been uncommon, understandably), the culture benefits less. When that is the general pattern, the culture is in a phase of decadence and stagnation. It grows weak and becomes vulnerable to being overtaken by its rivals.

The point needs to be emphasized because the prevailing theories about gender have come from a sort of clueless feminism that imagined men's lives from the perspective of female victimization. In that context, the life of a man was all about enjoying privilege. As we saw, Norah Vincent had thought that once she disguised herself as a man, she'd be mainly occupied with enjoying those benefits. But the feminist view of culture as a system designed to enable men to enjoy the sweet life is silly. A culture can function like that only if it has no rivals, and even then it can afford to let only a few men have such a life centering on leisure and luxury. If the culture is seriously competing against rivals, as has been the norm, then it cannot afford easygoing, unproductive men. Instead, it has to get the most out of everyone—perhaps especially the elite men who need to be coming up with the advances and innovations that will push the culture ahead of its rivals.

The toll of greatness is another paradoxical contradiction in the error we noted in the first chapter, namely the critique that the most powerful members of society are men and therefore society must be set up to benefit men at the expense of women. If you want to see someone with a fine life of pampered ease and luxury, it won't be the men at the top. If anything, look to the wives and children of these men. The pattern holds true even today. The men in the top echelons of the culture may amass fortunes and be able to buy beautiful houses with spectacular furnishings, but they have precious little time to enjoy them, because they are working long hours. More generally, the culture gets the most benefit if the topmost men work passionately hard to enrich it.

A recent conference took me to Sydney, Australia, one of the most breathtakingly fabulous cities in the world. The conference organizers booked a cruise around the harbor, so we could admire the stunning vistas. We cruised past some of the most expensive real estate in the world, the harbor front houses in this magnificent city. The psychology professors on the cruise fell silent looking at these amazingly expensive homes, with walls of windows facing spectacular views, even a couple of tennis courts overlooking the water.

But I also noticed that hardly anybody was to be seen in these magnificent, shockingly lavish homes. The tennis courts were empty, except for two women playing a friendly game in the afternoon sun. Maybe those two women were entrepreneurs who had amassed fortunes and bought these expensive homes. But I'll bet the fortunes were amassed by husbands who were still at work when we cruised by. That's how it is. To make that kind of fortune, you have to be a workaholic, and workaholics are mostly men. Being a workaholic means that you don't enjoy the fruits of your labor. However, your wife might.

Admittedly, the successful man's life is pretty good in many ways! But he just samples the luxuries and pleasures in between hard work. He can't ever really relax for more than a short time.

To achieve greatness is to contribute something to the society. The view of even the topmost male lives as ones of privileged luxury and indulgence may be correct in some cases, but these are not typical and not the point—rather, these are the men who exploit the system, such as corrupt rulers. The system is set up to get the topmost men to devote themselves to enriching the system and strengthening it. Calvin Coolidge once pointed out, "No person was ever honored for what he received. Honor has been the reward for what he gave." Some lucky men are able to claim honor while taking and receiving, but those who earn it do so by giving of their time, energy, money, talent, and other resources so as to benefit the culture and its society. Manhood means contributing.

The young male's first task is to prove himself a man. To become a *great* man requires several more big and difficult steps in the same direction. The criteria are similar. He has to earn respect by achieving things that the culture values, which tend to emphasize things that strengthen and enrich the culture.

There are exceptions. I confess to being unable to see precisely how throwing a basketball through a metal hoop enriches the culture, though

I have certainly enjoyed watching some games. Entertainment is now taking a central place in modern American culture, but that is perhaps historically unusual or perhaps characteristic of rich, successful cultures at their flowering peak and entering their declining stage, marked by rising self-indulgence. The strengthening and enriching part has been achieved and it is possible to relax and enjoy life, in modern America as in imperial Rome. The greatest men no longer have to do anything that actually benefits the culture. They can merely entertain it in superlative ways.

In a sense, the more men there are who strive for greatness, the better off the culture is. (In principle, this would apply to women also, but most cultures haven't used women in this way.) To be sure, many cultures have not afforded the majority of men much chance for greatness. This does not contradict the point, however. The cultures that do manage to get the most men striving for greatness are likely to become the most successful. The remarkable rise of the American society, from a baker's dozen of bedraggled backwater farming colonies into the world's greatest economic, military, and scientific power, owes much to the wide-open competitive opportunities for fame and riches that seduced countless men into giving it their best shot.

Let us acknowledge the facts. America became great mainly because of many American men who strove and competed and contributed. Many men tried and some of them succeeded, to varying degrees. It is a useful exercise to ask what, precisely, enabled America to become great. My answer is that it benefited from pushing lots of men to compete for big rewards. Some of these men helped the culture and, in the process, most of them got rich too. Plenty of other American men tried and failed, getting small or negligible rewards. Some women competed and contributed too, but the greatness of America was created mainly by its men.

As I said earlier, I like women more than men. Still, let's give credit where due. The fact is that America's greatness was propelled by its men more than its women. Maybe the women could have done just as well. Maybe not. We don't know. It is fair, and today it is politically correct, to assume that women can make a society great. In empirical fact, so far in world history, they haven't. What we know for certain is that American men made America great. Or, put another way, America became great because America found a new way of getting the most from its men.

The hankering to rise to the top is probably quite deeply rooted in the male psyche, thanks to evolutionary selection. Remember the harsh reproductive odds faced by past human men and, indeed, by males in the species from whom we evolved? Most males were biological dead ends. Only the men who made it to the top were able to have sex and reproduce.

Sure, there are easygoing, unambitious men. But in our evolutionary past, few of those were able to reproduce. Their more fanatically driven peers who strove for success were more likely to seize the top positions and impregnate the ladies. As a result, today's men are descended far, far more from those fanatically driven males than from the laid-back ones. This is crucial to remember, and it is quite different by gender.

Remember, most of the females have always reproduced—not just the highly ambitious, hard-working, talented ones. Most of the women who ever lived have descendants walking the Earth today. Moreover, regardless of their work-related talents and motivations, they left behind probably about the same number of offspring as other women of their time. If there was a selection so that some women had more descendants than others, being beautiful and lovable was the key to having the most and most successful offspring, not what the mother contributed to advancing the culture's wealth and knowledge.

In sharp contrast, we are descended from relatively few of the men, and these were disproportionately the most intense and driven ones. The blood of the bygone great men runs through the veins of today's baby boys.

Greatness is by definition a scarce commodity. All the sons of the alpha male horse may have his genes, but only one of them can be the alpha male himself. The pyramid of success is steep and cruel. Nature dooms most of the males to fail but impels each of them to try to be the one.

And culture can make great use of this. The drive that impelled the alpha male to fight off challengers to reach the top and stay there, and the drive that propelled some ancient conqueror to legendary conquests— that same drive lives on inside suburban high school boys. Over the centuries, it has been what propels a man to perform heroic acts on the battlefield or football field, to devote all his savings and many years of twelve-hour days to building up his business, to burn midnight lamps in his laboratory.

Our culture likes to recycle the success stories of how those exertions led to spectacular achievements. We must keep in mind that such stories, though true, are one-sided. Many men who worked just as hard or risked just as much did not achieve greatness. Some achieved modest success, and others ended in failure despite giving it all they had. The success stories are a vital part of the propaganda to keep the next generation of men from being discouraged by the long odds.

What About Women?

In the preceding section I focused on men and their strivings. One could reasonably ask, what about women? Why not women? A culture benefits from a new invention such as an electric can opener, and it doesn't really matter whether a man or a woman invented it. If anything, it would seemingly be to the culture's benefit to make the most use of all its talent, male and female.

Sure enough, this is the path our society has (finally) embarked upon: All opportunities are open to both men and women, and society seeks to capitalize on all their talents. I support this. It is the morally proper thing to do and seems pragmatically sensible as well. In that view, one wonders why it took so long. We may seek to understand why so many cultures have sought mainly to exploit male talent.

One answer, to be sure, is that social structure grew from the separate spheres in prehistoric tribes. Women were busy all along with the more important task of bearing and raising children, without which all cultural strivings are doomed and pointless. Cultures that exhorted their women to charge into battle or sail off on voyages of exploration instead of producing the next generation may not have survived. The women had plenty to do, in just making sure that there was a next generation.

Another answer, perhaps, lies in the long odds and seeming irrationality (for the individual) of striving for greatness. Perhaps women were less likely to fall for the seductive blandishments of the culture, the promises of rewards for greatness that are designed to make the many strive but that are ultimately given to only the few. Perhaps, to put it bluntly, women aren't suckers.

The biology behind striving for greatness is masculine. In our own prehistory, and in the lives of animals from whom we evolved, the females did not have to reach the top of the hierarchy in order to reproduce. The males did. Also—and crucially—any females who might have striven and reached the top of the hierarchy failed to get much reproductive benefit from doing so. Maybe their kids got a little better food and care. The top males had far more offspring than the bottom ones, whereas the top and bottom females probably had close to the same numbers. No human woman has ever had five hundred children, or even fifty.

In her bestselling *My Mother, My Self*, Nancy Friday struggled to understand what motivates women. She rejected the view that women are not competitive, which at that time was a standard impression of women. She said women compete for love. They want to attract the love of the most desirable men. In a further insightful comment, she suggested that women never feel there is enough love to go around, which I am suggesting corresponds rather closely to how men feel about respect.

One finding that greatly impressed Friday was the results of many surveys asking about hopes and dreams. She said many women's ideal was to marry a millionaire. In sharp contrast, and to her dismay, the surveys yielded rather few women who said they wanted to *become* millionaires. Friday was writing before the flowering of evolutionary psychology, but her impressions nicely foreshadowed that later body of work. Both men and women may desire and appreciate the value of having money, but they differ as to the tedious jobs, ugly compromises, and dirty sacrifices that may be needed to make money. The man sees no alternative to setting about finding some way to earn it. The woman's natural first impulse is to get it by being lovable enough to attract someone who already has it. Next best, marry someone who looks like he will get there.

This attitude has not disappeared, despite movement toward gender equality. There are certainly more female millionaires and would-be millionaires now than in the past. But still, many women regard marrying a rich man as the best strategy for getting rich. A recent popular book, *Smart Girls Marry Money*, by Elizabeth Ford and Daniela Drake, was successful precisely because it firmly endorsed the strategy for getting rich through marriage. The only novel twist of this book was its enthusiastic admiration for women who went on to divorce the rich men they married, in the process walking away with large amounts of the ex-husband's wealth.

When my wife was a schoolgirl, one of her girlfriends had an older brother who was accepted at Cornell. At the start of his freshman year, the family drove him there to help him move and get him settled in the dorms. The sister had scarcely ever been outside the small town where they lived, and the trip made a big impression on her. She was impressed by the university in many ways, including its beautiful campus and its atmosphere of thinking and learning. She came back full of excitement, which she shared with her friends. After a couple of days, she informed her parents that she wanted to go to Cornell too.

No way, they said. Cornell is expensive, and we are not rich. We can't send a daughter to a college like that. If you want to go to college, you should focus on Buffalo State or one of the other local opportunities. The girl, who had been a top student, was shocked and depressed by this, and she skipped school for almost a week.

I cannot defend the parents' decision. It was terribly unfair to the girl to be denied her chance to get a topnotch education and to reap the rewards that it can bring. Educating her to the best of her abilities could also be of considerable pragmatic benefit to society. She might have been the one to make a major discovery or technological innovation that would improve the lives of many people and enrich the culture as a whole.

America's Ivy League colleges (of which Cornell is one) provide some of the best educations in the world. The young men and women who are fortunate enough to attend these elite schools have their lives enriched in countless ways and gain credentials that can serve them well in many walks of life. A recent survey at another of these top schools asked the students what they hoped to do after graduating. A large number of the women said they wanted to stay home with a baby or work part-time at most. In essence, they wanted a relaxing life, enjoying the satisfactions of motherhood and, of course, of marriage to a loving man who would provide for them and their children.

Nor is this a matter of casual predictions. A national survey covered in *Time* magazine in 2004 found that 22% of women with graduate and professional degrees were currently staying at home with children rather than working at all. It found that one of every three female MBAs, as compared one of every twenty male MBAs, was working less than full-time. A 2001 survey of Harvard Business School graduates found that a third of the female graduates were not employed at all and another third were working only part-time or on contract. Graduates of that school are typically quite sought after, so it is doubtful that their low levels of work reflected being unable to get jobs. More likely, the women simply did not want their lives to revolve around a high-powered career.

One can hardly blame them. From the culture's point of view, however, there are costs associated with educating people who do not then use their education to benefit the society. To be sure, Cornell charges hefty fees to the students (or, more commonly, their parents), but most universities in the world charge lower amounts, and the cost of the education is born by the government (and thus, indirectly, by taxpayers). Either way, it is a rather considerable cost.

The costs extend beyond money. The number of quality faculty is limited, and so is their time. As a result, these intensely beneficial educational experiences are difficult to provide. In my field and many like it, graduate school consists of working one-on-one with professors, many of whom are active researchers and leading experts, and so each professor can work with only three to six graduate students at a time. There are also classes and seminars, but typically these have only a handful of students and are extremely costly to run. Hence the investment in each student is considerable. The cultural system as a whole struggles to provide these elite educational opportunities, and when people take them but then choose not to use them by working hard within the system, the system's investment is in a sense lost.

One of my favorite colleagues works at another university. I met her years ago when her research first began to have an impact on the field. We are about the same age and when we see each other, we like to compare notes on careers, students, journals, and all the other wonderful and aggravating aspects of academic life. She once said to me that one of her greatest frustrations was a pattern she had with multiple female graduate students. She said she had felt a particular responsibility to work with the female students, because there were more male than female professors and she thought she ought to serve as a role model. If she did well, she could help bring more female professors into the field.

She said that she would carefully comb through the applications and find talented students. There were plenty of women with excellent credentials. She would accept the most promising one, bring the young woman into her laboratory, teach her the skills and other tools for success, and work with her through her thesis and dissertation. Often they would publish research together. Then she would help the young woman find a good job as an assistant professor where she could put her skills to use. All of this takes a tremendous amount of the professor's time and energy. Each professor can do this with only a very small number of students.

But at some point along this cycle, said my friend, altogether too many of these promising young women would come in and say that they were getting married and had to move somewhere to be with the husband and would therefore have to put their careers on hold. Usually it never really came off of being on hold. The woman never got back to pursuing her research or fulfilling her promise. My friend who had lavished so much time and energy on these individuals felt that it had all been a waste.

What is most useful for society? That question is different from asking what is fair and right. It is colossally unfair to deny some women the chance to achieve and compete. But to take privileged places and resources like education, and then not use them, has some cost to society also. I cannot defend the decision of those parents who refused to pay for a Cornell education for their daughter, nor would I refuse to work with female students simply because they might be more likely than males to drop out of the field after years of training. Still, I can understand why a culture might produce people who have that policy. From the unfeeling perspective of the system, it could be worth it to restrict female access to education.

Nor can I blame these women, either. Striving for greatness is, in the final analysis, usually a fool's errand, a long hard slog that is likely to fail. Among those who reach the top, and among quite a few others who get close but ultimately fail to get there, most have paid a high price. They have had to work hard for long hours, day after day, year after year. The stereotype of successful men who feel they missed out on seeing their children grow up has more than a kernel of truth. And that's not all they missed out on.

In order to make a serious effort to achieve greatness, at least in today's highly competitive American society, one has to make sacrifices and risks that are out of proportion to the likely rewards, and in that sense it borders on irrational or pathological. Some men and occasionally women put forth that effort, and society benefits from their efforts, but we cannot properly hold them up as ideals of the good life.

For many people, the sacrifices needed to strive for greatness are not worth the effort. We should not be surprised that many women and many men too eventually decide not to devote their lives to trying to beat the odds and achieve greatness. If anything, we should be more surprised that so many people continue, somewhat irrationally, to try.

Why do so many men try so hard? The next section examines a big part of the answer, namely the male ego. But a deep part of the reason, and one that involves women, is rooted in the biological competition to reach the top because once upon a time only those males got to have sex—and men really want to have sex. For many men, success and sex are intertwined. Young men spend much of their time wishing and trying to have more sex than they can get. One reason they buy into the system of work and achievement and playing the game is the implicit promise that if they do become successful, they will finally be able to have the women and the sex they want.

They are not entirely mistaken, although I suspect most successful men would admit that their youthful hopes and fantasies about the sexual smorgasbord that is supposed to accompany career success were not realized. Women do, however, like great men, certainly more than they like losers, failures, mediocrities, and the rest.

At multiple points in this book I have presented the evolutionary point that successful men have more offspring than other men do. Although true, this is not what stands out in the consciousness of ambitious young men. They are not hoping to make boatloads of babies. Rather, sex is their goal and focus. They think, with partial justification, that their sex lives will improve if they become successful. In this way, the availability and the preferences of women support the male pursuit of greatness.

This too is something that is specific to men. There is little evidence that women who achieve high levels of career success will have more or better sex than other women. Even if they did, it is far from clear that that would motivate women to work harder and make more sacrifices to achieve career success. Women do not crave sex as much as men do, not least because they can usually get sex if they want it. Men pursue greatness partly because of the elusive promise of abundant sex.

Once again, we must object to the view of men and women as antagonists. From men's point of view, women are neither the competition nor the enemy: In an important sense, they are the reward.

Effects on Men: Male Ego

The pyramid of success is steep and the sacrifices needed to reach for the top are formidable. Why do so many men try? How can they not be discouraged?

The problem is not unique to modern American culture. It also applies to males of other species. The wild horses we talked about in connection with the most underappreciated fact about gender faced the same problem. The young males needed the confidence to challenge the alpha male. Those who lacked that confidence did not reproduce. To be sure, some who had plenty of (unwarranted) confidence challenged and lost, and they too failed to reproduce. Confidence alone was not enough. But without confidence, there was no success either.

These evolutionary pressures gradually stamped overconfidence into the male psyche. Underconfident males, who might have won the fight but failed to challenge, left no heirs. Overconfident males, who were not really strong enough to win but who challenged anyway, mostly would also end up defeated and sexless, but occasionally one would get lucky and win, perhaps because the alpha male was tired or injured or accidentally stumbled and broke his leg during the fight. Thus, for men, overconfidence probably paid off more than underconfidence did.

The male ego is nature's answer to the ultimate futility of most male lives. It enables each male to think that he is different, that he will not be one of the failing or mediocre majority.

Remember, too, that the genetic memory of male futility is rather thin. Instead, we are descended from the victors, the conquerors, the alphas. Only recently has the democratization of sex and marriage, most obviously in the form of laws against polygamy, made sure that the also-ran males can be husbands and fathers like the winners. We are descended mainly from many generations of males who thought they could make it to the top and who were right about that, at least for a little while—long enough to procreate.

Confidence is needed for more than ambition, though ambition is our concern here. But confidence is also necessary for sex itself. In our species, including today, the mating dance requires the males to take the initiative. If humans waited for women to initiate sex, it is doubtful that the species would reproduce itself. In the bars and mixers and apartments of the modern world, men ask and have to endure many refusals.

Norah Vincent, the lesbian who tried living as a man, said she thought dating women would be one of the most pleasant parts of her undercover life. As a lesbian, she had already dated women, but now there would be many more available to her, and she looked forward to the experience. She found it sobering and discouraging. As a man, she would approach women at the bar to try to chat them up, and more often than not she got a quick and unkind (sometimes downright humiliating) rejection. She soon lost her nerve and, were it not for the demands of her experiment, she says she would have given up. She wondered how men manage to do it, to persevere, to summon up their courage to approach women despite the expectation of being rejected most of the time and despite the accumulating history of bad outcomes. She said she did not know which was worse, the women who rejected you at a glance without giving you have a chance to prove yourself, or the ones who rejected you after a couple of dates and some degree of getting to know you.

There isn't much of an alternative. Nature needs for sex to happen, or else there is no reproduction. Women are selective, for strong biological reasons: A woman can have only a few babies, and so the best thing for her children is to choose a father with good genes. That leaves men the job of trying to be chosen. Men who do not have enough confidence to ask will join the majority who fail to pass on their genes. The men who live today are descended from the ones who did ask. As a result, they inherited that dogged spirit of confidence and initiative.

When a man asks for sex, his chances are vastly improved by having achieved some level of status. Men know this. Hence male ambition.

It is hard to be certain how much of the male ego is stereotype and hype, and how much is real. Questionnaire studies find that men score slightly higher than women on self-esteem and on narcissism, and moreover the difference seems biggest during adolescence and young adulthood, which is around the time of competing for mates and status (which is when the extra confidence is most needed).

There are also various signs that male egotism is bigger in interpersonal settings, suggesting that some of it may be an act rather than a deeply felt inner conviction. This too would be understandable. The male ego may be more a way of dealing with the rough social world the male faces than a requirement of his inner processes. When challenging another male, it is important not to show weakness or fear, but it may be all right to feel some of those if one can conceal it. Acting confident, in other words, may be more important than actually being confident.

Indeed, some of the male ego consists more of the desire to be great than of the actual belief that he is already great. The tension between motivation and belief has been apparent with the trait of narcissism (often considered the aggressive or obnoxious form of high self-esteem). Narcissists are characterized by thinking well of themselves, or at least by insisting that they do. Narcissists want everyone else to think well of them. Their wish to be admired is one of the most pervasive, best established aspects of the trait. It is possible to see narcissism as a kind of addiction to esteem.

As we have seen, nature has little use for males who do not strive for greatness, and most of those nonambitious men have ended up as reproductive dead ends. That means that natural selection has favored males with the male ego. The guys who had both the desire to achieve greatness and the confidence to enable them to try for it (and then to help them succeed) are the ones from whom today's baby boys are descended.

Our concern, however, is less with nature than with culture. What nature has prepared, culture can use. As we have seen, most cultures want many of their men to compete and achieve. The natural proclivities toward male egotism can be harnessed to yield the widespread striving for greatness on the terms that benefit the culture.

Cultural men need egotism to function in their large group. They need a self that can establish itself with special abilities and traits that will make it useful to the group and preferably hard to replace. They need a self that is confident enough to compete for those coveted slots. They need a self that is driven enough to want to surpass other men and climb toward the top of the hierarchy, where the women look for mates and where, therefore, a man has his best chances for sex.

Perhaps the optimal system for all concerned would be for only the most capable males to make the efforts and sacrifices necessary to achieve great things. The rest could take it easy. But the culture does not know who those most capable men are, and so the most effective (though wasteful) system is to have most or all of the men make such efforts and sacrifices, so that whoever is the best will come through. Note that this effective system requires some degree of overconfidence spread throughout the male population. In essence, every man has to act as if he is one of the gifted and talented ones, in order for the culture to benefit from the few who do turn out in fact to be those gifted and talented ones.

Man as Active Agent

The male ego is a controversial stereotype about which value judgments, mostly negative ones, are readily made. Let us turn to a possibly related and less contentious aspect of male psychology, called agency (as in being an agent, one who acts). The inclination to take action, to show initiative, to take charge and respond actively instead of passively is one of the core traits most commonly associated with men in research studies and in the opinions of expert researchers. Men have somewhat more of this trait than women do.

The theme of this chapter is the requirement that manhood must be earned. Agency is a useful and possibly necessary trait for the earning of manhood. Hence we should not be surprised that nature has selected in favor of agentic men and that culture reinforces and capitalizes on this trait.

The demands of male social life can offer ample explanation for male agency. Even the basic distinction between achieved and ascribed status invokes it. Manhood has to be earned, and so one has to take initiative in order to achieve something and prove oneself. Womanhood is ascribed without the young lady having to do anything, and so there is less need for her to have initiative.

Ditto for romance. It falls to the man to initiate love and sex. To be successful with women, even today, a man needs initiative as much as he needs the confidence that the male ego lends (see previous section). Indeed, his confidence is probably useful mainly in support of romantic initiative.

I have written this as if the social environment came first and the agentic aspect of manhood was a result. More likely, the two were intertwined. Nature required men to compete to reach the scarce spots at the top of the hierarchy, where the male's relatively few options for sex and reproduction were to be found. And each generation of baby boys was fathered by the men with the most agency. Human culture then could capitalize on this male trait and put it to work. Had nature bred men to be passive— for example, if the females had only been willing to mate with the quiet, unambitious, passive men—then culture probably could not have expected boys to have to earn their manhood by feats of active initiative.

I suspect one reason that men are liked and loved less than women has to do with the uglier sides of agency. Undoubtedly many men are bossy, domineering, stubborn loudmouths. Some women may also fit that description, but perhaps these traits are more common in men. Still, these can be understood as mere extensions of the traits that contribute to male success, as in being ready to take charge, to persevere despite setbacks, to step into leadership roles and dominate others, and to initiate and direct action. The difference between resolute perseverance and pigheaded stubbornness may often be no more than whether you agree with what the person is trying to do.

How Culture Gets What It Wants

With the combination of male ego and agency, a man is ready and well suited to operate in the kinds of social networks men create. In a sense, these are the raw human materials the culture has to work with. Let us now turn to consider how cultures adapt to capitalize on these.

Men have to prove themselves in order to qualify as men. The culture can set the terms by which they achieve that. In essence, the culture defines how they prove themselves. By doing this, it can steer men's efforts into excelling and achieving in ways that are most useful for the culture. In a fragile young tribe surrounded by enemies, it may emphasize valor and battlefield heroics as the test of manhood. In an isolated tribe where food is scarce, hunting may become the way to prove oneself. In an advanced industrial democracy, it may come down to making a substantial amount of money.

Just as culture sets the criteria for being a man, it also can set the definition of greatness, and it seems likely that greatness is often a matter of simply doing more and better along the lines of what was needed to prove manhood in the first place. If a successful hunt is required to prove one's manhood, then a long history of superior hunting results may be what qualifies one for greatness.

The extremity is required by the mathematics of greatness. All the adult males can prove themselves to be men, but the very definition of greatness limits it to the topmost few. If the average level of achievement rises, then the requirements for greatness must also rise.

Setting the criteria is not the only way the culture exerts its influence. By rewarding and celebrating great achievements, it can hold them up as examples to the other men, inspiring them to aspire to reach the same heights. We have seen that the contest for greatness is one in which the best interests of the individual man are not necessarily in line with the best interests of the culture. The culture benefits if many men pour their hearts and souls into striving to achieve things for the culture, seeking greatness for themselves, even though most of these strivings will end in failure. Hence a successful culture needs ways to motivate men to work harder than is good for them and to take risks and make sacrifices that are not really, objectively wise for them. These may range from sacrificing family time to the point at which the father misses out on his children's lives, to charging forward in the front line of an attack on a fortified enemy position.

Making a big fuss to reward and celebrate the top achievers is therefore a good investment for the culture. Strictly speaking, it may even justify rewarding the top achievers beyond the value of what they produce, even though this is precisely the sort of male privilege that draws the ire of the Imaginary Feminist and creates the impression that the culture is set up to shovel privileges and rewards to men. But rewarding those men is not the point. Motivating other men to strive is the point. The odds of being the successful one may be long, but if the rewards are immense, that may tempt many men into giving it a shot anyhow. The value (to the culture) of rewarding the top achievers lies not in what they get but in the effect it has on the rank and file. Showering the victorious warriors with gold coins is in essential part a way to motivate future warriors to be willing to risk their lives on future battlefields.

Turning to modern life, society needs men to do all sorts of work, and again by definition, work is not something that people are inherently motivated to do. Giving rewards such as pay is one widespread motivator. Beyond that, however, culture can motivate men to work by linking it to things people care about.

Theorists have distinguished three different major attitudes toward work, labeled job, calling, and career. The job is essentially a matter of performing the work for the pay or other extrinsic reward, and it does not have to have much involvement of the person's identity at all. The term *calling* was originally associated with priesthood or ministry (as in being called by God), but more recently it is associated with a calling based on one's inner aptitudes and possibly sense of destiny. Artists, physicians, writers, and others think of their work as a calling, and they may put more effort into it than the pay warrants. Callings can be effective ways to motivate men to work extremely hard, but because callings originate in inner promptings (even if they may be attributed to divine powers or other external inspirations), they are difficult for a culture to control.

The career is a relatively modern form of work. Its focus is on building the record of achievement, status, and success. Essentially, the careerist is motivated by what he or she can put on the resume. The work is not necessarily enjoyed for its own sake, but neither is it done merely for the sake of the paycheck. The career mentality looks at work as a way of glorifying the self. This can be an extremely useful attitude for the culture, because it motivates people to work hard at jobs that are not necessarily all that satisfying. The career mentality enables the culture to harness the male ego to serve that motivational function. One works in order to accumulate the record of promotions, awards, and other tangible or symbolic achievements.

A Shortage of Respect

Crucial to the way many cultures motivate and exploit men is maintaining a shortage of respect. Given the male ego and other factors, men want to be respected and want to do things that will earn them respect. Like most rewards, however, the value of respect rises with scarcity. It is therefore useful for a cultural system to maintain an environment in which there is not enough respect to go around, so that the men remain hungry for it and must fight hard for it.

We have already seen that greatness is itself necessarily limited to only a few, and that is one aspect of restricting respect. But the strategy may be applied more generally. In many male organizations, all respect may be in short supply. This can take the form of hazing new recruits, insulting them, calling them names, making them dress in unflattering ways. It may be reflected in titles and dress. (Whoever invented and who settled for the pathetically unglamorous title "Assistant Professor" to refer somebody who has gone through at least twenty years of schooling, earned a Ph.D., and is doing the same full-time work that a any level of professor does?) It may take the form of verbal putdowns.

Verbal putdowns are a common feature of male-only discourse. I remember when it was common in many organizations. In fact, my thesis advisor was fond of that kind of talk, though in a famous and powerful man it seemed to have a bullying edge, because not many of us students were willing to talk back to him the same way.

Verbal putdowns typically take the form of humorous insults. The target is expected to accept the disrespect in some gracious way. Among peers, the usual is to respond with a cleverly worded insult of your own. When these come from superiors, the only effective strategy is to join in by making a self-deprecating joke, thus weakening the insulting content by elaborating the joke aspect. Nonetheless, this pattern of response requires the man to say negative things about himself to others.

If the target fails to react well, such as getting upset or saying something inappropriate, the verbal assault gets worse. Showing signs that he is embarrassed or upset at the insulting comments is normally a serious loss of face, as well as an invitation to others to pile on and mock him more. To cry in response to such insulting treatment, which a priori would not be a completely shocking or unreasonable response to hearing unkind things said about you to your face, would be something the guy would not live down for years. A man who would cry in response to such comments obviously "can't take it," even when it is supposedly funny, and so obviously he is too weak and vulnerable to compete or to be taken seriously.

All of this is quite unfamiliar to women. My wife once sat at the end of a table of men and heard them talk to each other in this way, and afterward she told me how surprised she was, because women who spoke to each other like that would have quickly ceased being friends at all.

In fact, I suspect that this difference has produced many of the misunderstandings between men and women in the workplace, some of which no doubt resulted in lawsuits and dismissals and other severe outcomes. Users of verbal putdowns search for something vulnerable about a person and seize on it. When women entered the workplace, men did not know how to treat them, and some of them took at their word the liberated women's request to be treated equally, just like one of the guys. And so they directed some of their unkind, demeaning jokes at them. They would perhaps find something about the woman that invited or at least permitted ridicule. To the woman, this seemed like gender-specific sexual harassment, and probably when repeated in legal hearings it did sound like something specifically invented to make a woman feel bad. But the motive may often have been quite similar to how men had treated other men for decades, if not centuries.

Personally, I never liked that form of discourse based on competing to make insulting jokes at others' expense. Hence I do not mourn its gradual passing from the newly gender-integrated workplace. But I have wondered for years why it flourished in so many places and whether any function sustained it.

The answer, I suspect, is that it was part of the cultural system of maintaining the shortage of respect. It may be hard on the individual men, but it does benefit the system. Those little daily, hourly jabs remind the men of what it feels like to be disrespected and, in the grand scheme of things, motivate them to strive harder to succeed up to some level at which they will not have to endure disrespect.

In other words, the pleasures and benefits of respect are not necessarily enough for maximum effect. Bad is stronger than good. Given the choice between respect and nothing (i.e., neutral treatment), and given that one might have to work long and hard and take risks and make sacrifices to earn respect, some men might not find the reward worth the exertion. So the ante is upped by replacing the neutral treatment with regular disrespectful treatment. Until you prove yourself, you are ever vulnerable to having to endure humiliating treatment, and the vulnerability is half-jokingly enforced on a daily basis.

Moreover, proving himself is not a one-time, all-or-nothing matter, but rather a continuum. With each increment in achievement and status, the man reduces the amount of disrespectful or humiliating treatment he must endure. Perhaps it never entirely ends. (Our recently departed President George W. Bush, who in my impression seemed to have a men's club mentality in many unfortunate respects, is said to have favored the nickname "Turd Blossom" for one of his most influential advisors.) If he should slack off in his efforts to climb the hierarchy and achieve greatness—which also means reducing his efforts to produce things the culture values—the putdowns will remind him of the unpleasantness of not having enough respect.

Verbal putdowns may be a relatively informal and humorous version. Honor has traditionally been taken much more seriously, and it serves much the same function. We already covered how this was played out in duels. These were at bottom about the same thing: proving oneself worthy of respect.

Being worthy of respect is an important dimension of honor. As men are socialized to care about their honor, they learn to live by the culture's rules and to strive to excel by its criteria.

Honor was perhaps as much or more about morality as about achievement. Still, these were important too, especially in the olden days when there was less social mobility and so forth. Morally virtuous behavior was useful for society.

CHAPTER 10

Exploiting Men Through Marriage and Sex

I N 1978, a heap of Academy Awards, including the coveted ones for Best Picture and Best Director, went to *Annie Hall*. I was doing my dissertation that year and didn't see the film till several years later. That didn't matter, as much of the wisdom and humor are fairly timeless.

One part that still resonates today was the famous sequence in which the camera shifts back and forth between the psychotherapy sessions of Annie (Diane Keaton) and her live-in partner, played by the inimitable Woody Allen. The therapists ask each how often they have sexual intercourse. "Hardly ever. Maybe three times a week," complains the man. "Constantly: I'd say three times a week," complains the woman.

Surveys show that three times per week is indeed a fairly common habit for a sexually active young couple. As the film scene indicates, however, it may mean different things to the man and to the woman. Over the course of a long marriage, frequency of sex is often a difficult issue to negotiate and re-negotiate. And as the film scene implies, the difficulty lies in the common fact that men want sex more than women.

The male sex drive is a fact of nature, but it is one that presents culture with an assortment of problems and opportunities. In this chapter, we look at how culture can capitalize on male sexuality.

Mistaking the Beast

"There's a lot of anger in men. Anger at women." That sort of conclusion emerges over and over when women scholars study men's sexuality.

Nancy Friday, who compiled volumes of sexual fantasies, emphasized male rage at women as her main conclusion about men's fantasies. Even Norah Vincent said essentially the same thing after her forays (disguised as a man) into the back rooms of strip clubs.

Anger? What anger?

The conclusion has repeatedly baffled me. I read Friday's book, and was quite surprised by the conclusion about anger. I didn't see any anger in the stories she quoted. I've never heard men say they thought strip clubs were full of anger nor even heard them express anger about their own visits, except occasionally in connection with being overcharged or duped.

It's not anger. Women, perhaps especially thoughtful women, simply cannot fathom the strength of the male sex drive—and the ache of sexual frustration that pervades so many hours of a man's life.

We shouldn't entirely blame the female scholars for this inadequacy. Feminists told them, quite assertively, that the female sex drive is every bit as strong as any man's. Traditional folk wisdom held that women wanted sex less than men, but feminists angrily denounced this as another oppressive stereotype. If anything, the female sex drive was stronger than the male, they insisted. This went so far as to be cited as the correct view in some human sexuality textbooks.

But that's absurd. As one sign, when couples in marital therapy argue about sex, guess which spouse is the one wanting more sex? Almost never do couples report that the husband isn't willing to have sex as often or in as many different ways as the wife wants. Almost always, the husband wants more.

One research study tracked people who had been married for many years and asked them what their ideal amount of sex would be in a good marriage. Then it asked them how much sex they actually had. Wives reported that their ideal was almost exactly equal to the amount of sex they were having. To them, their married sex lives were essentially perfect, ideal, optimal.

Their husbands said the ideal was about 50% more than they were getting. And these were happily married husbands, middle-aged men, long past the overwhelming sexual frenzy of youth. Yet even for them, sex remained a source of recurring deprivation and frustration. They were getting considerably less than they wanted, unlike the women, who were getting precisely as much as they wanted. Just like the two characters in

Annie Hall, the couples agreed about the actual frequency of sex but disagreed about what the ideal would be. That's because the man wants considerably more sex than the woman.

The feminist insistence that women want sex as much as men do has created all sorts of mischief and misunderstanding. Many women object to pornography and erotica on the dubious assumption that media depictions of sex are somehow hostile to women. The arguments fall apart easily if examined (why would a picture of a man and woman having sex be degrading to the woman but not to the man?), but one can understand how women got there. The intelligent woman sees men wanting to watch pornography and thinks, I don't want pornography, so why do men want it? She thinks, it can't be because men have a stronger desire for sex than I do, because my sex drive is just as strong as men's. Therefore there must be something else, something oppressive and hateful.

She thinks, porn can't be what it looks like: just pictures of sex. But that's precisely what it is. She thinks that all the time, effort, and money that men spend to see porn can't be just a reflection of their desperate, endless craving for sex. But that craving for sex is precisely what is behind those acts.

The fancy theories about how men are engaging in oppression of women when they masturbate to porn are all an attempt to paper over one of the gaping holes in the feminist analysis, all stemming from the fundamental lie that says women want sex as much as men. But many well-intentioned people were fooled into accepting that lie as truth, and so they were at a loss at how to explain the obvious facts.

Some Facts and Findings on Sex Drive

The problem of recognizing the reality of the male sex drive was brought home to me in a rather amusing experience I had some years ago. I was writing a paper weighing the relative influence of cultural and social factors on sexual behavior, and the influence consistently turned out to be stronger on women than on men. In any scientific field, observing a significant difference raises the question of why it happens. We had to consider several possible explanations, and one was that the sex drive is milder in women than in men. Women might be more willing to adapt their sexuality to local norms and contexts and different situations, because they aren't quite so driven by strong urges and cravings as men are.

When I brought this up in the paper as one possible theory, reviewers reacted rather negatively. They thought the idea that men have a stronger sex drive than women was probably some obsolete, wrong, and possibly offensive stereotype. I wasn't permitted to make such a statement without proof, which they doubted could be found. And when I consulted the leading textbooks on sexuality, none of them said that women had a generally milder desire for sex than men. Some textbooks explicitly said that that idea was wrong. One, by Janet Hyde and Richard DeLamater, openly speculated that women actually had a stronger sex drive than men, contrary to what I thought.

Two colleagues and I decided to see what information could be gleaned from all the published research studies we could find. This meant a long process of slogging through hundreds of scientific journal articles reporting scientific studies of sexual behavior. One colleague, Kathleen Catanese (now a professor of psychology at a Midwestern college) started out as a strong feminist with the party-line belief that there was no difference in sex drive. The other, Kathleen Vohs (now a professor of marketing), was undecided. My hunch was that men had the stronger sex drive. Thus, at the outset, we held an assortment of views, but we all decided we would just follow the data and revise our opinions as the evidence came in.

The task was considerable, and I at least was nagged by the fear that this point was so obvious that no one would want to publish our research. One colleague heard we were reviewing the literature to see whether men wanted sex more than women, and she commented acidly, "Of course they do. Everybody who's ever had sex knows that!" Well, everybody, apparently, except the expert researchers on sexuality and authors of textbooks.

There is no single, clear measure of sex drive. So we approached the problem like this. Imagine two women (or two men for that matter), such that one of them has a truly stronger sex drive than the other. What differences in preferences and behavior would you expect to see between the two of them? For example, the one with the stronger sex drive would presumably think about sex more often; have more fantasies, desire, and actual sex more often; have more partners; masturbate more often; and devote more effort to having sex than the other. The reverse is quite implausible. That is, it is hard to imagine the woman with the weaker sex drive having more frequent sexual fantasies than the woman with the stronger sex drive.

And so we searched for studies that compared men and women on these types of behaviors.

After months of reading and compiling results, the answer was clear. There is a substantial difference, and men have a much stronger sex drive than women. To be sure, there are some women who have frequent, intense desires for sex, and there are some men who don't, but on average the men want it more. Every marker we could think of pointed to the same conclusion. Men think about sex more often than women do. Men have more sexual fantasies, and these encompass more different acts and more different partners.

Men masturbate more than women—much more. Masturbation is considered by sex researchers to be one of the purest measures of sex drive, because it is not much constrained by external factors (such as the need to find a partner, or the risk of pregnancy or disease). Some people say that women feel guilty about masturbation, but that's not what the data say, at least not any more. In fact, it's mainly the (few) nonmasturbating men who associated masturbation with guilt. Nonmasturbating women generally say they just don't feel any inclination to do it. They don't need guilt to resist the impulse, because they aren't resisting—because they don't have the impulse.

There's plenty more. Men take more risks and incur more costs for sex. (Remember President Clinton!) Men want sex more often than women, whether one is talking about young couples or people who have been married to the same person for forty years. Men also want more different partners than women want, and men like a greater variety of sex acts than women do.

Men initiate sex often and refuse it rarely. Women initiate it much more rarely and refuse it much more often than men. Given an opportunity for sex, men leap at it, while women say no. One classic study sent student research assistants out on campus to approach fairly attractive people (of the other gender) at random with the line, "I've been noticing you around campus and I think you're attractive. Would you like to go to bed with me tonight?" More than three-quarters of the men said yes. Not a single woman did.

Women find it easier than men to go without sex. An adult woman who is between relationships can easily go for months, sometimes even years, hardly thinking of sex and not minding if she doesn't have it. Men go nuts without sex (or at least some do). A man who loses his girlfriend will often start masturbating by the next day or two.

Even when both men and women make a heartfelt, sacred vow of chastity, the men find it much harder to keep than the woman. Catholic priests have much more sexual activity than the nuns, even though both have committed themselves to the single standard of complete abstinence and have backed this up with a sacred promise in the context of the most important beliefs and values in their lives.

In short, pretty much every study and every measure fit the pattern that men want sex more than women. It's official: Men are hornier than women.

Living with the Beast

Flipping channels one time I heard on Bill Maher's *Politically Incorrect* show the remark "For me, a day without great sex is a wasted day." The audience laughed, but I knew exactly what he meant, and I felt the same way, or at least did through several decades of manhood until the beast quieted down a bit when I reached my 50s. I think most men resonate to the same feeling.

That's the level of interest we are talking about. A man in love may feel sexual desire for a specific, particular woman, but most men also have plenty of free-floating sexual interest in other women, all women, any woman, at least in the broad set of "reasonably attractive" ones (e.g., the top 90% of women in their twenties, etc.). Part of him can't help wanting her, wanting to look at her, to see a glimpse of her flesh. He always wants it, and he knows he will hardly ever get it. Having one partner for sex only slightly reduces the desire for every other possible one. This is normal.

A few lucky or worthy men (kings, movie stars, top athletes) reach positions that enable them to have whatever sort of sex lives they want. It is revealing to see what they choose. In general, they do pick a favorite partner, such as a wife. But they also generally have plenty of others on the side: mistresses, groupies, concubines. Today most such men feel pressure (despite their high status, and even because of it) to settle down with one wife and be faithful to her. Even so, they often find ways to enjoy others. If their choices were truly up to them, we would see more of the harems and other such systems of rotating bedmates.

Remember the psychology experiment described in the previous section, in which a set of female research assistants approached attractive males walking across campus and asked to have sex with them that evening? The research assistants were of average attractiveness, so they were approaching men who were better-looking than they were. (Hence you might expect many males to say no.) The request came out of the blue, and we can assume that most of the guys already had some plans for what to do that evening. Yet three-quarters of the men said yes. They were willing to cancel their other plans for the chance to have sex with a woman they didn't know and who was only moderately attractive. Even the ones who said no typically showed signs of cognitive dissonance: They apologized, offered explanations ("I have a girlfriend"), or suggested alternative times ("I really can't tonight, but how about tomorrow?").

The men's willingness to scrap most other plans and activities in order to have sex with a willing, average-looking partner is as revealing as anything about the high priority that sex holds in the minds of young men. Women don't have the same feelings. When that experiment was run with the genders switched, not a single woman agreed to have sex with the average-looking male stranger who politely asked her to go to bed with him that evening. But most of the men said yes to the female stranger, and many of the others wanted to.

Even the most pliable, civilized, well-behaved little boy finds at some point in his teen years that his mind has been invaded by a relentless beast. His vague romantic thoughts about the cute little girls in his class have mutated into endless wishes and imaginings, of a nature he cannot tell anyone. He swallows hard and tries to put these thoughts out of his mind to focus on his math homework or whatever. But sex is never far from his thoughts, and if out of the blue a woman were to stop him to invite him to her bed, he doesn't have to ponder the request for very long.

He may wish it worked the other way: that he could ask an attractive stranger for sex and she would say yes. But it doesn't. He tries everything he can think of, from crude advances to flowery romantic courtship. The modern young man has heard all the talk of equality and can't understand why the women insist on playing these games and saying no. It is hard for him to accept that she does not sex as much as he does—or, more likely, if he instinctively understands this, he cannot reconcile it with the rhetoric of equality and sameness.

A startling yet revealing observation was made by Norah Vincent, after she had lived as a man for some months. She said that when she got men to open up and talk about their sexual feelings, most confessed that at some point they had done something of which they were now ashamed, motivated by their sexual desires. She did not elaborate on what these were, and one does not know even whether they men told her the specifics. And despite my extensive reading of research on sexuality, I have not seen any systematic data on this question. But let's suppose that she's right. What would that tell us?

Certainly anyone who watches the news knows that many men, even highly respectable, prominent, successful men, have done sexual things of which they were ashamed. We have seen presidents and presidential candidates admit to sexual misdeeds that compromised their careers. We have seen senators and congressmen admit to doing things in public restrooms or in their offices that have made them laughingstocks. Are these men somehow atypical? More likely these incidents are the tip of the iceberg. These men were caught because they were such public figures that when they do what many other men do, the media are eager to report on them.

There are many things men could mean when they say they have been ashamed by something sexual they once did. It is not just having sex with the wrong person or wrong type of person. It may include making inappropriate advances. It may include misleading a woman such as by pretending to be in love with her in order to convince her to have sex. It may have been trying again after she said no once.

Before we condemn men as hopeless sinners, however—and I suspect many men regard themselves as such, at least when they reflect on their attempts to come to terms with the inner sexual beast—we might feel a moment of sympathy for their unrewarded successes. How many times on the dance floor, possibly head swimming with too many drinks, did he want to reach out and touch some woman's derriere, and yet he resisted? How many times did he stop as soon as the woman with whom he was necking said to stop? (Research has suggested that most women have said "no" when they meant "yes" at least occasionally, which introduces a further element of confusion to even the most well-intentioned young man.)

He doesn't get any credit for all the times he stifles his desires, despite all the struggle and sacrifice that they cost him. Daily he wrestles with the beast, and mostly he keeps it controlled, even though it is part of him and, crucially, when he does manage to give it the sex it wants, the result has been some of the most glorious moments of bliss he has ever known. Mostly he succeeds in restraining himself. Out of every thousand times he has to deny himself and stop himself from acting on his feelings, once or twice he slips up, and these can be enough to shame him. In fact he's lucky if their only lasting effect is painful memories tinged with shame, embarrassment, and guilt. These little slip-ups could ruin him, costing him his career, his marriage, his happiness, even his freedom.

To be sure, young men in Western countries today have far more and better opportunities for sex than most young men have ever had. Premarital sex has become common, even expected. Men still do not get all they want, but they get much more than has been the norm, and at much less risk. Through most of history, most young men either had no sex at all, or they had rare and furtive opportunities that were attended by substantial risks of pregnancy (which would often trap the man into marriage) and nontrivial risks of disease. Even most married men did not get all that much sex. Oral sex was not usually a viable substitute or even an accepted possibility. Intercourse carried a risk of pregnancy, and so either your wife was pregnant much of the time (itself reducing sex) or one had to abstain in order to avoid pregnancy.

Yes, in relative terms modern men live in an age of sexual opulence, yet satisfaction remains elusive. It is probably not in the nature of the male sex drive to be satisfied for more than a short time. Nature saw no point in letting men be happy with the sex they've already had. Over the ages, the male population descended from the most insatiable ones, who continued to pursue every opportunity for sex and who spent their lives trying to rise to the top of the social hierarchy so they could have more sex.

Sex Can Be, uh, Useful

Sex is a consuming concern of many people. It is a source of passion, ecstasy, misery, risk, disaster, craving, worry, and much more. But let us set aside the human dimension and look at sex from the unfeeling, amoral perspective of a cultural system.

Sex presents both challenges and opportunities. Sex can be disruptive, causing people to do irrational and violent things, bringing babies into the world with no one to care for them, spreading disease, making enemies, and more. Hence it is vital for a culture to control sex. It is not surprising that all known cultures have rules and regulations about sexual behavior.

On the positive side, if sex is managed reasonably well, it is vitally important to the culture and can be beneficial in all sorts of ways. Most obviously, it creates the babies needed to make the next generation and keep the culture alive. Moreover, as we have seen, cultures compete partly by means of population, and so making plenty of babies has usually been seen as a positive good in most civilized cultures.

The greater sex drive of males is almost certainly a result of nature, not culture. Culture can try to change this, but as I have said repeatedly, culture usually has to work with what nature gives it. It can build on or weaken the natural patterns, but it cannot easily reverse them. There is no known culture in which the women are the ones eager for sex at every opportunity, while the men resist and refuse. If there ever were, it would be a most unusual one. Plenty of cultures have tried, after all, to bring up their boys not to become sex-crazed adolescents. Plenty of parents in other cultures have also tried. They can make a dent in the male sex drive, but they can't really kill the beast. And none of those cultures have managed to bring women up to want sex more than men. Au contraire, the best strategy for keeping the male sex drive under control is to keep the guys from being exposed to anything that could stimulate sexual thoughts. That usually means keeping the girls covered up and preferably out of sight. I believe that, incidentally, is the motive behind those head-to-foot shapeless coverings for women favored by some cultures. The Imaginary Feminist says those are a ploy to subjugate women. More likely, I think, they were designed to prevent men from getting turned on by seeing the curves and flesh of the female body.

Still, why would culture want to reverse the natural order? That's not what cultures need in order to prevail over their rivals.

The male sex drive can be used to motivate men. It is probably an almost universal truth that plenty of men will do whatever is necessary to get sex. Women are attracted to successful and rich men, and the culture can make the rules about how men become rich and successful. In that way, it can get men to produce the things it needs.

This list is far from exhaustive. Sex in advertisements helps sell all sorts of products. Sex provides material for conversation and jokes. It helps people express affection and cement commitments to each other. Sex itself can be bought and sold as a commodity. My point is just that cultural rules about sex typically serve an assortment of functions. Despite the impression one gets from America's Puritan heritage, sexual rules are not all merely designed to prevent people from having any fun.

Thus, sex is useful for a culture. Let's look at how it finds men useful in connection with sex.

Somebody Has to Start the Ball(ing) Rolling

Before we get to the more complex and interesting uses of the male sex drive, let's start with the obvious. A culture won't survive unless it produces babies, and for that, sex is generally necessary. Somebody has to initiate sex. This job usually falls to the men.

Many research studies have found that lesbian couples have sex less frequently than other couples, especially after the first phase of intense passion is over. The cessation of sex in these couples has sometimes gone by the uncharming name of "lesbian bed death." The women themselves are (understandably) reluctant to say that it's because they are not interested in sex. They do, however, often cite the difficulty of initiating it. They want it to happen "spontaneously," which is perhaps a quaint way of saying that sex should occur without either of them having to make the first move or risk rejection by asking for it. Many researchers have interpreted this to mean that the sticking point with lesbian sex is that no one wants to take on the role of initiating sex, because that it typically a man's role, and there is obviously no man in a lesbian relationship.

Why men initiate sex has been explained in various ways. Sometimes culture and socialized roles have been invoked. There is indeed some socializing in the process, but I suspect it builds on nature. Because men want sex so much more often than women, it will inevitably fall to men to initiate it. They are the first to ask because they want it more. When asking becomes institutionalized, the culture will build on the male tendency to initiate it and define it as a man's job.

The Male Sex Drive Isn't Just for Sex

Men have more desire for sex than seems absolutely needed to perpetuate the species. Why? Is this just nature's surplus, like every oak tree making thousands of acorns? Indeed, wouldn't women have possibly preferred men who weren't pawing them all the time and wanting to have sex twice a day, year in, year out? One could make a case that evolution, with women as agents of selection, would have favored men with less sex drive.

More likely, the male sex drive isn't just for sex. It's to motivate all the heroic and risky behavior that men perform to get sex.

The difference in sex drive stems partly from the hormone testosterone. Men have about ten times as much of this as women. Higher testosterone predicts higher sex drive within either gender. Sometimes people get shots of testosterone to increase their sexual desire.

But testosterone does more than fuel the person's desire for sex. It contributes to an assortment of behaviors—indeed most of the ones we associate, for better or worse, with manliness. Men with high testosterone get into more fights than other men. They take more risks and chances. They compete more readily and harder. They are more restless and more prone to look for novel experiences, including thrills but even just curiosities. Professor Jim Dabbs, whose research on testosterone contributed extensively to the scientific understanding of the psychological effects of that hormone, said that one amusing problem was that the research participants with high testosterone levels did not like to sit still, and when they finished their questionnaire they would get up and wander around the lab, unlike other men. (Women who were given testosterone shots showed similar patterns.)

In other animals, the male sex drive motivates mainly competing for dominance, maybe also some risky sex (trying to screw one of the alpha male's consorts when the alpha male isn't looking). But culture can put this male sexual desperation to multiple uses. Men will do all sorts of things the culture might want, as long as there is promise of sexual rewards. And since women respond to status, culture can deliver the women by according status.

Men clearly have much more sex drive than is absolutely needed to perpetuate the species. Why? Why should nature have created this monster sex drive that leaves so many young men suffering endlessly over unfulfilled cravings?

The answer probably begins with the most underappreciated fact about gender that we saw earlier. Most men who ever lived did not pass on their genes. The reproductive odds are sharply against individual men. To succeed at reproducing, men had to be driven. Partly this meant wanting sex relentlessly, so that they would seize any opportunity. Partly this meant being willing to strive, risk, fight, and achieve in all the difficult and dangerous ways that have often been necessary to make it to the top, where the women will finally smile back.

We are descended from the men who fought their way to the top. They had to outdo other men. The desire for sex was part of what drove them to do that.

Culture and Sex

Thus far the point has been that nature has made the genders unequal on at least one dimension: Men want sex far more than women.

What can culture do with this?

Let us return to what cultures do need, as we saw in the chapter on culture. In general, they want their populations to increase, because the larger group tends to dominate the smaller one, militarily or economically. Sex is useful for making babies, but of course the culture's needs are not met merely by creating pregnancies. Babies have to be fed, cared for, raised, and molded by education and socialization into useful citizens. Inevitably there will be some children whose parents cannot or will not provide for them, and the culture must then take over the responsibility, if those children are to grow up to be useful adults.

So, sex is useful for making babies, but a culture needs to harness sex and surround it with rules so that the babies that come from sex will get what they need in order to become productive citizens.

Culture also needs a fair amount of order. Chaos is bad for culture, and a culture engulfed by chaos will not dominate its rivals or even be much good at resisting their efforts to take over. On this score, sex is potentially dangerous. Sex can disrupt families, set friends against each other, even produce violence and murder. Unregulated sex creates all sorts of social problems: children with no one to care for them, violence, and disease.

Cultures that have property and wealth need to manage how it is transferred from one generation to the next. Sex creates the inheritors, but unrestricted sex can muddy the waters as to who is descended from whom and who should inherit what from whom. In particular, in many societies, men create most of the wealth, but they cannot be certain whether any given child comes from any specific man's sperm. Prior to the recent advent of DNA testing, there was simply no foolproof way at all to ascertain who the father was.

Thus far we have focused on what cultures must do in order to control sex. There are opportunities beyond just regulating sex, however. The male sex drive can potentially be harnessed by the culture to produce more behavior of the sorts that it values.

Essentially, men want sex badly enough that they will do whatever it takes to get it. This affords the culture an opportunity to get the men to produce for the culture. In other words, cultures can potentially use sex as an incentive, to control men. Most cultures value the creation of wealth, for example, and so if wealthy men get more women and more sex than other men, then men will strive to create wealth. Today's United States gets considerable wealth from its entertainment industry. American sports and films and music are purchased and enjoyed throughout the world. One reason men go into those fields is for money, but another is sex, and indeed the sex lives of musicians, film stars, and top athletes are envied by other men. If the culture insisted that athletes must remain celibate, the talent pool would likely be far less.

Money, Women, and Children

As we have seen, cultures benefit by the creation of wealth. And throughout history, most wealth has been created by men.

Culture needs for some of this wealth to be channeled to women and especially directed to support the children that represent its future. Some men naturally are inclined to devote their money to taking care of their children. Others seem not to have this inclination.

Moreover, some men who happily spend money on their children while living with them may cease to want to send money to ex-wives and other partners to spend on children, especially given that the ex-wife is free to spend it on herself or whatever she chooses and so the children may not get any benefit. The moral issues here are complex and I do not intend to take a position on them. We are merely considering the pragmatic concerns that a cultural system needs to solve to ensure that children are supported. The most effective method is to get the fathers to pay for the children. Otherwise, the money has to come from elsewhere, which ultimately means other people, usually other men, must create money that is then spent on those children.

Marriage serves many functions, but one of them undoubtedly is to transfer money from men to women and children.

Sexual Economics

That men want sex more than women is not just an inconvenient fact of life. It becomes a driving force in gender politics and male–female interactions. It creates the basis for a marketplace, in which men compete for women's affections and offer them inducements to interest them in sex.

In many cultures, wealth is mainly created by men. But women need to get a share of it. Wealth buys food, shelter, clothing, and other necessities and luxuries. No culture allows men to keep it all while women starve and freeze. There has to be some mechanism for transferring wealth from men to women.

Wealth is increased by trade and exchange. Many men have made fortunes by means of trade. To move wealth from men to women, some form of exchange would be a helpful mechanism. To be sure, cultures can just require men to give money to women. Many modern societies do this, such as by taxing men and giving money to women. (Women who earn are taxed too, though I believe every society in the world taxes men more than women, if only because men work more and earn more than women.) But this is not easy and it requires a complicated enforcement and distribution system. Direct exchange works much better, because individuals will arrange it themselves.

But what would women have to offer in exchange for male wealth? Especially women who have no job and no marketable skills? The culture must find a system to get money to these women and their childen.

What do women have that men want?

Sex is one answer. I freely acknowledge that this is not a highly romantic or idealized view of how men and women relate to each other. Indeed, the theory I am about to sketch out may be accused of being terminally unromantic. But it is supported by a vast amount of evidence. Also, to avoid misunderstandings, let me say straight out that I am a strong believer in romance and the magic of love and all that. Still and all, alongside those sweet and high-flown sentiments, the pressures of the sexual marketplace do affect the choices people make.

Sexual economics theory is based on the idea that men want sex more than women. As a result of this difference, men find themselves in a weak bargaining position vis-à-vis sex. They may have to offer a woman something more than sex in order to induce her to engage in sex with them. Hence the male desire for sex impels men to ascertain what women want and find ways of giving it to them.

The makings of an exchange, and of a marketplace, are thus there. Both sides (men and women) have something the other wants and want something the other has. The men have material and cultural resources. The women control access to sex.

I am not speaking strictly of the so-called oldest profession of prostitution here. To be sure, prostitution is an explicit trade of money for sex. The fact that it has been found all over the world in widely different cultures and circumstances attests to the near-universal appeal of the bargain. At least, it is something both men and women can understand. The gender roles are remarkably stable. A researcher will have to search long and hard to find any culture in which prostitution is mainly a matter of women paying men for sex. Here and there one can occasionally find a (usually well disguised) example of a woman paying a man for sex, but these are quite rare, and even in those cultures, the reverse is more common.

Rather, we speak here of marriage and other heterosexual relationships throughout the world. We should not here be misled by the ideals of equality in the most modern and progressive societies. In most cultures, and throughout most of our own history, marriage consisted of a deal in which the man provided wealth and other resources, while the woman provided sex and a few other services (e.g., cooking, child care).

It is not usually an exchange of cash for intercourse on a pay-as-you-go basis. Rather, sex commences when the man has committed himself to provide material support over a long period of time. (That's the essence of marriage.) In many cases, the man will have expended resources in advance with no explicit return, such as by paying for dates or expensive gifts.

Even modern, progressive societies are hardly immune. When was the last time you asked a man what his girlfriend gave him for Valentine's Day? And who pays for dates? All women seem to have heard the benchmark that engagement is celebrated by a man giving the woman a ring equivalent to two months' worth of his salary. Why are there no protests from feminists insisting that, for the sake of equality, the woman should give the man a comparably expensive gift?

Whether we speak of prostitution, dating, marriage, or other arrangements, women do not pay for sex. *Because they don't have to.* Women can get sex for nothing. Men usually can't. More precisely, women can easily get all the sex they want. Men cannot get all that they want.

Hence female sexuality has value in the way that male sexuality does not. (Nobody prizes male virginity, for example, whereas in some cultures female virginity is extremely precious and strenuously guarded.) A man who wants to pay off his debts by money earned from getting women to pay him for sex had better have a Plan B ready. Likewise if he wishes to have women offer him career advancement, better grades, preferential treatment, or other goodies in exchange for his having sex with them, he will be disappointed.

Both men and women fantasize about having sex with celebrities, but only women can do it. Women can offer sex to male celebrities, and that offering has sufficient value that sometimes the famous men will accept the offer. Male fans who offer sex to female celebrities will find themselves angrily rebuffed. Male sexuality has no value that can be exchanged for the time and attention of someone famous.

The exchange of money for sex, via marriage and other customs, is one of the foundations of most cultures. One reason for this is that cultures need to transfer money from men to women. Thus, the male sex drive can be recruited by the culture to bring about the transfer of money from men to women.

Divorce laws and practices are revealing. From the perspective of the culture as an abstract system, here is the problem of divorce. Marriage is an effective means of transferring money from men to women. Sex gets men willing to make the deal of getting married in the first place. But when marriages go bad or the wife loses her sexual desire or interest, the man may start to think the deal is no longer good. He wants a new deal with a new partner (and new sex). Yet if he leaves his wife, who will provide for her? In particular, if he leaves her and her children, who will pay in order for them to grow up into healthy, productive citizens who can keep the culture going?

Some cultures have dealt with the problem by prohibiting divorce. This has obvious drawbacks in terms of long-term marital unhappiness, but remember that cultures don't care much whether people are happy. Still, they may rebel if they become too unhappy.

Others have dealt with the problem by permitting polygamy. The man (if he can afford it) can add a new wife to satisfy his sexual wishes, but he continues to provide financial support for his older wife and her children.

Monogamy presents a particular challenge, however. The man may not marry a new wife unless and until he divorces his old one. If both husband and first wife are young and childless and can find new partners, the system can cope with this fairly well. But suppose she cannot easily find a new partner. Perhaps she has lost her sex appeal. Perhaps she has several children, and potential new husbands do not want to take them on. Perhaps there are not enough available men to go around, especially in her age group.

The solution most modern cultures reach is to require the man to continue shipping wealth to his former wife (and her children), even after he divorces her. This can work almost as well as polygamy, insofar as the man's earnings go to support both the new and the old wife. He simply loses most of his rights as husband with the former wife.

Even in supposedly enlightened and gender-egalitarian societies, alimony and child support remain primarily something that men pay to women, far more than the reverse. My point is not to bemoan the unfairness. My point is simply that this practice shows the pragmatic operation of the cultural system. Marriage is for transferring money from men to women, and it is useful for the culture to ensure that this continues even after divorce. Only if the woman is fully able to provide for herself and her children can the culture let the ex-husband off the hook. (Even then it does not always do so.)

Modern societies extol the power and value of love. Songs, films, books, and other sources repeat endlessly the theme that love will last forever. This is itself somewhat odd because most research shows that the passionate, romantic form of love is at best a temporary phase that is likely to subside in a matter of months or at best a couple years.

The fiction of everlasting love is important, though. The cultural system functions best if people marry and stay married. If a man realized that his feelings for this particular woman, suffused with sexual desire, will likely subside before long, he might balk at signing the long-term commitment to share his earnings with her forever. The culture promotes the belief that love will burn strongly and passionately for the rest of your life, in order to get men to agree. When he makes the deal, he is high on love, and sharing his earnings for life seems a reasonable price to pay for having this wonderful feeling (plus great sex) forever. He does not realize that his commitment to pay will likely last far longer than the elation of passionate love.

This has proven to be a highly effective system for many cultures. Too bad for the men who realize, upon coming down off their passionate high, that they have made a very costly deal.

Reluctance to Commit

Trends in recent years have seen people marrying later and later. Men who reached maturity in the 1950s and early 1960s typically married in their early twenties. Now, the late twenties or early thirties is more common. More men resist marriage for a long time, in some cases forever. This pattern of postponing marriage has given rise to a stereotype of modern men as afraid to make the commitment to marriage. On talk shows, advice columns, and other female-dominated media, the complaint that men are reluctant or afraid to commit will be heard over and over. Thus, we have yet another bad thing to think about men: Supposedly they are afraid of a healthy, loving relationship.

The discourse about whether to get married, sooner versus later, is dominated by females and therefore sees things through their eyes. The male attitudes are distorted.

Assume, for the sake of argument, that there is some truth to the behavioral pattern: that men are in fact reluctant to commit. The women will label this as fear of commitment. It is treated as a character flaw common to men.

One could just as well look at it all differently. I suspect the men-are-flawed view is biased and possibly unfair. The alternate could also be characterized as biased and possibly unfair, which makes them equal.

The alternate view is that women are trying to hustle men to do something against their best interests. The men sense at some point they are being taken advantage of. They prefer to slow down and wait. The male reluctance to commit could be a rational response and a reluctance to be exploited.

After all, do the talking heads and other purveyors of cultural wisdom complain about women waiting a bit longer to have sex? When it is a matter of getting into bed, the men are in more of a hurry than the women. But it makes rational sense for the women to slow things down. The reverse is true with making a lifetime commitment centered on the man's financial earnings. Now she tends to be in a hurry and he wants to slow things down. This makes rational sense too.

The issue is whether to rush ahead and marry now, or leave this till later. There is no question which gender has more reason to hurry. Getting married early is more urgent for women than for men. This is not just a reflection of the so-called biological clock, though that is undeniably a factor. Many women think they need to have their babies before the age of 30 or 35, while men can father children for several decades beyond that.

Above and beyond that, though, there are other reasons for women to be in more of a hurry than men to get married. Sexual economics theory depicts many romantic pairings as exchanges in which the man brings money and other resources, while the woman contributes sex. Her sexual desirability is based partly on her looks. These resources change over time in a way that is not kind to women. If a man and a woman wait five years, as compared to marrying now, things likely change in different directions. His salary and bank account are likely to increase over those years. Her face and body may lose some of their bloom. Hence when they revisit the marriage market, his appeal and his options will have increased, while hers have decreased.

The deal he can get will improve over time; the deal she can get will get worse over time. I sympathize with her predicament, but that's not our concern here. It's whether his reluctance to get married right away reflects some character flaw in him or simply a very sensible, rational strategy. He has no hurry.

Again, this is the mirror image of the decision whether to have sex. Women can always stand to wait a bit longer to let the man prove his commitment more strongly, before getting into bed. He is the one in a hurry to have sex. Her reluctance is understandable, and for same reasons (fear of being exploited, or simple rational assessment that she doesn't lose out on much by waiting).

Many of us men were told when young that yes, it will seem for a long time that the dating game is against you, and the woman has all the power and advantage, but at some point that will switch over. We doubted this was true, and even if it would be, the time of our advantage seemed impossibly remote. But it is correct nonetheless. The young woman holds all the cards over the young man, but by age 30 if not earlier, the man has more cards, and on average the woman is increasingly anxious to close the deal. This is all based on rational calculation of one's appeal in the mating market and how to get the best deal. Other considerations certainly operate. Still, the calculation of rational advantage has a way of bringing people around, to some extent at least.

All the talk of men's fear of commitment can thus be seen in another light. It is a bit like a marketplace in which all the sellers are urging the buyers to buy now, hurry, sign right now! The sellers know the prices will be dropping severely next week. So of course they want to sell as soon as possible. The buyers do not know quite what the hurry is. In reality there is no hurry as far as their prospects are concerned. Sellers point out that some sales have been made, some properties thus off the market, and they imply that if you do not buy quickly, you will miss out. Some of the buyers heed the warnings and buy rapidly. But it is the sellers who have to hurry. The buyers can wait till next week, when the sellers who have not yet sold will be cutting their prices, and new sellers will be entering the market. The buyers themselves may even be better off next week, because they will have more money.

Understood in this way, what does the culture want? It is probably not best for the culture to let the men understand that things will go their way in time. In many cultures, the men create much of the wealth, and the culture needs significant chunks of it to be transferred to the women, partly for raising children. It is fine for the culture if the men marry early and start supporting families. If the men marry late, there may be fewer families, and the size of the next generation could be smaller. Hence the interests of the culture are in this case mostly aligned with the goals of the women.

The culture and the women need to work together to take advantage of the men when they are most vulnerable, namely when they are at the height of passionate love. They need to maintain the men's illusion that this love they have is precious and will last forever if they are willing to make a permanent financial commitment. Likewise, they should sustain his illusion that this one woman is his soul-mate and that if he loses her by failing to offer marriage in a suitably manly manner, she will go off and marry someone else, and he will have lost his best and perhaps only chance at happiness.

The Imaginary Feminist, and plenty of non-imaginary ones (e.g., *Smart Women Marry Money* by Ford and Drake), have said that the social myths of romance and love are aimed at deceiving and exploiting women. Maybe. But perhaps they are aimed at exploiting and deceiving men. It is men who must be induced to fall prey to romantic mythology, so that they will enter into marriage, where their money can be tapped to support a woman and her children for a very long time, regardless of how their relationship to that particular woman unfolds.

The Impossible Promise

In bygone eras, only a few lucky people could marry. In the modern world, most people marry. At their weddings, most people promise to be faithful. That means they promise never to have sex with anybody else, ever.

Is that a reasonable promise? People are frequently shocked and hurt to find that their spouses have had sex with someone else after all. I used the word "frequently" on purpose: It happens fairly often. So often, in fact, that one has to question whether all those people should have made that promise of fidelity in the first place.

Actually, the frequency can be argued either way. According to the best available data, in an average year, well over 90% of husbands remain completely faithful to their wives. In that sense, adultery is rare. Then again, if you aggregate across all the years, something approaching half of all husbands will eventually have sex with someone other than their wives. Husbands avoid or resist many temptations, but eventually many of them do succumb to one, perhaps more. The glass is most full but partly empty, and it is empty enough to make the promise of total, permanent, complete fidelity dubious if not absurd.

The marriage institution in Western culture was developed during earlier eras, when life expectancies were considerably shorter. Most marriages lasted fifteen to twenty years, a long time to be sure, but nothing like what is possible today. When two twenty-five-year-olds promise to be true "till death do us part" (admittedly, euphemisms are popular, given that people are skittish about saying the word "death" aloud at a wedding), given the strong chance that both will live till at least eighty, they are making a sixty-five-year commitment. Whoa. What person in his or her right mind would make any sort of binding sixty-five-year promise? Not that people in the throes of passionate love are "in their right mind!" Culture takes advantage of the craziness of passionate love to sign people up for permanent family commitments. It's a bit like getting a tattoo when you're really drunk.

At least it's fair. Husband and wife make the same promise.

But wait: it's only fair if all else is equal. And in sex, all else is decidedly not equal.

As we have seen, men and women have serious differences in their desires for sex. It is much harder for men than for women to keep almost any known promise of sexual abstinence. Remember the priests and nuns: There is a single standard for both, and both make their heartfelt vows based on the sincere and earnest faith in their God. Both mean it. But by any measure, the men are far less able to keep such a promise than the women.

This is the first thing to realize about these wedding vows. If he promises lifelong sexual fidelity to his wife, in effect he is making a promise that he may find much harder to keep than she will.

So what happens? What ought to happen?

Nature plays a dirty trick on men here. Culture compounds it. Men may be fooled into making the promise of eternal sexual fidelity. They marry an illusion. Women in love do typically have high rates of sexual desire. When she wants the man to make the promise, the woman actually changes, not in a sneaky or manipulative way, but rather because her own feelings sweep into stronger sexual desires and responses than she is ever likely to have again. Many a man thinks he has found his sexual soul-mate, whose desires match his. But when the romantic passion wears off after a year or two, they revert to their quite different baselines. Most husbands discover that their wives want sex far less than they themselves do.

The woman is likely fooled also. She knows her future husband wants sex with her often, but she likes this and thinks it suits her. Then her feelings subside and she finds herself stuck with a partner who is pressing her for more sex than she wants to have. In some times and places, women have simply accepted that providing her man with sex was part of her duty as a wife. Nowadays, however, she is far less likely to think this way.

The Imaginary Feminist tells women that they should not have sex unless they really desire it. This includes in marriage. A husband is therefore expected to wait until his wife wants sex. This is the proper, gentlemanly thing to do.

Unfortunately, in practice it means that year in, year out, if he wants sex four times a week and she wants it twice a month, he will spend most of his adult life in a state of unsatisfied sexual longing. His feelings, wishes, and desires don't count. He has unwittingly agreed to this. But he still can't help having those feelings and wishes and desires.

If children come, the problem typically gets worse. Many women report that their sexual desires diminish greatly after childbirth. The mother is focused on her children. She may be tired from getting up at night to care for them and from not sleeping enough in general. She may find that spending the day cleaning up spilled milk and changing diapers is slightly gross and unpleasant and therefore not conducive to wanting sex with her husband that evening. She may feel that her children's clinging and pawing her body all day makes her want to spend her quiet evening time with no one touching her.

Regardless of the cause, the pattern is common. Nearly all studies show that husbands want sex more than wives. Remember the study we cited earlier in which long-married couples were asked what was the ideal amount of sex in marriage and how much sex they had. Wives gave about the same answer for both questions. For them, their own marriages had achieved just about the optimal balance, the right amount of sex. Their husbands, however, reported wanting twice as much sex as they were getting. Thus, husbands are mostly respecting the new feminist ideal that the man should wait until his wife is ready. She's just not ready very often.

Another study tallied up the sexual problems of couples in marital therapy. Many had arguments about sex. In general, these arguments boiled down to the man wanting something more than the wife, either more total sex, or more varieties of sex. This pattern was not just a simple majority: it fit *all* the cases. The opposite, of a wife wanting sex more than the husband, did not show up at all in this sample. I'm sure there must be some cases somewhere, but they are quite rare. In general, marital arguments about sex reflect the husband wanting more than the wife.

The married man has thus put himself in a bind. He promised to refrain from sex with anyone else but his wife. And now she doesn't want him, at least not very often.

Let us consider another possibility. Suppose his desire for her diminishes. Many women gain weight as they get older. Does the bridegroom realize that he is promising never to have sex with anyone but her, even if she were to double her weight and become unappealing to him?

In recent weeks the advice column in my local newspaper has had a series of letters from readers about prenuptial agreements that include specifications about weight control. The columnists, a pair of women, were predictably indignant about such a legalistic requirement. They thought that trying to control someone's weight is a ridiculous thing in a marriage. In fact, they seemed skeptical of prenuptial agreements generally.

Such views are understandable from women. And perhaps it *is* unreasonable to divorce somebody because he or she put on weight. Then again, people are allowed, even expected to divorce partners based on having sex with someone else. If the two are related, why is one the norm and the other unreasonable?

The fashion industry and mass media emphasize the ideal of slim women as sexually attractive. Countless pages have been written about how difficult and tragic this is for ordinary women, who cannot live up to those ideals and therefore must feel bad. I have not seen many pages devoted to sympathy for the husbands of those women. But the media's ideals of thinness affect men too. The men see those same commercials with the attractive models. That makes it harder for them to desire their own sagging, thickening wives. You think men don't notice or don't mind?

Weight is not the only culprit, of course. Very few women look better at thirty-five or forty-five than they did at twenty-five. Most lose some degree of sex appeal. The bridegroom looks at his bride, all lovely and slender in her white dress, and he feels a surge of desire. He is thus able to make the promise that she is the one for him, for now and forever. He should look at the older women in the group, perhaps her older female relatives, or indeed middle-aged women in general. Not just the pounds, but the wrinkles, the downward drift of loosening flesh, the other inevitable parts of aging.

Aging must be accepted, of course, especially if marriage is to survive. The problem is that sex must be accepted too, somehow. The bridegroom may promise to desire only his wife, but this is an unrealistic promise. Both parts are difficult. It may be difficult to continue desiring her, and it is surely difficult to avoid desiring anyone else.

One stereotype of forty-something married men is that they go through a midlife crisis and either buy a fancy car or have an affair with a beautiful young woman. The conventional wisdom is that this reflects man's insecurity and immaturity. He cannot accept getting older, so he does these silly things.

Maybe they are silly and immature. But these are culturally loaded value judgments. If we were to say, simply, that at some point many a married man acts on his sexual desires for other women, it would not seem surprising.

Another problem comes from the modern practice of expecting the father be present at childbirth. How much these husbands help the process is debatable, and if they make it better for the mother, there is certainly benefit. On the other hand, I've heard multiple men say that the experience was so thoroughly disgusting at a visceral level that it produced long-term changes in their ability to feel sexual desire for their wives. As one man told me, "The thought of having oral sex with your wife after you've seen that (her give birth) is just out of the question." Even television sitcoms have begun to make jokes about the reduced scope of desire for a wife after seeing the placenta.

Disgust is a powerful antidote to sexual desire. When I reviewed the empirical literature on rape, I found multiple stories about women who successfully prevented themselves from being raped by vomiting on the attacker. I recall one woman who said that the man hit her, and she vomited, and he stopped fighting, looked down at the puke, and just ran away. If you want to prevent sex, disgust really works well. Unfortunately it works on helpful fathers too.

In many of these cases, of course, a husband may continue to love his wife and be devoted to her. She may make a fine wife and a good mother to his children. He does not want to leave her. But he may have lost his sexual desire for her.

And losing his desire for her does not mean that he loses all interest in sex. This is the tragic part. He is still a man, with a man's desires. He wants sex. Just not with her. He cannot will himself to desire her.

What should he do?

Moralists (though few sex researchers) may be surprised that many men eventually have sex with someone other than their wives. They "cheat," to use the popular but strongly evaluative term. Society condemns these men, even though many surveys have found that half the married men have already engaged in sex with someone other than their spouse, and more will do so. Some experts are surprised that the rates are not higher yet. Indeed they may be: some men who have sex on the side decline to say so on surveys.

Men will get no sympathy from women on this. Most women cannot imagine how much men want sex, as I have already said earlier in this chapter. One can try to make an analogy. Tell a woman that she is allowed to see her children only three times a month, for 10 minutes each. Most people would see that as cruel. Indeed, such a heartrending thought is partly why the courts let divorcing women have their children, regardless of what the father wants or feels. But people refuse to see the parallel to the similar and endless sexual deprivation that is the lot of many married men.

What does the future hold in this regard? This problem is one that I anticipate will become quite intensely worse. For one thing, opportunities for extramarital sex are on the rise, as typically both spouses work and travel on business, and are thus away from their partners and encountering potential new partners.

Personality changes are likewise not conducive to fidelity. Young people today are raised, in America at least, with support for self-esteem, with the result that they become more narcissistic than ever. That means they are taught to be oriented toward their own means, selfish, feeling entitled to have what they want. Meanwhile, discipline is out of fashion, and self-control is probably weaker than in the past. Hence even if all else were equal, today's young men would be (even) less likely than previous generations to be able or willing to put aside their own sexual feelings and desires for the sake of marital stability.

To make matters more difficult, premarital sex has now become the norm, and for a gradually lengthening period of time. Take a young man who started having sex at perhaps age 16 and who has gone for ten to fifteen years having a series of exciting sexual liaisons with a variety of women, some of whom he hardly knew. Then convince him to settle down and promise to have sex with only one woman for the next sixty years. Then let that woman grow older, plumper, less attractive, and let her sexual desires wane significantly while his desires remain close to what they were. Last, surround him at work and in his other activities with attractive younger women, some of whom are willing to have sex with him now and then. That will be the norm in the foreseeable future. What do you predict?

I see two directions that society is likely to change. One is that marital stability will decline further. Husbands will have more affairs, wives will kick them out, and more children will grow up without seeing their fathers. Alternatively, some new methods will emerge to accommodate male sexuality in marriage so that husbands can stay with their wives for the long haul without living in chronic sexual deprivation.

My thought is just that a man should not promise something that he cannot be sure he can deliver. Everything conspires to make the young man promise eternal sexual fidelity. Masses of evidence show that relatively few men can actually deliver on such a promise. When contemplating marriage, the young man should perhaps refrain from self-deception and honestly ask himself what he is going to do in twenty or indeed ten or perhaps even five years, when his wife no longer wants sex with him more than once a month, or when he no longer desires her (but still wants sex). Is the only solution to divorce her, at a huge financial cost, and start over with another, younger woman?

CHAPTER 11

What Else, What Next?

THIS BOOK STARTED WITH THE QUESTION of whether there was anything good about men. It soon moved into the related question of what men are good for, especially from the perspective of a large, cultural system that competes against other systems. We have seen plenty of answers. They are not the entire story, but they are a big part of it.

I have repeatedly argued against views that set up men against women, as if the two genders were rivals or enemies. David Buss, the pioneering thinker who has influenced me in many ways, even objects to the term "opposite sex," because men and women are not opposites. "Complementary sex" would be a better phrase. Men and women are different, but the differences are there for valid reasons, and both genders are better off because of them.

I have resisted attempts to depict one gender as better than the other. Arguments that one gender is better off than the other are equally dubious, despite all we have heard to the contrary. Here and there, to be sure, the disadvantages associated with gender are overwhelming. On the *Titanic*, for example, being a man was such a huge disadvantage that no amount of wealth, status, or male privilege would offset it. But that same year, if a student wished to study at Harvard or Princeton, being a female would have ruled out her chances.

Nonetheless, we do have to acknowledge that culture has in general placed more value on men and the things men do than on women and their contributions. Some modern Western societies seem hell-bent on leaning over backwards to create the opposite bias in favor of women, but in the long run, the cultural bias in favor of men seems unlikely to disappear entirely. Culture has been largely created by men, and it relies on the large-group activities, elaborate systems, and large networks of relationships that men favor more than women. To be sure, part of what makes culture value men is that it regards men as expendable, and so many individual men will find themselves ill used by the culture. As the opening chapter of this book explained, there are more men than women at both the top and the bottom of society. Don't expect that to change.

One can think of the maleness of culture as balanced against the femaleness of nature: Mother Nature meets Father Culture. As we have seen, nature favors females in many ways. Throughout human history (and prehistory) and a long way further back in evolutionary history, females have faced much better reproductive odds than males. Yes, the fortunate few males enjoy privileges and successes beyond what most females can attain, but the majority of males face a rough life of hard competition against long odds and, ultimately, biological failure.

Nature favors women in other ways. Women can have more orgasms than men, though not all women are able to take advantage of this. Women live longer than men these days, though possibly this is a result of cultural developments that have increased the stress on men. Now that high-powered, high-stress careers are open to women, it will be revealing to see whether these women live longer than their male peers. Probably the stress will have some impact, but it may not entirely erase the difference. For the present, the bottom line is that women live longer than men, and that is a biological victory no matter how you spin it.

Undoubtedly some of the longevity enjoyed by today's women is a result of the scientific work by men, instituting medical advances and public health improvements, not least including the improvements in the rates of surviving childbirth. It would be nice if women, collectively, could do something equally beneficial for men, something that would extend men's lives, but don't bet on it. Women do not work together in large groups or networks very much, and certainly not for the benefit of men. But countless individual women have done much to make the lives of individual men better, happier, and probably longer and safer too. That's how women work, at the individual, one-on-one level. That is one of the wonderful things about women. It's also one of the reasons they have always been at best junior partners in large cultural systems.

To be sure, nature does not favor all women, nor does culture favor all men. Indeed, as we have seen, cultures use plenty of men in ruthless and destructive ways. Both nature and culture view men as more expendable than women. Men go to extremes, not just in terms of natural endowments but also in terms of cultural activities. More men than women create vast fortunes, but more men also end up in prison or executed. Still, in general and on average, cultures place somewhat more value on men's than on women's activities, while nature allows more women than men to survive and reproduce.

A World Without Men?

At the start of the book I mentioned the recent fad of books and articles asking whether men could be dispensed with entirely. Some of these are little more than vehicles for the authors to vent their antimale prejudices. As such, we can expect them to continue: Nobody is censuring female bigots yet. A feminist colleague recently showed me a book of feminist cartoons, most of which had no humor but merely bitterness, but the last one in the book did have an amusing caption. It read as follows: "Imagine a world without men—no crime, and a lot of fat, happy women."

Ha, right. These days the world is filling up, but up until recently there was always plenty of empty space. If women really would have been happier without men, they would have moved into some of those open areas and set up shop there. They could have created the wonderful utopia envisioned in that cartoon and in the other books and articles that muse on how perfectly lovely life would be without men. They haven't. That should be enough to discredit those ideas. In terms of how women vote with their feet, the historical record is overwhelming. Women stick around men.

I recently attended a university discussion on the future of the world. Some women stood up to proclaim that if women ran the world, there would be no war. Probably that is an overstatement. Still, it seems quite fair and reasonable to speculate that if women were in charge everywhere, there would be less war and less violence generally. This is the utopian fantasy of the Imaginary Feminist.

But there would be less of other things too. Look at what men have created and women have not. If you want to imagine a world without men, you have to subtract more than violence. Subtract electricity, computers, cars.

Subtract universities. Subtract flush toilets. Subtract hospitals and all the medical knowledge men have created. And on and on. No wonder women stay near men.

We saw that according to U.S. Government statistics, men are responsible for well over 90% of the patents that introduce new products to our society. They also make up more than 90% of all the people killed on the job. Until these ostensible hordes of happy women are ready to risk their lives in dangerous jobs and to devote years of their lives working long hours to pursuing novel ideas that may or may not lead to innovations, we all need to count on men to do these things.

Men contribute in other, perhaps less important ways. A recent summary of research on laughter found that all over the world, men make jokes more than women do, and women laugh more than men. There has been a recent upsurge in female comediennes, but many of them rely on making jokes about men. A world without men would have much less laughter.

Music, too. Like laughter, music appeals to women but is created mostly by men. Women can play the music that men write, using the instruments that men invented and built. But in a world without men, there would probably be only a few songs.

Probably the single biggest thing that would be missing, or mostly missing, in a world without men is progress. That is ultimately why the women's sphere fell behind the men's sphere over and over, all around the world, even though the two spheres started off as prehistoric equals. Progress depends on the things men do: compete, take chances, innovate, develop, build large. My guess is that if it is ever possible to test what happened to matriarchal and female-dominated societies in world history, it would be that they started off doing fine but then fell behind rival cultures because of their lack of progress.

In general, the idea of a world without men is a silly and pointless exercise. Both men and women prefer to live in worlds where they have some contact with the other gender. As just one of many signs, single-sex universities are rapidly dwindling and closing. The male-only colleges were mostly wiped out by government edict, but even before that they were declining in popularity. Female-only colleges have been permitted to continue existing, but they attract fewer and fewer students. More broadly, women have hardly ever created any sort of major cultural system that was viable.

Men have made a few male-only cultures, sometimes by necessity because the risks and hardships discouraged women from being there, but in the long run the men there too wanted women around. Not only did men try to get women to join them as soon as they could. Men also invented monogamy, as a way of making sure that there is a woman for every man. That's another sign that men don't really want to live without women.

Yet one more way for a social scientist to consider life without men is to look at individual households (rather than search for those elusive female-only communities). Lately our society has found it fashionable to promote female-headed households. In general, though, these do not live as well as households with men. True, there are plenty of exceptions, particularly highly successful single career women. But on the whole, a household without a man is poorer and worse off than one with a man. As we have seen, many women, especially young mothers, prefer not to work at a job. Many married women can do this, but the single ones usually need to be subsidized by the government or another source. The official, politically correct line that children can grow up just as well without a father as with one has increasingly been exposed as a harmful fiction. Fatherless children do not thrive as well as children with fathers, on average. Lesbian couples tend to be poorer than gay male couples. Thus in all these ways, when women live without men, they do not live as well.

Let us therefore set aside these pseudo-utopian single-gender ideas and get real. Men and women want each other around. And for good reasons: Social groups are more likely to flourish if they have cultural systems that can benefit from the activities of both genders.

Men as Symbols

I put "What else?" in the title of this chapter for a specific reason. The preceding chapters focused on several ways that culture finds men useful. But these were not all a complete list.

Yet another way that culture uses men more frequently than women is for symbolism. Cultures have values, and they hold up individual persons or events to express those symbols. Doing that is probably an effective way to help the culture succeed, not least because it reminds everyone what the culture values as right and good.

Being used as a symbol can be good or bad. For the individual who happens to be used as a symbol, the result may be an intensification of what would have happened otherwise. It amounts to being pushed to the extreme. And, as we have seen, cultures push men to the extremes more than women, partly because men lend themselves to extremities.

Becoming a symbol can help put a man into the presidential office— or into prison. Some men who became symbols have experienced both extremes. Nelson Mandela was imprisoned by his culture for a quarter of a century, after which he was released and elected president. He was a huge symbol. Saddam Hussein likewise hit both extremes, but in the opposite order. He ruled Iraq for several decades, after which his society put him in prison and then hanged him.

The role of symbolism was well illustrated by the career of Oliver Cromwell. He was a general in the English civil war, on the winning side. After his victory, he had a hand in having the king put to death, which is of course powerful symbolism. Cromwell resisted offers to become king himself, but he accepted the title of Lord Protector over a king-less country. He retained that position until his death, whereupon he was buried with honors that resembled those of the kings of yore. After he died, however, his republican government crumbled. The royalists returned to power and invited the dead king's son to return and ascend the throne, thus restoring the monarchy.

The new king ordered Cromwell's corpse to be dug up. First he had it subjectd to a public hanging for the better part of a day, so anyone could see its desecration and humiliation. Then its head was chopped off as public spectacle.

What's the point of chopping off a corpse's head? Cromwell had been dead for a couple of years already. Pragmatically, he suffered nothing from this punishment. But the symbolic point was important. The king and his minions showed the country that beheading was the proper punishment for a traitor and regicide, even if it came a bit late. Let the young lads be warned. The punishment was aimed at the future as much as the past.

Political careers turn on symbols. Minor offenses can be forgiven and forgotten—or can become symbols that snowball into career-wrecking events. Two American presidencies in recent memory were severely affected by the men's misdeeds that seem quite trivial in comparison with what countless rulers throughout history have done. The first, Watergate, involved a bungled and futile burglary by some of Nixon's underlings in a pointless attempt to gain information about the opposition in an election that was already going Nixon's way. Nixon won the election by a landslide, without any help from the silly burglary. Yet the revelation of this crime and his attempts to cover it up destroyed his credibility and led to his resignation. The second was Clinton's brief sexual affair with a member of his staff, spread over about a dozen encounters, most of which did not even include full sexual intercourse. The scandal (again including his attempt to cover it up) led to impeachment, which was unsuccessful, but after which he was never again a fully effective president.

We have become accustomed to such scandals involving the symbolic sacrifice of men. What about women? A revealing case occurred in Great Britain while I was researching this book. It involved the culture secretary Tessa Jowell. Her husband had been involved in several shady deals, and he was involved in some investments that may have profited from her ministerial position. She had covered up, or at least neglected to disclose in accordance with legal obligations, some conflicts of interest and some deals that had benefited her. The escalating revelations filled the news for weeks. Most seasoned pundits recognized this as a familiar story that would end, inevitably, with her resignation: "the ritual dance that ends with the offering up of the minister's head to propitiate the capricious media gods," as one news magazine put it. The ritual dance, or the script, was familiar from many previous instances—but those all featured men as the symbolic sacrifice.

And then things took a peculiar turn. The *Daily Mail* ran a front-page story asking, "How much more can Tessa take?" Abruptly, instead of a scandalous wrongdoer, she was seen as a woman in distress, a victim of harsh and possibly unfair treatment. Using her first name evoked sympathy. The colleagues calling for her resignation stepped back, and several others spoke out in her defense.

This was not a matter of new information that reduced her guilt. Rather, it was a shift in sympathy and sensitivity. Nobody wanted to be seen as picking on the poor woman. She kept her job and was even rewarded with a new post, in charge of reducing the pay differential between men and women.

It is hard to escape the impression that had Tessa been a man, her career would have been over. She had done wrong and covered it up, and the media had found her out. This process—again, the "ritual dance"—was something that has been repeated over and over. The difference was that when the media monster got a woman rather than a man in its claws, it lost the stomach for the endgame and instead discovered that the person whose life and career were being destroyed was, after all, a human being.

This case is not alone. In *The Myth of Male Power*, Warren Farrell noted the parallels and contrasts between two major news events that occurred while he was preparing his book. In one, the (male) captain of the *Exxon Valdez* made a mistake that caused an oil spill. The man's name was revealed to the world and was made the butt of jokes on the *Tonight Show*. His reputation was destroyed and his career was ruined. He was put on trial, fined, and imprisoned. There was no sympathy for him, despite the fact that the accident had occurred following a last-minute schedule change that had required him and his crew to continue working past the point of exhaustion.

In the other story, a female air traffic controller made a mistake that caused an airplane crash. This time the deaths were human, not wildlife as in the *Exxon Valdez* case, and they ran to several dozen. Her colleagues spirited her away to a hotel to protect her from the media. Her name was never revealed. Instead of trial and imprisonment, she was given therapy, paid for by her employer and thus, ultimately, by taxpayers.

As I was researching this book, in fact, there were two local events. In one, a teacher at my daughter's school was investigated for something, and some downloaded pictures of nude children were found on his home computer. This ran afoul of the child pornography laws. The man's career was ended and he was sentenced to fifteen years in federal prison—very hard time. Yes, of course we need to protect children from sexual abuse, but he had never abused any children. In fact he had taught for many years in an exemplary fashion, inspiring many children, including my daughter, to become scientists.

Meanwhile, at a nearby school, a woman was found to be having a sexual affair with one of the boys at her school. She spent about a month in the local jail, a low-key affair, and was sentenced to probation. That's all. And remember, she actually had engaged in sex with children, unlike the man, who had merely owned some pictures.

One can see these examples as illustrating bias against men. Instead, however, I want to use them to suggest that women tend to be treated more as real people instead of symbols. Our culture, like many others, has few scruples about ruining or ending a man's life to make a symbolic point. Somehow women do not lend themselves to symbolism as easily.

Feature-length obituaries are more frequently written about men than about women. Such articles, discussing the meaning of a recently ended life, do little for the person featured in them, because the person is dead, but they help the culture appreciate the symbolic significance of the person's life.

In his book, *Manliness*, Harvey Mansfield, a noted Harvard professor, concluded that men are more likely than women to stand for something. Manliness to him meant in part taking some broader symbolic meaning onto oneself. Men, with their orientation toward broad systems, are perhaps more prone than women to lend their identities and lives to such symbolic usages.

Is it good to be a symbol? The examples I have given should suffice to show that it can be good, bad, or indifferent. Becoming a symbol can make or break you. After you are dead, becoming a symbol has no pragmatic impact on you. It is something the culture does for the sake of the system and for those who remain alive, something aimed at the future.

For better and for worse, culture uses men as symbols more than it uses women. This is thus another thing that, apparently, men are especially good for.

Building Big

One of the major obituaries of 2007 marked the death of the fashion designer Liz Claiborne. Her accomplishments were impressive. Among them was the fact that her company, Liz Claiborne, Inc., was the first firm ever founded by a woman to be included in the Fortune 500 list of most successful firms in the United States (based on how much money it made). It broke into the list in 1986 and was still there, at number 440, when she died. Claiborne herself was also the first woman to be CEO of a Fortune 500 company.

As the obituaries sometimes celebrated, Claiborne's success proved that a woman can indeed achieve success in business at the highest levels. Anyone who founds a company and builds it up into the Fortune 500 deserves to be recognized as a huge success, and she was.

Yet her success can be viewed another way. If women can achieve at that level, why don't they do so more often? Oppression, says the Imaginary Feminist, but that argument seems weak. Does anyone seriously imagine that customers in stores refuse to buy products because they were manufactured by companies founded by women? It is somewhat embarrassing to report that no company founded by a woman had made it to the Fortune 500 until 1986.

As we have seen, the difference has less to do with discrimination or "glass ceilings" or other barriers than with the ambitions and efforts of women themselves. Women found plenty of businesses, indeed more than men. But women do not turn these into large, successful companies.

For present purposes, the point is that the culture needs men to do this. A modern culture depends for its lifeblood, or part of it, on large corporations and other large institutions (e.g., universities, banks). Few women will create these, even given various advantages and encouragements. No doubt there are several reasons for this, but I have suggested that the most telling reason is that women are more interested in close, one-to-one relationships than in giant systems and large social groups.

Thus, the culture really needs men to create its large social structures. Here and there, a remarkable woman such as Liz Claiborne will have both the ability and the drive (and probably a few other ingredients) to accomplish this. In general, though, this is men's work. For the foreseeable future, the culture will depend on men to build these organizations.

Men Supporting Women

One theme of this book is that nearly all cultures have recognized the need to transfer wealth from men to women. Like it or not, the creation of wealth has been mainly the job of men, whether by engaging in trade, building up a business, creating new knowledge and products, or whatever.

It is open to debate how much our own society's future needs to keep relying on men for this. On the one hand, women are now much more active in business and research than ever before, and so much of the work that goes into building wealth comes from women. On the other hand, as we have seen, the bigger and riskier leaps that do the most for creating wealth are still taken far more by men than women. Men earn the vast majority of patents and scientific prizes for major innovations, despite policy efforts designed to bring women along quickly and thus effectively overvaluing women's work. Men still start and build most of the big corporations, even though women start and operate plenty of small businesses.

Moreover, as we have seen, men earn more money than women, and that is not going to change in the foreseeable future. Even if we were to adopt radical measures to erase the pay gap in the workplace (see below for one suggestion), there would still be plenty of women who choose to spend their days with their children, and they will not themselves earn enough money to support themselves. They need to get money from somewhere, and presumably from men, regardless of whether these men be current or former husbands or high-earning taxpayers.

Thus, one could argue either way whether future policy should be based on the assumption that men create most of the wealth and so society needs to redistribute it to women. What is probably less debatable is the greater number of women needing financial support. From the perspective of the culture, someone has to pay for the expenses of raising children who will form the next generation and sustain the culture's very existence. When we look at the category of parents who do not earn enough to provide for their children, this category is likely to remain predominantly female.

Moreover, even if we decide to let individuals go their ways and present the bill for underfunded children to the taxpayer, this again will mean transferring money from men to women. In the United States, a few taxpayers carry most of the load. A recent report calculated that out of all the income tax money the government gets each year, 40% comes from just 1% (!) of the people who file income tax returns. And who are those people? Although I have not found a breakdown of the American taxpayers by gender, a recent Australian report was revealing. Australian tax laws ask companies to list their five highest-paid employees. A survey of these found that—you guessed it—they are mostly men. Across all firms, 89% of the top earners were men, and if one focuses only on the biggest and richest companies, then 93% of top earners were men.

Thus, any tax on the top money-makers in such a society will mainly take money from men.

I'm not saying we need to feel sorry for these men. Few of them will be reduced to living in a one-room shack on diet soda and peanut butter.

To be sure, if they are working 60 hours a week to make money that is mostly spent by ex-wives and tax collectors, they may feel justified in a bit of self-pity now and then.

The point is simply that, issues of justice and fairness aside, the cultural system will look on these men as important sources of money. In Chapter 9, I quoted Steve Nock's formulation that being a man means producing more than you consume. Among these top producers, the culture is likely to find a way to get its hands on large chunks of that surplus—and to make sure that some of it is quickly shifted to various women.

The bottom line is that moving money from men to women is going to remain a goal of the culture. Marriage is one of the most efficient means of doing this, and so it is in the culture's interest to encourage marriage. The recent trend toward marrying later is not necessarily a problem, as long as the men do eventually marry. But it contains risks. Older men have more money and perhaps more sense than younger men, and so they may be more likely to wed only with carefully arranged prenuptial agreements that allow them to take much of their wealth with them in the event of divorce. The culture's best interest is to discourage that practice. After all, from the perspective of the cultural system, divorcing parents present the problem of how money is to be found to provide for the children. Often the woman has poor skills or qualifications (relative to those of her departing husband) or indeed simply does not want to work. If the ex-husband does not pony up the money, the taxpayer must step in, which is inefficient and brings a host of other problems, such as making the child's welfare somewhat dependent on government budgets and politicians' decisions.

Thus, the culture will need to continue getting money from men to support women with children. As for other women, the case is fuzzier. In principle, marriage allows two people to take different roles, so that one can live off the other's money. In practice, few men think it is realistic to live off their wife's earnings, so it is mainly women who can take advantage of this aspect of marriage.

Schoolboys Today: Raising Boys Like Girls

Concern about America's schools has been a perennial theme of national debate as long as I can remember and probably much longer. Recently these worries have gained urgency as increasing numbers of international tests show American education to be falling behind that of many other countries. American colleges and universities continue to be among the world's best, despite their apparent decline. Other countries never seem to have the political will to implement the competition between public and private universities that propelled American higher education to the top. From kindergarten to high school, however, the United States no longer leads the world.

Another theme that has escalated in recent years is that boys are doing worse and worse in schools. The problems of boys are mentioned only occasionally and hesitantly, because the official concern is still focused on girls. The view that girls are victims of the system, including educational systems, became dominant in the 1970s and has made it politically incorrect even to ask whether the system is bad for boys, because the female victimization story is based on the assumption that everything is set up for the benefit of boys.

The data are piling up, however. Boys get lower grades than girls. Boys are more likely to drop out of school than girls. Boys outnumber girls in special education and other classes for problem students. Boys are disciplined far more than girls, up to ten times as much. Boys are put on Ritalin and other behavior-control drugs far more than girls.

People are reluctant to acknowledge, however, that these statistics imply there is a problem. Many like to look at them as showing the innate superiority of girls. The Imaginary Feminist continues to insist that schools are biased against girls, and the fact that girls do better than boys in schools is simply proof that girls are superior beings, triumphing over adversity, while the evil conspiracy to favor boys is gradually failing.

To appreciate the bias in this view, it is useful to imagine what people would say if the genders were reversed. Suppose all those statistics about lower grades, higher dropout rates, more severe discipline, and so forth were reversed, such that girls came out worse. Everyone would be up in arms and there would be strident demands that the system must change at once.

Around the 1970s, schools began to accept the idea that girls were at a disadvantage. They embraced the principle that it is vitally important to treat boys and girls exactly the same, out of fairness. Then, however, arose a series of specific choices to make, in which one style of teaching or discipline or policy was better suited to boys and a different one was better suited to girls. These included such everyday things as framing a writing assignment in terms of preparing for battle or in terms of preparing for a dinner party. What do you think happened? Each time such a decision was faced, it would seem that to do what is best for boys rather than for girls would be sexist. Therefore, time after time, the school would settle on doing things the way that was best for girls. This probably would have been the logical outcome for each decision maker, but it had plenty of help from the fact that there were many voices speaking for the interests of girls, while nobody speaks for boys. Feminist watchdog groups oversee and scrutinize policies to make sure they are female-friendly, but there are no such groups to watch out for boys. Most teachers and other school administrators are women, so it was easier for them to figure out what was best for girls and easier to sympathize with the need for systems to be well suited to girls. Plus, especially at the lower levels, girls tend to be the model students, partly because of their faster maturation, so gearing the system toward girls brings quick rewards.

Thus, over time, schools have been reformed to make sure that everyone is treated in the way that is most congenial to and most effective for girls. It is therefore hardly surprising that today's schools get better results with girls than with boys.

Let us return to the idea that the basic drives of males and females are somewhat different as a result of the big difference in reproductive odds. Specifically, let us consider the idea that males have a stronger urge to strive for greatness than females. The competitive drive to achieve something that outperforms everyone else, along with perhaps the cocky confidence that oneself can do it, may be stronger in the boys than in the girls.

What are schools like these days? One theme that has been discussed a great deal is grade inflation. Teachers now give higher grades than in the past, for the same quality work. Hence plenty of students get A's. We already talked about this in connection with the fact that males go to extremes on ability more than females. But another, more insidious result of grade inflation is that there is no recognition for greatness, maybe even no chance for it. Grade inflation undercuts the boy's motivation to want to be the best.

Let us take seriously the idea that boys have more of a desire than girls to achieve at an extremely positive level that will stand about above all others. Girls may be reasonably content to get an A even if plenty of others also get an A. For a boy, however, the appeal of getting an A is diminished if plenty of others do. Grade inflation thus does not mesh well with the male striving for greatness. It fails to harness the boy's motivation to excel.

Another big change in American schools since the 1970s has been the self-esteem movement. This was driven in part by trumped-up statistics and irresponsible misinterpretations claiming that girls suffered a crisis of self-esteem in adolescence and needed drastic interventions to save them. So schools started programs to promote self-esteem. Many other policies, such as not keeping score in soccer matches, giving prizes to everybody rather than just the single champion, reducing the use of red ink for marking mistakes on student papers, and, yes, grade inflation, probably also were encouraged by this unwarranted concern with maintaining self-esteem, especially girls' self-esteem.

A major impetus for this concern over girls' self-esteem was an alleged research study by the American Association of University Women documenting that adolescent girls suffered from low self-esteem. The report was never published and thus never subject to scientific peer review. (That means we have no idea whether it was properly done; most experts have little faith in unpublished work.) The report itself was not even made public. Instead, the AAUW issued press releases to get the mass media all talking about a crisis among girls. One careful scholar, Christina Hoff Sommers, managed with considerable difficulty to obtain a copy of the report. She noted that much had been left out of the press releases. Yes, white girls had lower self-esteem than white boys, though the difference was not large and could just as well have been interpreted as indicating adolescent cockiness among the boys as low self-esteem among the girls. She also read that black girls had higher self-esteem than white boys. Black boys had the highest self-esteem of all. The press had not been told about the racial differences, or about black girls having higher self-esteem than white boys.

Crucially, Sommers pointed out a severe lapse in logic behind the claim that the girls needed help in the form of self-esteem bolstering. She said that if you looked at school performance, the ordering was exactly the opposite of the self-esteem ordering: white girls did best, followed by white boys, then black girls, with black boys doing worst. Why, she asked, did everybody think that the system needed to change to bolster the self-esteem of white girls? Instead, based on school performance, it would seem that the logical course would be to change all the other groups to be more like them, possibly including bringing their self-esteem down a notch.

For better or worse, our schools have embraced the idea of boosting everyone's self-esteem. I think it is for the worse. The boys may find this appealing, possibly because it caters to their budding male egos and adolescent vanity, but it is not likely to bring out the best in them. You get the best out of a boy by stimulating his desire for greatness and then telling him he has a long way to go: that he can perhaps achieve something marvelous but he must be humble and work hard for it. Telling a boy he is already great, and that so is everybody else in his class, seems a perfect recipe for ruining any inclination he has to work hard at school.

My sense is that the spread of video games and Internet has contributed to the problem, though I am generally favorably disposed toward both video games and internet. But let us think back a moment to what boyhood was like in the 1950s and 1960s. What avenues were available to strive for greatness? Athletics were there, of course, as they still are. But mostly the jocks were not the ones who were also going to be the star students. The quiet, physically slight, nerdy types were never going to be gridiron heroes, and so excelling at schoolwork was their main option.

Today, however, such boys can excel at video games. They know how much their peers play these games and what they score. Just when our society closed down the pursuit of greatness through schoolwork (by grade inflation and so forth), it offered boys an alternate pathway to feel great, namely by heroic feats of video gaming. I should know; I have enjoyed video games and experienced the seductive thrill of spectacular achievement one gets after breaking through to a higher level. It takes hours and hours of practice to get there, but, again, boys are willing to put in the hours in order to achieve greatness. (Incidentally, has anyone noticed that boys' self-esteem is not ruined by the many failures they encounter while playing video games?)

So the result is that our smartest and most talented boys find their desires and motivations engaged by the video game subculture much better than by the schools. If anything the schools seem to work at cross purposes. In a nutshell, we are trying to raise boys like girls while letting the video game marketplace be the main outlet for boy qualities. This is not going to work all that well.

Reducing the Quality of Men?

Is our society producing a lower quality of men than previous eras? Perhaps we should ask, is our culture producing lower quality men than its foreign rivals? The second question is more important because it points to possible risks: What if our culture were to be surpassed, supplanted, and superseded by others?

Our culture has spent several decades trying as hard as it can to reform all its institutions to make them more hospitable and suitable to women. This has undeniably involved making them somewhat less hospitable to men. Assuming these policies have had some success, then it would be a fair guess that today's women are stronger, more capable, and otherwise superior than their grandmothers were—while today's men would be psychologically weaker, less capable, and otherwise inferior to their grandfathers.

The changes to the schools (see preceding section) would be one major contributing factor. To get the most out of girls, we boost their self-esteem and rely on guilt to keep them behaving well. A bit of guilt is all the girls need to foster self-control. Guilt tends to be effective in girls, given that they are not generally bursting with antisocial impulses and desires.

But thanks to the commitment to treating all children the same, our society now wants to use that same strategy on boys too. Like it or not, boys are different. They are naturally more egotistical than girls, so bolstering self-esteem gives rise to narcissism—and narcissism has been rising alarmingly in recent decades, as careful research by Professors Jean Twenge and Keith Campbell has confirmed. Hence the boys become complacent, self-centered, and indeed just plain selfish. Guilt doesn't work as well with boys as with girls, as their narcissistic tendencies make them unwilling to accept responsibility for failures and misdeeds, so instead they blame others. Boys have stronger impulses and desires than girls, including antisocial ones, and so undermining their self-control while telling them they are great and hence entitled to do whatever they want seems a dangerous recipe likely to make them indulge those impulses. We may see more male misbehavior of all sorts.

Meanwhile, the male striving for greatness is sidetracked or ignored by a system that is oriented toward girls. It will not disappear from the male psyche, but it will probably not work as well for the cultural system, and it may get directed in useless or even unsavory ways. Narcissistic men may not want to toil for years to achieve greatness, because they think they are already great. They may simply expect to be treated as if they are already great.

The effects of this procedure will gradually spread through our society. The adult men may become increasingly reluctant to take on the burdens and responsibilities of traditional manhood. Recent reports of the increasingly unrealistic expectations of America's young people about their first jobs confirm that the products of today's self-esteem-boosting schools do not want to work their way to the top over decades. They expect a reasonably easy path to the top in a fairly short time. Dissatisfaction with actual jobs may increase, and productivity may decline, although technological improvements could offset that.

The long-term demands of marriage and family may not sit well with the narcissistic, undercontrolled men we are producing today. Narcissists don't go in for self-sacrifice. They may postpone marriage for longer and longer and, once they are married, may be ready to bolt as soon as the opportunities for self-fulfillment seem to grow dim.

The modern style of producing men may ultimately come into conflict with the culture that requires its young males to earn manhood. I have already remarked that the phrase "Be a man" is going out of style. Possibly it is losing popularity because today's males do not want to have to earn manhood. Brought up on praise, self-esteem, and indulgence, they expect to be acclaimed as men automatically.

In an earlier chapter, I said that the call to "be a man" often meant doing what needs to be done, regardless of your feelings or preferences. Nobody wants to fight the dangerous attacker, or get up in the cold night and go investigate mysterious noises from downstairs, or kill the ugly bugs, or do the messy jobs. That's why most societies teach men to stifle their feelings, so that feelings don't prevent the men from doing what has to be done. In today's America, however, we raise boys like girls, including encouraging them to explore and share their feelings. Boys raised like that may not turn into men who will put aside their feelings to do what is needed.

Remember, though, that these arguments are speculations that take current trends and extrapolate. Other things might counteract or offset them. It is entirely possible that schooling doesn't much matter and that when men grow up they will rise to the occasion, accept and face the challenges as always, and turn into the sorts of men who do their bit for society, the same as always.

The worst effect may be that as the schooling system increasingly fails boys, our culture will have fewer and fewer well-educated men. It is quite possible that women will step up and take over many of the jobs that highly educated men have done in the past. The culture would not suffer inordinately—indeed perhaps not at all—if the highly educated work is done by women instead of men.

Gender Politics

Now let's step way back for a moment and try to discern the broadest trends as to how men and women have collectively related to each in recent years. Most of the people who argue these points have strong axes to grind and take one side, so they focus on particular issues to say that their preferred gender is unfairly getting the worst of it: Women earn less money than men, say, or men have hardly any reproductive rights. But instead of a partisan and specific view, let's try to see the big picture. I see a tradeoff. Both men and women have given up some things and gained some things.

Women now enjoy significant advantages in the major institutions of society. The laws favor women. Indeed, as some legal scholars point out, each new law relevant to gender is carefully scrutinized by many individuals and interest groups to ensure that it does not cause any harm or disadvantage to women, but nobody pays attention to whether it is bad for men.

Likewise, in corporations, universities, and other large organizations that employ many people, there are many policies to protect women and advance their interests. Most organizations have some offices that watch over women's needs and interests, but none to take care of men. Many have women's groups or women's organizations, while men's groups and men's organizations are forbidden. When important jobs are to be filled or prizes to be awarded, part of the policy is to make some extra efforts to ensure that any eligible women get full and careful consideration. I have never heard anyone ask whether the applications contained some good male candidates, or say that we need to be sure to give the best men a fair shot. (Advertisements for faculty positions at my university, like most others, state explicitly that they encourage women to apply. When there was an opening in my group, which already had more women than men, I mischievously inserted the words "and men" next to "women" in the ad, so it read that applications from women AND men were encouraged, but the administrators quickly deleted that!)

What have the men gained? Sex. That is, the past half-century's changes in sexual behavior seem largely favorable to men. Although official pronouncements keep saying how great the Sexual Revolution was for women, in fact it seems to have gone much more the way that men wanted. Today's young man faces a sex life that probably would have exceeded the most optimistic imagination of most men throughout history. He can start having sex in his teens, in some communities even in his early teens. He can continue having sex with a revolving series of partners through his teens and twenties, and longer if he is willing to postpone marriage.

Moreover, this sexual smorgasbord is available to him without most of the costs that traditionally accompanied sex for men. He does not have to make long-term commitments: Sex can be gotten after a few dates or, depending on how lucky and non-choosy he is, sometimes after just a few drinks. There are reliable means of avoiding pregnancy, unlike through most of human history. If pregnancy does occur, it can be terminated swiftly or, if the woman prefers to have the baby, he may be able to get away without moral, legal, or financial obligation. Remarkable varieties of sexual adventure are there to be found, ranging from seeing pictures on the Internet to threesomes, sadomasochism, and more.

The rich and varied sex life of today's young man seems an exceptionally poor preparation for marriage and long-term fidelity, to be sure. (More on that later.) Perhaps when he falls heavily in love he can persuade himself that, after having had a couple dozen sex partners in a decade of adventure, he will be able to manage to desire only this one woman for the next half century and that she will always be as exciting to him as she is now. But a long period of indulgence is a poor foundation for an even longer period of abstinence. Yet even if and when he does find himself shackled to one partner while overflowing with further desires, the modern Western man again has more options than most of his predecessors: erotica widely available, plenty of chances for discreet affairs, and of course divorce and re-entry into the wide-open world of being single, where the newly divorced man will find that the odds have shifted increasingly in his favor as he became older and wealthier, at least up to a point.

Indeed, the opportunity to trade in your old wife for a new, younger and slimmer one, is a major benefit that the feminist movement unwittingly bestowed on men. Whether women also benefit from this is hard to say. Many feminists thought of men as the enemy, and so they pushed hard to liberalize divorce laws. This was supposedly done under the guise of enabling women to escape from abusive relationships. How much it helped is debatable: American women could generally get a divorce from an abusive husband long before 1970. What's new is the easy, no-fault divorce that one can get simply because one is tired of the old spouse and would like a new, possibly better one.

The feminists believed that liberalizing divorce was good simply because it got women out of relationships with men. There may be something to that argument, especially if you accept the premise that it is generally better for women to be on their own rather than attached to men. But not all women feel this way. Many women would rather remain married to men, even imperfect men, than be alone for the rest of their lives. And though some women remarry, many don't. Divorced men are much more likely than the women to remarry. Only some of that difference is due to personal preferences.

The giant trade, thus, was that women got career advantages and benefits, while men got more sex.

Who got the better of this trade? That is not so easy to say. In a sense, both genders got what they wanted most. Many young men put sex above most or all other goals, and so they would gladly accept some career disadvantages in order to enjoy the greater sexual freedom. Meanwhile, for women, getting access to and preferential treatment in such a wide range of organizations is a huge benefit, and it is probably worth whatever they give up in order to have sex more on men's terms. One could even argue that women have not lost anything, since they get to have plenty of sex too, unlike their grandmothers, and they do not suffer the costs in bad reputation and unwanted pregnancies and the like that plagued most sexually active unmarried women throughout history. More likely, though, the modern sexual norms do favor men in meaningful ways, and many women must engage in more sex with more different men than they would ideally like, in order to get the relationship they want.

Looking ahead, the women's advantages seem a bit less solid than the men's. Sexual freedom seems unlikely to reverse in a big way. In past centuries, shifts away from sexual liberty toward more prudish norms were often supported by waves of religious enthusiasm, and it is hard to envision such a trend sweeping through Western civilization any time soon. Moreover, at the upper levels of society, such as the highly educated, women will soon outnumber men, and a surplus of women typically contributes to loosening of sexual morality.

In contrast, the structural advantages of women in the workplace are possibly at risk of being eliminated. At present they are based on a giant falsehood, namely the idea that organizations discriminate against women and therefore affirmative action and other policies are needed to overcome them. Sooner or later the truth will get out. At that point several different things might happen.

Equal Pay for Less Work?

One possibility is that the laws and policies that require preferential treatment for women will be overturned. Society might realize that the lower earnings of women are caused by the choices women make, not by oppression and discrimination. As a result, it may decide that no corrective action is needed. The day of realizing this is a long way off, as long as women and in particular feminist spokespersons dominate the discussion of gender policy. They can perhaps sustain for a while the false belief that male oppression and patriarchal conspiracy hold women down. But my guess is that it is difficult to sustain a convenient fiction forever. A century from now, when women still earn less than men, will people still claim that it stems from a conspiracy by men?

Another possibility would be to shift the terms of the debate. In my view, the core issue for women's welfare will be persuading the culture at large to embrace the principle of equal pay for less work. That is, laws could be passed requiring organizations to pay women on average the same amount as men. Some such laws and policies have been proposed, but nowadays they are usually cloaked in rhetoric about discrimination and oppression. In the future it will be necessary to recognize that, in a totally free market with no discrimination, women will still earn less than men on average. The culture could embrace the value of eliminating that difference.

Remember, there are places where it is already clear that that is the eventual outcome. Catherine Hakim's research (among others) has pointed to the American pharmacy industry as one field that is essentially free from gender or other forms of discrimination, simply because there is a chronic labor shortage. Pharmacists can have whatever careers they choose. Both men and women go into that field, with no obstacles. But once in it, they make different choices. Many more women than men choose low-pressure, family-friendly positions with regular and convenient hours, low stress, and no travel. Meanwhile, more men than women choose the ambitious jobs that make more demands but offer more opportunities for advancement and ultimately pay more money.

That is a microcosm of what is likely to be the future for workplaces in general, and it ends with men earning more money, mainly because men work harder than women. (Again, not all men, and not all women, but enough to perpetuate inequality.)

Creating a formal policy of equal pay for less work would have a variety of advantages. It would allow culture to shift money from men to women without having to accuse men of being evil. It would give men respect for creating wealth while also putting more money into female hands. It would create a sustainable long-term arrangement, unlike the present one which is based on false assertions of male oppression and discrimination.

There are some women who achieve and excel at the same level as the top men. They do not really need affirmative action or other policies. Their work is not less than men's. A policy of equal pay for less work might take away some of their credit. Still, it might be worth it to them. These women do benefit from the preferential treatment that women now get in organizations. Perhaps the best way to put it is that for a man, to get to the top requires being both very good and fairly lucky. Given that organizations are extra considerate of the best women, these high-achieving women do not need as much luck: being good is enough. They get the rewards they deserve. Many high-achieving men do not get the rewards they deserve.

Still, one can make a strong case that lavishing some extra benefits on high-achieving women is good for society. These women are exceptionally valuable, indeed perhaps more valuable than their high-achieving male peers. If the society is to get the most out of all its talent, this requires cultivating both male and female talent, and because males are generally more career-motivated than females, extra encouragement and recognition may help foster the female talent. It is also possible that men and women have somewhat different perspectives or insights, and so a field will flourish most if it gets contributions from both genders. Again, outstanding female achievement is rarer than male achievement, and so giving it extra encouragement may be useful. In short, high-achieving females are a particular treasure to culture and society, and so rewarding them handsomely may pay off.

The only downside of a policy of equal pay for less work is that it makes the companies somewhat less profitable. Essentially it means that they shift pay from some of the more productive workers to some of the less productive ones. That would reduce the competitiveness of those companies. If this principle were accepted nationwide, then the less of competitiveness would show up only at the international level. Possibly other countries would adopt the principle too, and then it would not be a problem for anyone.

Battles, Babies…and Science

It is an entertaining intellectual game to ask who is better off, men or women. Likewise, to forecast who will have the advantage in the future is interesting to speculate about. But I said back in the first chapter that we must always consider the third party: the cultural system. The welfare of both men and women depends on the culture being able to keep functioning well enough to work its magic and confer its benefits.

To the system, it doesn't matter very much whether men or women do particular jobs, as long as the jobs get done. Policies may be unfair to individuals, as in forcing women to take care of children or forcing men to risk life and limb in battle. But systems aren't moral beings. The system will survive if the children get fed and cared for, and if warriors defend it against its enemies, and in principle it doesn't matter who does those jobs.

The culture can get into trouble if it assigns important jobs to people who are unwilling or unable to do them. Through much of history, military combat meant fighting with spears and swords. Men's superior upper-body strength gave them an advantage over women at this. A culture that insisted that women do its hand-to-hand fighting might lose too many battles to survive. Today, however, the highly technological nature of warfare means that most jobs do not depend on upper-body strength.

At present, the most interesting debate from this point of view concerns the movement to "Title IX" science classes. That is, many are arguing that America should do to science what it has done to college sports—namely pass laws and enforce policies that prevent men from doing any more than women. This is being ardently promoted in some circles based on feminist arguments about gender equality. As usual, the argument says that the reason for the lack of women's success is male conspiracy and oppression, and so stringent laws are needed to counteract that imaginary bias.

The application of these laws to college sports resulted in widespread cutbacks and cancellations of men's sports teams. The underlying assumption behind the laws and policies was that women want to play sports as much as men, and so if the colleges treated both equally, then both genders would have all the opportunities for playing sports that they want. The assumption is false, of course. Men like to play sports more than women. Hence the only way to make the opportunities equal was to eliminate them for men.

But sports don't really matter. The culture can survive and function just as well if the quality and quantity of college sports declines. I realize this is heresy to many sports fans, but nothing of substance is actually at stake in a ball game. One may debate the moral issues of whether it was unfair to men to cancel their sports teams so as to bring down the male sport participation to the level of the female. But in terms of the effect on the culture of this practice, it essentially led to a small decline in quality and quantity of sports playing among college students, and it is hard to see how that would really affect our culture in a consequential matter. Neither the Gross Domestic Product, nor the nation's ability to defend itself against enemies, nor the rate of technological innovation, nor the any other measure of societal well-being is likely to change.

Science is rather different. Science has been one of the three or four keys to America's prominence in the world, and science has helped the nation to advance and thrive. If we cut men out of science at the same rate we have cut them out of college sports, then our culture's well-being depends on women taking the men's places. Yet there is no sign that that will happen, and in fact there is plenty of evidence that it won't. As I said earlier, all the evidence indicates that the lack of women in science is mainly based on their own lack of interest in that kind of work.

Our society already faces a shortage of scientists. Hence the proposal to turn away many of the young men who would like to pursue careers in science seems dangerous. The advocates of this policy claim that turning men away will free up spots for women. I think there are already spots available to women who want them, but not many women want them. If women do replace men in science, the culture will continue just fine. If they do not, American science will deteriorate.

Certainly one cannot point to any society anywhere in the history of the world where the majority of scientific research was carried out by women. Maybe America can be the first, but it seems a dangerous gamble to stake our nation's competitive future on that chance. Rigging the system to make science less appealing to young men could be very costly.

Comparing Options

In nearly every culture in the history of the world, the life paths that were open to people depended rather heavily on their gender. Whether you were born male or female dictated what sort of work you would be doing, how much and what kind of schooling you got, whether you would be sent into battle, whether you would be taught various crafts and skills, how much say you would have in your marital decisions, and many other things. Unlike most of those cultures, modern Western civilization has sought to make gender into a nonfactor, so that all paths would be open to both men and women.

Yet the men of today still face a selection of life paths that is not quite the same as the women's. Many of those differences are likely to persist tomorrow. Some of those differences favor women with more options than men have, but there is at least one important option that is still more available to men than women.

In terms of mixing career and marriage, modern women can have almost any option they choose, at least if they plan well. I mentioned Catherine Hakim's research that lists the three main types of life path: career first, family first, and balanced. Women's preferences are divided among all three. More important, women's actual lives are also divided among them. At the extremes, some women pursue high-powered careers while leaving family in the background, and others devote themselves to family while having little or no career at all.

For the modern man, in contrast, the career-first option is pretty much the only available choice. The opposite choice, of being mainly a homemaker, is not really an option, though few men seem to want it anyhow. (It is conceivable that if it were genuinely available, some men would opt for it, but I find little evidence that many men would.) Hakim finds that many men would like the balanced option, in which a low-powered, casual career is pursued to accommodate heavy involvement in family—but few men are really able to make it work in practice.

Thus, our culture still requires men to earn their manhood by their work. Most men understand this and build their lives on that basis. Our culture believes that a woman is entitled to stay home and raise her children, financially supported either by a husband or by the government's tax dollars. Whether our culture will ever come around to thinking that men are equally entitled to that sort of life is debatable, but it is not going to happen soon. In that respect, women's options are better than men's.

On the other hand, there is one form of having it all that still seems to elude women but remains possible for at least some men. Men can build their lives around a high-powered career but still have a thriving family life. In contrast, most women who want to have intensive careers find it difficult to reconcile them with raising several children. Many successful women (in career terms) remain childless, and others wait a long time and have one or at most two children after their careers are well grounded. Even they tend to say it was a struggle.

The difference is the mirror image of the career options. Having it all (i.e., high-powered career plus rich family life) depends on marrying someone who will take over most responsibilities for home and family. Most of those "someones" are female. Because some women but very few men can build their lives around family, with little or no career, then men but not women can find a partner of that sort. Some women mate with other women and can manage this, and some women can even find a man like that, but most cannot.

Young Men Today and Tomorrow

To close, let us consider an average baby boy born in the United States today. What does the future promise him? What are the prospects for American manhood in the coming decades, as he moves through the stages of his life?

In some respects, they are great. Being born in the United States at this time, almost regardless of the details and specifics, is a huge blessing in comparison to most other times and places in the history of the world. Opportunities and options are extraordinary. The likelihood that this baby boy will find himself in a situation like my father and countless other young men in history encountered—drafted against his will and marched off to die for his country in a hopeless cause—is slim. The prospects for a pleasant, comfortable life, with a cozy home, reasonable job, family, and a goodly assortment of pleasures to fill his leisure time are quite good, especially if the young man manages to finish his education. He may not live as long as the baby girls who lie next to him in the hospital maternity ward, but he will probably live longer than most men have in almost any other place and time in world history.

He will also find, to his pleasure, that the biggest concern of young men's lives, namely sex, also goes better than it has for the vast majority of his ancestors. He can start having sex in his teens and can find a series of willing partners. The dangers of unplanned pregnancies and shotgun marriages are vastly reduced. He mainly has to fear his own mistakes, such as getting a sexually transmitted disease, or being swept away by his own passionate love to marry the wrong person and, especially, doing so without a prenuptial agreement to protect him from the ruinous ravages of divorce, or damaging his reputation by a sexual misdeed that gets found out.

In other respects, though, problems and dangers loom. His society may not march him off to death against his will, but it has other uses for him. Its attitude toward him *as a man* is mixed at best. He will find things subtly stacked against him everywhere, as schools and corporations and other institutions everywhere follow policies officially designed to favor women and girls.

Respect, the centerpiece of men's strivings for centuries, is allotted to modern man in erratic ways. On the one hand, he finds organizations now insist that everyone is entitled to respect, and so he shares in the devalued respect that is doled out to everyone free of charge. On the other hand, he as a man is not respected. He lives in a society that regards women as superior to men, a message echoed everywhere from the private prejudices of individuals, to entrenched biases in the legal system, to the news and entertainment media. If he extends the male role by becoming a father, he will find that the avalanche of disrespect gets worse.

Furthermore, he will be expected to shoulder a large amount blame that is not really his. It is a remarkably impressive trick that men have been made to feel guilty and responsible for some women's low achievements. For example, women earn less money than men. Why is this fact held up to make men feel bad, instead of proud? In Chapter 7, the creation of wealth by men was cited as a main cause for gender inequality. Yet an influential handful of women have deftly managed to make men feel guilty rather than proud of many of their greatest achievements.

The result is that tomorrow's men will likely find a paradoxical, confusing situation. Unearned respect is cheap, and they can claim their free dose of it just like anyone (although perhaps not as much as women). When they strive and earn, however, they will find that the rewards and recognition are erratic. Their very success brings guilt rather than respect. The expanding population means that reaching the top of the pyramid is harder than ever.

Can we reasonably expect that these next generations of men will continue to solve society's problems, even as our society pressures them to step aside and let women and a few favored minority groups take all the leadership positions they want? Remember, men don't just walk into success, as the Imaginary Feminist supposes—they have to fight long and hard for it. Maybe the discouraging signals will tell men not to bother. Can we expect them to continue doing the crucial and sometimes dangerous tasks that society needs somebody to do but that somehow women mostly don't do, even as we tell the men that everyone is equally valuable?

Can we expect the men to provide for their children, even as we tell them that fathers aren't needed and as we bombard them with media depictions of fatherhood as a sucker's job fit for buffoons and losers? Can we expect men to accept the responsibilities of fatherhood despite a lack of rights—including the right to help decide whether a pregnancy should be completed or terminated, to be informed of medical evidence that a particular baby is not biologically related to him (contrary to what its mother might say), or to have even a sporting chance to keep his children in the event of divorce?

Can we expect men to continue to believe that their own success, brought by their own hard work, is actually the result of unfair preferences in their favor? Can we make them continue to think that they are responsible for the failings of others, and that they should accept lesser rewards on that basis?

One irony we have seen is that culture values men's activities more than women's but treats individual men as more expendable than women. Culture was created by men, and for good reason. It depends on men's strivings and social networks men create. Yet it also progresses by using men in a heartless manner that sometimes extends to sacrificing them. Being expendable is part of what makes men useful to culture.

All his life, he will likely hear the messages that most of us are familiar with. Society will tell him that men are fools and pigs, are interpersonally inept, are wicked oppressors who enjoy unfair advantages, are dangerous and possibly obsolete creatures filled with violent tendencies and other undesirable impulses, and are inferior to women in countless small ways. It will remind him that his fortunes and his life are less precious and more expendable than those of other people, especially women and children. And then it will remember it needs him to strive, to risk, to achieve, to produce, to provide, to protect. It needs him to solve specific problems, to shoulder responsibilities, and to create wealth and share it with others. It needs him to work with other men (and women too) and against other men to drive the progress of culture forward. It needs him to be a man.

Will he play along? The future of the culture depends on his answer. In many crucial ways, the culture depends on men more than on other people—even women and children.

Toward a Better Future

Long ago I stopped reading college student newspapers, but every so often one falls into my hands while I am enduring a boring wait at some campus event, and so I thumb through it. The last time, about two years ago, one full page was devoted to a write-in poll that had asked the paper's readers whether they preferred male or female roommates. This high-spirited and good-natured survey of personal preferences had however deteriorated into a somewhat acrimonious outpouring of bruising complaints and enumerations of the shameful failings of former roommates, here attributed to their respective genders.

Amid this wave of gender-bashing, I was struck by one letter that actually expressed itself well, had a restrained and even rather nice tone, and was surprisingly free of grammatical outrages. The author said she had lived with both men and women and thought they could both be pretty good. There were differences, but they balanced out. She said she liked living with women because you didn't have to deal with all the constant mess. She liked living with men because you didn't have to deal with all the constant drama.

People used to say there was very little difference between men and women, but *vive le difference!* That saying and the sentiment behind it have gone very much out of fashion. Today there is strong ideological pressure to deny that there are any differences and if any are found to erase and eliminate them, rather than to value them.

Let's re-think this and lighten up. There are in fact some differences between men and women, and as I have said these have more to do with wants and likes than with abilities. Let men and women do what they want. Among other things, they want each other. They will work it out. They generally have.

Most of the history of the human race has involved men and women living and working together. As partners they have each contributed vitally to the flourishing of humankind. Partnerships work best with a bit of specialization. That's ultimately why nature made men and women different.

Maybe one day we could learn to value both men and women for what they do, instead of wishing that they wanted to do something else. Men and women could thank each other. Now, wouldn't that be something?

Sources and References

T his book was intended as an essay, not a scholarly work. In fact, as I did the background reading for it, I was struck by the very wide range in scholarly discipline exhibited in previous works. Some did a terrific job of documenting other points. Others cited many sources but did so frivolously and carelessly, so that the appearance of careful scholarship was an illusion.

What also struck me was that the difference between serious versus apparent versus nonexistent scholarship seemed to make little difference in terms of what impact the book had. Hence it hardly seemed worth exerting myself to fill this book with a plethora of research citations, as I normally do in my scholarly and scientific writings.

Nonetheless, it is hard to break the habit entirely. More important, I know many people will want to check some of the original sources for the important claims and statistics that fill this book. Plus, it is possible that people will expect more scholarship from a professor than from other sources.

Therefore, here are the major sources behind various specific statements in the book. Some of the names were mentioned in the text, and so here I merely provide the full reference for anyone who wants to look it up. In other cases, where names were not mentioned in the text, I provide some indication of what the text material was and where to find the original sources. I hope this will enable readers who want to go beyond my writings to look up the basis for my claims. I encourage anyone who is interested to read these sources and continue on from there.

Chapter 1

Patai, D., & Koertge, N. (2003). *Professing feminism: Education and indoctrination in Women's Studies*. New York: Lexington Books.

Sommers, C. H. (1994). *Who stole feminism? How women have betrayed women*. New York: Simon & Schuster.

On salary differences, see Shackleton, J. R. (2008). *Should we mind the gap? Gender pay differentials and public policy*. London: Institute of Economic Affairs. (Available for download on the Internet.). Another good source is Furchgott-Roth, D., & Stolba, C. (1999). *Women's figures: An illustrated guide to the economic progress of women in America*. Washington, DC: AEI Press. (Online see http://www.aei.org/book/292). On difference in negotiation, see Balcock, L., & Laschever, S. (2003). *Women don't ask: Negotiation and the gender divide*. Princeton, NJ: Princeton University Press.

On numbers of women in Senate, Congress, etc., this information is readily available online anywhere from dozens of sources.

On imprisonment, see the site of the US Bureau of Justice Statistics: http://www.ojp.usdoj.gov/bjs/gcorpop.htm#CorrPopGender.

On anti-male bias in the justice system, such as men getting longer sentences for identical crimes, see Warren Farrell (1993). *The myth of male power*, Part III, especially Chapter 11. New York: Berkley Books.

On death on the job, there are multiple publications by the US Department of Labor with relevant statistics. See "Women experience fewer job-related injuries and deaths than men," the title of which says plenty. Also "Occupational injuries, illnesses, and fatalities among women" (Anne B. Hoskins for U.S. Dept of Labor). There are also breakdowns by years, but the pattern does not seem to change much.

On deaths in battle, the 2,938 to 62 difference was much in the news and official reports when the 3,000th death was tallied. The ratio stayed about the same at 4,000, in other words 98% male and 2% female, as reported in *USA Today*, March 18, 2009. Note that these tallies involve all deaths of American service personnel in Iraq, including many killed in ordinary traffic accidents (which should be an equalizing force). About one-fifth of the deaths were from non-hostile causes.

Vincent, N. (2006). *Self-made man: One woman's journey into manhood and back again*. New York: Viking/Penguin.

Chapter 2

Stephenson, J. (1993). *Men are not cost-effective*. New York: HarperCollins.

Dowd, M. (2005). *Are men necessary?* New York: Putnam.

Fendrich, L. (2009). Who needs men? *Chronicle of Higher Education* (July 16). Accessed online at http://careernetwork.com/blogPost/Who-Needs-Men-/7034/.

Several quotations taken from *The Economist*, April 15, 2006, A guide to womenomics, pp. 73–74.

The designation of the "WAW effect" (short for "women are wonderful") was mentioned by Dr. Eagly in her talks during the 1990s, as possibly her in-house designation. A good example of the data on which that designation was based can be found in Eagly, A. H., & Mladinic, A. (1989), Gender stereotypes and attitudes toward women and men. *Personality and Social Psychology Bulletin, 15,* 543–558. See also: Also Eagly, A. H., & Mladinic, A. (1994). Are people prejudiced against women? Some answers from research on attitudes, gender stereotypes, and judgments of competence. In W. Stroebe & M. Hewstone (Eds.), *European Review of Social Psychology* (Vol 5, pp. 1–35). New York: John Wiley & Sons.

On persistence of false statistics in feminist writings, see C. H. Sommers, "Persistent myths in feminist scholarship," *Chronicle of Higher f Chronicle Review,* June 29, 2009. Online version at http://chronicle.com/article/Persistent-Myths-in-Feminis/46965.

Farrell, W. (1993). *The myth of male power*. New York: Berkley Books.

Brizendine, L. (2006). *The female brain*. New York: Random House.

The gender difference in variability of IQ scores has been found many times. For an early source, see Roberts, J. A. F. (1945). On the difference between the sexes in dispersion of intelligence. *British Medical Journal, 1,* 727–730; for discussion and overview, Jensen, A. R. (1998). *The g factor*. Westwood, CT: Praeger; also Lehrke, R. (1997). *Sex linkage of intelligence: The X-factor*. Westport, CT: Praeger. For one of the most dramatic studies on it, based on giving an IQ test to almost everyone born in Scotland in 1921, see Deary, I. J., Thorpe, G., Wilson, V., Starr, J. M., & Whalley, L. J. (2003). Population sex differences in IQ at age 11: The Scottish mental survey 1932. *Intelligence, 31,* 533–542.

On accuracy of stereotypes, an impressive review of the literature is available here: Jussim, L., Cain, T. R., Crawford, J. T., Harber, K., & Cohen, F. (in press). The unbearable accuracy of stereotypes. In T. Nelson (Ed.), *Handbook of prejudice, stereotyping, and discrimination.* Mahwah, NJ: Erlbaum. Another useful source is Jussim, L., & Harber, K. D. Teacher expectations and self-fulfilling prophecies: Knowns and unknowns, resolved and unresolved controversies. *Personality and Social Psychology Review,* 9(2), 131–155.

Chapter 3

Maccoby, E., & Jacklin, C. (1974). *The psychology of sex differences.* Palo Alto, CA: Stanford University Press.

One influential application of meta-analysis to gender differences was by Aries, E. (1996). *Men and women in interaction: Reconsidering the differences.* New York: Oxford University Press. The quotation is from page 6.

Tannen, D. (1990). *You just don't understand.* New York: William Morrow.

Gray, J. (1993). *Men are from Mars, women are from Venus.* New York: HarperCollins.

Hyde, J.S. (2005). The gender similarities hypothesis. *American Psychologist,* 60, 581–592.

My point that modern America has made men and women relatively similar, as compared to other societies, is a common-sense argument but is not a proven fact. Indeed, there is a contrary suggestion in recent work by Schmitt et al. (2008), who found that men and women's personalities were relatively more different in advanced cultures where women presumably had more opportunities than in traditional societies with more fixed gender roles. This finding has inspired some controversy and plain puzzlement, partly because there is no very satisfying explanation for it, and it may be linked to the particular traits and measured featured in that study, but it remains a throught-provoking challenge to common sense and something for future research to tackle. See Schmitt, D.P., Realo, A., Voracek, M., & Allik, J. (2008). Why can't a man be more like a woman? Sex differences in Big Five personality traits across 55 cultures. *Journal of Personality and Social Psychology,* 95, 181–196.

For quotations by Hausman, these are taken from: Hausman, P. (2000). A tale of two hormones. Presented at the National Academy of Engineering SE Regional Meeting, Atlanta Georgia, April 26.

Eccles's work has been published in many places. My source was the overview she gave here: Eccles, J. (2007). Motivated behavioral choices. Presented at the American Psychological Society 19th Annual Convention, Washington, DC, May 25.

For the recent and authoritative overview on women and science, see Ceci, S.J., Williams, W.M., & Barnett, S.M. (2009). Women's under-representation in science: Sociocultural and biological considerations. *Psychological Bulletin,* 135, 218–261. There are a couple other issues worth mentioning here to anyone interested in delving deep into the topic. These authors noted (as have others) that, first, more men than women score in the top levels of math ability and, second, among those in the top range of math ability, the women are more likely than men to be good at many other things (e.g., high verbal ability). This enables the math-talented women to choose non-math careers, which they seem to prefer anyway. That finding also suggests that being good specifically at math is a male thing. Women who are good at math are good at it because they are all-around brilliant. Some men fit that description too, but the surplus of men at the top may be due to men (but not usually women) being specifically good at math.

One other point, this article did not have much to say about women being steered away from math or the field being prejudiced against them, but they did note some evidence that women with children had lower promotion rates in some math-oriented fields. That pattern could obviously be explained in multiple ways.

On people overestimating their own work relative to a partner's, the classic source is Ross, M., & Sicoly, F. (1979). Egocentric biases in availability and attribution. *Journal of Personality and Social Psychology,* 37, 322–336.

The survey indicating inflated self-reports of work: Robinson, J.P., & Godbey, G. (1997). *Time for life: The surprising ways Americans use their time.* Pennsylvania State University Press.

On the preponderance of men among people who work long hours, see "Stress: Never a dull moment," in *The Economist,* August 28, 2004. It was on page 29 of the European version of the magazine. The specific finding quoted was "'four out of five of those working 48 hours or more per week are male."

Machlowitz, M. (1980). *Workaholics*. Reading, MA: Addison-Wesley.

On the pharmacy industry, including the figue of 27% pay gap, see Hakim, Catherine. (2006). Women, careers, and work-life preferences. *British Journal of Guidance and Counselling*. 34, 279–294. That paper is also a useful overview of male-female differences in career attitudes and preferences.

On salary differences, see Shackleton, J.R. (2008). *Should we mind the gap? Gender pay differentials and public policy*. London, England: Institute of Economic Affairs. (Available for download on internet.). Another good source is Furchgott-Roth, D., & Stolba, C. (1999). *Women's figures: An illustrated guide to the economic progress of women in America*. Washington, DC: AEI Press. On difference in negotiation, see Balcock, L., & Laschever, S. (2003). *Women don't ask: Negotiation and the gender divide*. Princeton, NJ: Princeton University Press.

Chapter 4

The wild horses story is standard stuff. I do not recall where I first read this, but there is a nice account of life among bighorn sheep that makes the same points, see Gould, J. L., & Gould, C. G. (1997). *Sexual selection: Mate choice and courtship in nature*. New York: Freeman/ Scientific American.

The DNA studies on how today's human population is descended from twice as many women as men have been the most requested sources from my earlier talks on this. The work is by Jason Wilder and his colleagues. I list here some sources in the mass media, which may be more accessible to laypersons than the highly technical journal articles, but for the specialists I list those also.

For a highly readable introduction, you can Google the article "Ancient Man Spread the Love Around," which was published September, 20, 2004 and is still available (last I checked) online. There were plenty of other stories in the media at about this time, when the research findings first came out. In "Medical News Today," (www.medicalnewstoday. com), on the same date in 2004, a story under "Genes expose secrets of sex on the side" covered much the same material.

If you want the original sources, read Wilder, J. A., Mobasher, Z., & Hammer, M. F. (2004). Genetic evidence for unequal effective population sizes of human females and males. *Molecular Biology and Evolution,* 21, 2047–2057. If that went down well, you might try Wilder, J. A., Kingan, S. B., Mobasher, Z., Pilkington, M. M., & Hammer, M. F. (2004). Global patterns of human mitochondrial DNA and Y-chromosome structure are not influenced by higher migration rates of females versus males. *Nature Genetics,* 36, 1122–1125. That one was over my head, I admit. A more readable source on these is Shriver, M. D. (2005), Female migration rate might not be greater than male rate. *European Journal of Human Genetics,* 13, 131–132. Shriver raises another intriguing hypothesis that could have contributed to the greater preponderance of females in our ancestors: Because couples mate such that the man is older, the generational intervals are smaller for females (i.e., baby's age is closer to mother's than to father's). As for the 90% to 20% differential in other species, that I believe is standard information in biology, which I first heard in one of the lectures on testosterone by the late James Dabbs, whose book *Heroes, Rogues, and Lovers* remains an authoritative source on the topic.

On Genghis Khan, see Weatherford, J. (2004) *Genghis Khan and the making of the modern world.* New York: Three Rivers Press/Random House.

The many modern descendants were mentioned by Wilder, J.A., Mobasher, Z., & Hammer, M. F. (2004). Genetic evidence for unequal effective population sizes of human females and males. *Molecular Biology and Evolution,* 21, 2047–2057.

On the Crusades, a thorough and highly readable account, albeit hardly the most recent, is by Runciman, S. (1951–1954). *A history of the Crusades* (3 vols.) New York: Cambridge University Press. Also highly worth reading, Maalouf, A. (1987). *The Crusades through Arab eyes.* New York: Schocken.

Chapter 5

The specific finding that interacting with a woman had a carryover effect to produce positive mood for the rest of the day and perhaps the next day, whereas interacting with a man had no such effect, I recall from a presentation by Harry Reis at the Society for Experimental Social

Psychology conference in the 1980s. I have not been able to find that specific source, including from contacts with Dr. Reis. Still, similar findings are available. Wheeler, L. & Nezlek, J. (1977). Sex differences in social participation. *Journal of Personality and Social Psychology,* 35, 742–754, report that men find opposite-sex interactions more satisfying than same-sex ones, whereas for women the difference is considerably smaller.

Hopkins, J. (2006: August 24). "More women of color take lead on path to entrepreneurship." *USA Today,* 3B.

"Researchers identify 'male warrior effect'," *Yahoo! News,* September 8. 2006.

See the journal article also: Van Vugt, M., De Cremer, D., & Janssen, D. P. (2007). Gender differences in cooperation and competition: The male-warrior hypothesis. *Psychological Science,* 18, 19–23.

On empathy differences being found mainly with self-report measures, see Eisenberg, N., & Lennon, R. (1983). Sex differences in empathy and related capacities. *Psychological Bulletin,* 94, 100–131.

See Baron-Cohen, S. (2002). The extreme male brain theory of autism. *Trends in Cognitive Sciences,* 6, 248–254.

Cross, S. E., & Madson, L. (1997). Models of the self: Self-construals and gender. *Psychological Bulletin,* 122, 5–37.

Need to belong: Baumeister, R. F., & Leary, M. R. (1995). The need to belong: Desire for interpersonal attachments as a fundamental human motivation. *Psychological Bulletin,* 117, 497–529.

Baumeister, R. F., & Sommer, K. L. (1997). What do men want? Gender differences and two spheres of belongingness: Comment on Cross and Madson (1997). *Psychological Bulletin,* 122, 38–44.

On female aggression in close relationships, there are important early findings reviewed in Baumeister & Sommer (1997), but the definitive review of the literature came out a few years later: Archer, J. (2000). Sex differences in aggression between heterosexual partners: A meta-analytic review. *Psychological Bulletin,* 126, 697–702.

Subsequent work: See Gabriel, S. & Gardner, W. L. (1999). Are there "his" and "her" types of interdependence? The implications of gender differences in collective and relational interdependence for affect, behavior, and cognition. *Journal of Personality and Social Psychology,* 75, 642–655. Also see Benenson, J. F., & Heath, A. (2006). Boys withdraw more in one-on-one interactions, whereas girls withdraw more in groups. *Developmental Psychology, 42,* 272–282.

There have been many studies indicating higher emotional expressiveness and empathic responding in women. One particularly compelling investigation showed that women report stronger emotions than men in an empathic context (i.e., witnessing emotionally evocative films), but on physiological measures of responding there was no difference: Kring, A. M., & Gordon, A. H. (1998). Sex differences in emotion: Expression, experience, and physiology. *Journal of Personality and Social Psychology, 74,* 686–703.

Benefits of anger in negotiations:

Van Dijk, E., Van Kleef, G. A., Steinel, W., & Van Beest, I. (2008). A social functional approach to emotions in bargaining: When communicating anger pays and when it backfires. *JPSP, 84,* 600–614.

Van Kleef, G. A., De Dreu, C. K. W., & Manstead, A. S. R. (2004a). The interpersonal effects of anger and happiness in negotiations. *JPSP, 86,* 57–76.

Van Kleef, G. A., De Dreu, C. K. W., & Manstead, A. S. R. (2004b). The interpersonal effects of emtions in negotiations: A motivated information-processing approach. *JPSP, 87,* 510–528.

Tannen, D. (1990). *You just don't understand.* New York: William Morrow.

The example of requesting more water was taken from Vincent, N. (2006). *Self-made man: One woman's journey into manhood and back again.* New York: Viking/Penguin.

The finding here from the research literature is well summarized in the first few sentences of Major, B., & Adams, J. R. (1984). Situational moderators of gender differences in reward allocations. *Sex Roles, 11,* 869–880.

They cite, for systematic reviews, Major, B., & Deaux, K. (1982) Individual differences in justice behavior. In J. Greenberg & R. Cohen (Eds.), *Equity and justice in social behavior.* New York Academic Press. Also Kahn, A., Nelson, R. E., & Gaeddert, W. P. (1980). Sex of subject and sex composition of the group as determinants of reward allocation. *Journal of Personality and Social Psychology, 38,* 737–750; Kahn, A., Lamm, H., Krulewitz, J. E., & O'Leary, V. E. (1980). Equity and equality: Male and female means to a just end. *Basic and Applied Social Psychology, 1,* 173–197.

On hierarchy, my colleague and friend Jetse Sprey remarked to me once that equality is inherently problematic for sociological theory, because it leaves no easy way of making decisions and controlling actions. The idea that hierarchy is natural and equality had a bit more of a struggle to emerge is discussed at length in Boehm, C. (1999), *Hierarchy in the forest: The evolution of egalitarian behavior.* Cambridge, MA: Harvard. Boehm's thesis, however, is that the historical record is not one of hierarchy being found everywhere. He notes that hunter-gatherers (especially the men) were far more egalitarian than what came after. This argument does however link hierarchy to cultural progress, which is the crux of my argument.

On gender differences in personality traits, including assertiveness (higher in men) and nurturance (higher in women), see Feingold, A. (1994). Gender differences in personality: A meta-analysis. *Psychological Bulletin,* 116, 429–456. The difference in agency and communion has become such a standard finding and assumption that it is difficult to list a single source, though Feingold's meta-analysis says his more detailed findings are quite consistent with the characterization of males as agentic (also instrumental) and females more communal (also nurturant). The original distinction is generally attributed to Bakan, D. (1966). *The duality of human existence: An essay on psychology and religion.* Chicago, IL: Rand McNally.

On moral reasoning:

Gilligan, C. (1982). In a different voice: Psychological theory and women's development. Cambridge, MA: Harvard University Press.

There are many sources on Kohlberg's work. Try Kohlberg, L., Levine, L., & Hewer, A. (1983). *Moral stages: A current fomulation and response to critics.* New York: Karger.

The definitive review of research subsequent to Gilligan's book was by Jaffee, S., & Hyde, J. S. (2000). Gender differences in moral orientation: A meta-analysis. *Psychological Bulletin,* 126, 703–726.

They concluded that most studies found no significant gender differences in moral reasoning. If results from large numbers of studies are combined, a significant but small effect emerged, indicating that women think more in terms of caring and men more in terms of justice. But the small size and rarity of such differences induced these researchers to conclude that "although distinct moral orientations may exist, these orientations are not strongly associated with gender" (p. 719).

On different brain reactions to norm violators, see Singer, T., Seymour, B., O'Doherty, J. P., Stephan, K. E., Dolan, R., & Frith, C.D. (2006). Empathic neural responses are modulated by the perceived fairness of others. *Nature (Letters),* 439, 466–469.

Chapter 6

The potato washing story has been widely repeated. I have it from De Waal, F. (2001). *The ape and the sushi master: Cultural reflections of a prima-tologist.* New York: Basic Books. He cites as the best known original source, Kawai, M. (1965). Newly acquired pre-cultural behavior of the natural troop of Japanese monkeys on Koshima islet. *Primates,* 6, 1–30.

On traits required for culture, see Baumeister, R. (2005). *The cultural animal: Human nature, meaning, and social life.* New York: Oxford University Press.

For a highly readable introduction to Zulu history, featuring the life of Shake, see Morris, D. R. (1965). *The washing of the spears: The rise and fall of the Zulu nation.* New York: Simon & Schuster.

On systematizing versus empathizing as emphasis in brain design, see Baron-Cohen, S. (2002). The extreme male brain theory of autism. *Trends in Cognitive Sciences,* 6, 248–254.

McNeill, W. H. (1982). *The pursuit of power.* Chicago, IL: University of Chicago Press.

For the Pew surveys about luxuries versus necessities, see http://pewsocialtrends.org/pubs/733/luxury-necessity-recession-era-reevaluations

http://pewresearch.org/pubs/323/luxury-or-necessity.

Chapter 7

On gender equality in prehistoric societies, there are many sources, and recent work has (as usual) focused more on variation and complexities than the overall pattern. But for influential sources, see Cashdon, E. A. (1980). Egalitarian among hunters and gatherers.

American Anthropologist, 82, 116–120; also Woodburn, J. (1982) *Egalitarian societies, Man*, 17, 431–451.

There are also many sources on the relative caloric contributions of men and women, but for one good and fairly recent study, see Marlowe, F. 2001. Male contribution to diet and female reproductive success among foragers. *Current Anthropology*, 42, 755–760.

On reproductive dangers, see Cott, N. F. (1977). *The bonds of womanhood*. New Haven, CT: Yale University Press. Also the highly readable works by Shorter, E. (1975). *The making of the modern family*. New York: Basic Books, and Shorter, E. (1982). *A history of women's bodies*. New York: Basic Books.

For the data on patents, see *Buttons to Biotech: U.S. Patenting by Women, 1977 to 1996*. It is readily available from the U.S. Patent Office to anyone who wants a copy.

On the investment banking, see Sapienza, P., Zingales, L., & Maestripieri, D. (2009). Gender differences in financial risk aversion and career choices are affected by testosterone. *Proceedings of the National Academy of Sciences*, early edition online publication August, 2009. Doi: 10.1073/pnas.0907352106.

The quotation by John Putnam is taken from Cott, N. F. (1977). *The bonds of womanhood*. New Haven, CT: Yale University Press. See p. 109 of her book.

Patai, D., & Koertge, N. (2003). Professing feminism: Education and indoctrination in Women's Studies. New York: Lexington Books.

The comparison to master-slave relationships was from Farrell, W. (1993). *The myth of male power*. New York: Berkley.

Systematizing brain, see Baron-Cohen, S. (2002). The extreme male brain theory of autism. *Trends in Cognitive Sciences*, 6, 248–254.

Chapter 8

The information on the British mining laws and so on is standard stuff. I first read this in some pop history sources. Wikipedia and other online sources confirm the facts.

See Summers, C. H. (1994). *Who stole feminism? How women have betrayed women*. New York: Simon & Schuster. She quotes Steinem, G. (1992), *Revolution from within: A book of self-esteem*. Boston: Little, Brown, and Wolf, N. (1992) *The beauty myth: How images of beauty are used against women*. New York: Doubleday. Summers said she contacted Wolf about the error, and Wolf said she would correct the false statistic in subsequent editions of her book.

The statistic about the discrepancy in execution rates in the German Wehrmacht in the Second as opposed to the First World War came from a lecture by Martin Irle at the University of Mannheim in 1991.

On the Russian army, Merridale, C. (2006). *Ivan's war: Life and death in the Red Army, 1939–1945*. New York: Holt/Metropolitan.

The Horatio Nelson story is from Toll, I.W. (206). *Six frigates: The epic history of the founding of the U.S. Navy*. New York: Norton.

On unrequited love, see Baumeister, R. F., & Wotman, S. R. (1992). *Breaking hearts: The two sides of unrequited love*. New York: Guilford Press.

Also see Baumeister, R. F., Wotman, S. R., & Stillwell, A. M. (1993). Unrequited love: On heartbreak, anger, guilt, scriptlessness, and humiliation. *Journal of Personality and Social Psychology, 64*, 377–394.

Vincent, N. (2006). *Self-made man: One woman's journey into manhood and back again*. New York: Viking/Penguin.

The insurance study: Bernheim, B. D., Forni, L., Gokhale, J., & Kotlikoff, L. J. (2003). The mismatch between life insurance holdings and financial vulnerabilities: Evidence from the health and retirement study. *American Economic Review, 93*, 354–365.

Scarry, E. (1985). *The body in pain: The making and unmaking of the world*. New York: Oxford University Press.

Okun, A. M. (1975). *Equality and efficiency: The big tradeoff*. Washington, DC: Brokkings Institution.

Chapter 9

On the so-called but mostly illusory double standard, see Smith, T. (1994). Attitudes toward sexual permissiveness: Trends, correlates, and behavioral connections. In A. S. Rossi (Ed), *Sexuality across the life course* (pp. 63–97). Chicago: University of Chicago Press; Sprecher, S. (1989). Premarital sexual standards for different categories of individuals. *Journal of Sex Research, 26*, 232–248; Handy, B. (1998: Aug. 31). How we really feel about fidelity. *Time, 152* (9), 52–53; on reverse double standard, see Sprecher, S., McKinney, K., & Orbuch, T. L. (1991).

The effect of current sexual behavior on friendship, dating, and marriage desirability. *Journal of Sex Research,* 28, 387–408; on greater support from women than from men for conventional double standard, see Oliver, M. B., & Hyde, J. S. (1993). Gender differences in sexuality: A meta-analysis. *Psychological Bulletin,* 114, 29–51.

Many cultures require boys to do stuff before they are men. See Gilmore, D. D. (1990). Manhood in the making: Cultural concepts of masculinity. New Haven, CT: Yale University Press.

For laboratory tests, see Vandello, J. A., Bosson, J. K., Cohen, D., Burnaford, R. M., & Weaver, J. R. (2008). Precarious manhood. *Journal of Personality and Social Psychology,* 95, 1325–1339.

On dueling, including the duels of Alexander Hamilton: Freeman, J. B. (2001). *Affairs of honor: National politics in the new republic.* New Haven, CT: Yale University Press. See also Kiernan, V. G. (1989). *The duel in European history.* Oxford: Oxford University Press.

Vincent, N. (2006). Self-made man: One woman's journey into manhood and back again. New York: Viking/Penguin.

Nock, S. L. (1998). *Marriage in men's lives.* New York: Oxford University Press.

Unemployment increases erectile dysfunction: see Morokoff, P. J., & Gillilland, R. (1993). Stress, sexual functioning, and marital satisfaction. *Journal of Sex Research,* 30, 43–53.

Friday, N. (1977). *My mother, my self:* The daughter's search for identity. New York: Dell.

On Ivy League educated women opting for part-time work or for not working at all, see Story, L. (2005: September 20), Many women at elite colleges set career path to motherhood. *New York Times* (accessed June, 2006 and July, 2009 at nytimes.com). http://www.nytimes.com/2005/09/20/national/20women.html.

Regarding the *Time* magazine survey, my source was O'Beirne, K. (2006), *Women who make the world worse,* New York: Sentinel/Penguin. She cites "The case for staying home" in *Time,* March 22, 2004.

Ford, E., & Drake, D. (2009). *Smart girls marry money.* Philadelphia: Running Press.

There is a large literature on narcissism. For excellent discussion of the motivational aspect, see Morf, C. C., & Rhodewalt, F. (2001). Unraveling the paradoxes of narcissism: A dynamic self-regulatory processing model. *Psychological Inquiry,* 12, 177–196. For the point about addiction to esteem, see Baumeister, R. F., & Vohs, K. D. (2001). Narcissism as addiction to esteem. *Psychological Inquiry,* 12, 206–210.

The difference regarding agency was discussed in Chapter 5; see the sources cited there, with Bakan as the original theorist, and Feingold's meta-analysis being one authoritative confirmation of it.

On the three meanings of work as job, calling, and career, see Bellah, R. N., Madsen, R., Sullivan, W. M., Swidler, A., & Tipton, S. M. (1985). *Habits of the heart: Individualism and commitment in American life.* Berkeley, CA: University of California Press.

Bad is stronger than good: See review article, Baumeister, R. F., Bratslavsky, E., Finkenauer, C., & Vohs, K. (2001). Bad is stronger than good. *Review of General Psychology,* 5, 323–370.

Chapter 10

On rage, see Friday, N. (1980). Men in love: The triumph of love over rage. New York: Dell. Also Vincent, N. (2006). Self-made man: One woman's journey into manhood and back again. New York: Viking/Penguin.

The study that compared ideal to actual marital sex lives by gender was by Ard, B. N. (1977). Sex in lasting marriages: A longitudinal study. *Journal of Sex Research,* 13, 274–285.

A substantial amount of research is covered in this chapter. Readers interested in the question of gender differences in sex drive are referred to my review of the scientific literature: Baumeister, R. F., Catanese, K. R., & Vohs, K. D. (2001). Is there a gender difference in strength of sex drive? Theoretical views, conceptual distinctions, and a review of relevant evidence. *Personality and Social Psychology Review,* 5, 242–273. Essentially all the work discussed is covered in that article.

The famous study in which research assistants approached random (but attractive) strangers on campus and offered to have sex with them that night was by Clark, R. D. & Hatfield, E. (1989). Gender differences in receptivity to sexual offers. *Journal of Psychology and Human Sexuality,* 2, 39–55.

The finding that many women say no to sex when they mean yes was this: Muehlenhard, C. L., & Hallabaugh, L. C. (1988). Do women sometimes say no when they mean yes? The prevalence and correlates of women's token resistance to sex. *Journal of Personality and Social Psychology*, 54, 872–879.

On the shortage of sex in lesbian couples and the idea that one cause is the lack of a man to initiate sex, see Blumstein, P., & Schwartz, P. (1983). *American couples*. New York: Morrow.

On testosterone, see Dabbs, J. M. (2000). *Heroes, rogues, and lovers: Testosterone and behavior*. New York: McGraw-Hill.

Ford, E., & Drake, D. (2009). *Smart girls marry money*. Philadelphia: Running Press.

Meanwhile, for the theory of sexual economics, including an extensive review of research relevant to that, see the following article: Baumeister, R. F., & Vohs, K. D. (2004). Sexual economics: Sex as female resource for social exchange in heterosexual interactions. *Personality and Social Psychology Review*. 8, 339–363.

There was a reference to the textbook by Hyde, J. S., & DeLamater, J. (1997). *Understanding human sexuality* (6th ed.). Boston: McGraw-Hill. It is possible that they have revised their statements in light of our work, and I would hope they have.

The idea that women lose little but gain something by delaying sex, whereas contingencies differ for men, was well articulated in this article: Haselton, M. G., & Buss, D. M. (2000). Error management theory: A new perspective on biases in cross-sex mind reading. *Journal of Personality and Social Psychology*, 78, 81–91.

There are many sources on adultery and extramarital sex. The best available data are in Laumann, E. O., Gagnon, J. H., Michael, R. T., & Michaels, S. (1994). *The social organization of sexuality: Sexual practices in the United States*. Chicago, IL: University of Chicago Press. For an older, but thoughtful and readable introduction, see Lawson, A. (1988). *Adultery: An analysis of love and betrayal*. New York: Basic Books.

On duration of marriage, I have simplified the rather chaotic history here. For excellent historical sources, see the following: Stone, L. (1977) *The family, sex and marriage in England* 1500–1800. New York: Harper & Row; Shorter, E. (1975). *The making of the modern family*. New York: Basic Books; Macfarlane, A. (1986). *Marriage and love in England: Modes of Reproduction* 1300–1840. Oxford: Basil Blackwell.

On marriage, the Nock book cited earlier is useful, as is Wilson, J. Q. (2002). *The marriage problem.* New York: HarperCollins.

Chapter 11

Cartoon quoted from R. Warren (1991) (Ed.), *Women's glib: A collection of women's humor.* Freedom, CA: Crossing Press. Page 74. Original may have been by Nicole Hollander.

On gender differences in laughter: Provine, R. R. (2004). Laughing, tickling, and the evolution of speech and self. *Current Directions in Psychological Science,* 13, 215–218.

On the Tessa Jowell case, see Bagehot, *Tessa's not (yet) for burning,* The *Economist,* March 9, 2006. That magazine, like most British-based media, ran several other stories on the case, but that one captures the gist.

Farrell, W. (1993). *The myth of male power.* New York: Berkley Books, pp. 209-210.

Mansfield, H. C. (2006). *Manliness.* New Haven, CT: Yale University Press.

Claiborne's obituary in *The Economist* was how I learned about her career, but the same information is readily available from multiple sources, including Wikipedia.

On top earners and the taxes they pay. The gender distribution of top earners was from *Gender income distribution of top earners in ASX200 companies: 2006 EOWA census of women in leadership.* Published 2008 by Australian Government, Equal Opportunity for Women in the Workplace Agency.

On the finding that 1% of US taxpayers pay 40.4% of all taxes in 2007, up from 39.9% the previous years, see page 4 of *The Kiplinger Tax Letter,* 84(16), August 7, 2009. It notes that those folks earned 22% of all the income, which is pretty hefty too, and so paying 40% of the taxes should be seen in that context.

Much has been written about how badly boys are doing these days. Gurian, M. (2005). *The minds of boys: Saving our sons from falling behind in school and life.* San Francisco, CA: Jossey-Bass/Wiley. Sax, L. (2007). *Boys adrift: The five factors driving the growing epidemic of unmotivated bys and underachieving young men.* New York: Basic Books.

Sommers, C. H. (1994). *Who stole feminism? How women have betrayed women.* New York: Simon & Schuster.

On the self-esteem movement, see Sommers, C. H. (1994). *Who stole feminism? How women have betrayed women.* New York: Simon & Schuster.

On increase in narcissism, Twenge and Campbell have published a series of studies in the research journals. For most readers, the most easily accessible source will be their recent book: Twenge, J. M., & Campbell, W. K. (2009), *The Narcissism epidemic: Living in the age of entitlement.* New York: Free Press.

Hakim, C. (2006). Women, careers, and work-life preferences. *British Journal of Guidance and Counselling.* 34, 279–294.

On the movement to "Title IX" American science, there are several excellent recent articles on it. See C.H. Sommers, "A threat in Title IX," *Washington Post,* April 14, 2009 (and easily available on the web) for recent version. The original article, which anyone who cares about American science and America's future prosperity would find of interest, was C.H. Sommers, "Why can't a woman be more like a man?" *The American,* March/April 2008 issue. Again, easy to find online.

Index

THE PURSUIT OF POWER
MCNELL   P.126